How to Save Gasoline: Public Policy
Alternatives for the Automobile

Sorrel Wildhorn
Burke K. Burright
John H. Enns
Thomas F. Kirkwood

Ballinger Publishing Company ● Cambridge, Mass.
A Subsidiary of J. B. Lippincott Company

This book is printed on recycled paper.

International Standard Book Number: 0-88410-453-2

Library of Congress Catalog Card Number: 75-26641

Printed in the United States of America

Library of Congress Cataloging in Publication Data

Wildhorn, Sorrel.
  How to save gasoline.

  Includes bibliographical references.
  1. Transportation, Automotive—United States. 2. Energy Policy—
United States. 3. Automobiles—Fuel consumption. I. Title.
HE5623.W48 1975   388.3'2   75-26641
ISBN 0-88410-453-2

Contents

List of Figures

List of Tables

List of Abbreviations

CVT   = Continuously Variable Transmission
EPA   = Environmental Protection Agency
ICE   = Internal Combustion Engine
NAV   = New car sales/Auto ownership/Vehicle miles traveled, an econometric model developed for this study
NO_x = Nitrogen oxides
OAP   = Identifies an urban and rural driving cycle developed by the Office of Air Programs of the EPA
SFC   = Specific Fuel Consumption
SIE   = Spark Ignition Engine
VMT   = Vehicle Miles Traveled

Preface

This book is unusual in that it relates a policy study to a context in which that study can be evaluated by the reader. Part I presents the study evaluating certain public policies for conserving energy used by automobiles. Part II, a record of the ensuing public dialogue flowing from the study's release, provides a context in which to evaluate Part I.

Part I and the Appendixes present a study conducted by the authors at the Rand Corporation.* It is a part of Rand's continuing research program in *The Evaluation of Measures to Conserve Energy*, supported by a grant from The National Science Foundation. (Views or conclusions expressed in this study should not be interpreted as those of the NSF.) This program's general focus has been on the growth in demand for energy in all sectors of the U.S. economy, the conflict between this demand and the national goal of reducing our dependence on foreign energy supplies, and the implications of this conflict for governmental policymaking.

The study has two purposes. One is to develop analytical tools to help evaluate national energy conservation policies for private auto transportation. The other is to apply the tools in a systematic analysis and comparison of several alternative policy instruments. The study focuses on two classes of policy instruments: those that raise the price of driving and those that aim to improve average auto fuel economy through regulatory means. Part I and The Appendixes summarize the methodological approach and present the findings and tentative policy implications.

After the study's release in early November of 1974, the senior

*Sorrel Wildhorn, Burke K. Burright, John H. Enns, and Thomas F. Kirkwood, *How to Save Gasoline: Public Policy Alternatives for the Automobile*, R–1560–NSF, October 1974.

author was invited by the United States Senate Committee on Commerce to submit written testimony on our work at their Hearings on the Committee's *Energy Conservation Working Paper* held in November and December of 1974. Chapter Eight of Part II contains the written testimony he submitted. Automobile industry witnesses also testified at those Hearings. During their testimony the auto industry witnesses were asked to comment in writing on, among other things, several statements in the published study and written testimony. Chapter Nine of Part II contains the auto makers' comments on our work. All four of the major U.S. auto manufacturers—General Motors, Ford, Chrysler and American Motors—responded to the Committee's request.

Upon receiving the auto companies' comments, the Committee asked for a response in writing to the auto companies' views of the study. Chapter Ten of Part II, prepared by three of the authors, contains the response. All of the public dialogue presented in Chapters Eight, Nine, and Ten are also part of the public record of the Committee Hearings *(Hearings before the Committee on Commerce, United States Senate, Ninety-Third Congress, Second Session on Energy Conservation Working Paper, November 26, December 10 and 11, 1974, Serial No. 93-128).*

Finally, the senior author was also invited to present oral and written testimony at Hearings held on April 2, 1975, by the California Assembly Committee on Energy and Diminishing Materials on bills relating to auto fuel economy regulation and taxation. Chapter Eleven contains this testimony.

Sorrel Wildhorn
Santa Monica, California

November 12, 1975

Acknowledgments

Many persons in various organizations provided valuable assistance in this study. We had helpful discussions during the course of the study with R. L. Strombotne of the Office of the Secretary, Department of Transportation, and with R. G. McGillivray of the Urban Institute. Charlotte Chamberlain, of the Transportation Systems Center, Department of Transportation, provided early drafts of her work on the demand for gasoline and commented on preliminary drafts of our econometric work on the demand for motor fuel. D. Rubin and J. K. Pollard, of the Transportation Systems Center, supplied us with a variety of auto transportation data and early drafts of their energy conservation studies.

Philip Verleger, of Data Resources, Inc., provided us with an advance copy of his econometric study of gasoline demand. Frank Wykoff, Professor of Economics at Pomona College, supplied us with a data series on permanent income. W. J. Page, of the Program Management Division, Federal Highway Administration, supplied data on average fleet fuel economy by state. And John L. Smith, Manager, Car Engineering Division, Product Planning Office, Chrysler Corporation, discussed the relationships between employment in the auto manufacturing industry and technical characteristics of automobiles.

We are indebted to Peter Huntley, Vice President, Orshansky Transmission Corporation, for helpful discussions about continuously variable transmissions and for supplying us with papers reporting on their development and performance. C. E. McInerney, of the AiResearch Industrial Division of the Garrett Corporation, supplied us with information on turbosuperchargers and their effect on fuel economy. Derek P. Gregory, of the Institute of Gas Technology, provided papers on methanol and hydrogen. D. Gartner, of the

Du Pont Corporation, supplied information on the cost and energy consumed in manufacturing methanol. Under subcontract to Rand, LeRoy H. Lindgren, Director of Technical Services, Rath & Strong, Inc., supplied us with information regarding automobile component weights and costs. And J. Witzky, of Southwest Research Institute, P. Breisacher, of The Aerospace Corporation, and A. Amito, of Honda, supplied information on stratified charge engines. Finally, T. Sebastyan and S. Lucther, of the Advanced Automotive Power Systems Division of the Environmental Protection Agency, supplied information on advanced engines.

Several Rand colleagues and consultants provided valuable assistance. Loanne Batchelder and Marianne Lakatos provided excellent programming support. We had helpful substantive discussions with K. Anderson, F. S. Hoffman, M. Kamins, D. N. Morris, and F. Welch during the course of the study. Finally, G. H. Fisher, F. S. Hoffman, M. M. Lavin, D. N. Morris, G. Nelson, and G. K. Smith reviewed and made helpful comments concerning an earlier draft, Part I.

How to Save Gasoline: Public
Policy Alternatives for the Automobile

Summary of the Study

PURPOSES

The ubiquitous automobile consumes more than half the fuel used in transportation, or roughly 13 percent of the total direct energy used in the United States. Moreover, the share being consumed by automobiles has been rising over the past decade. If we can devise policies that save even modest percentages of the fuel consumed by automobiles, the absolute savings in energy will be very large.

This study had two purposes. One was to develop analytical tools to evaluate the effects on private transportation of national energy conservation measures. The other was to apply these tools in a systematic analysis and to compare the effectiveness of several alternative policy instruments, or combinations of policy instruments, and to draw broad policy implications useful to governmental policymakers.[a] Beyond these general policy conclusions we sought to assess, in some detail, the implications of specific policy decisions: what policy components or combinations of components achieve what results over what period of time.

To forecast gasoline consumption by automobiles, we have linked together several complex models. Then we use them to make a series of forecasts for the period 1975–1995; the forecasts involve different

[a]For the reader interested in a summary of the analytical framework used and the tools developed in this study, Chapter Three and Appendices A through G provide such an overview. A detailed discussion of the major tools developed is found in Rand Corporation reports R–1561–NSF, *Econometric Models of the Demand for Motor Fuel*, by Burke K. Burright and John Enns (forthcoming), and R–1562–NSF, *A Generalized Model for Comparing Automobile Design Approaches to Improved Fuel Economy*, by Thomas F. Kirkwood and Allen D. Lee, January, 1975.

1

assumptions about the price, technology, and weight of new cars and about the price of gasoline. These forecasts have led to a series of findings that we believe will help decisionmakers select policies to reduce gasoline consumption by automobiles over the next twenty years.

Because the subject is very complex, we concentrated our study resources on policies that have a *direct* impact on the demand for gasoline; we have not tried to deal with policies that would encourage or limit importation, refining, or production of petroleum or petroleum-based products in the United States.

Our forecasts of the impacts of government policies and our conclusions about the relative attractiveness of policy instruments are strongly dependent on simplifying assumptions with respect to a number of factors. These include the elasticity of supply of gasoline and the willingness of automobile manufacturers to adopt new technologies and variations in the product mix in response to price changes and/or taxes on gasoline or new cars. These assumptions and their impacts are discussed below.

Finally, our forecasts are based in part on econometric estimates of the price elasticity of demand for gasoline; the estimates used in our forecasts are considerably larger than short-term estimates obtained in other studies but are of the same order of magnitude as other long-term estimates of demand elasticities. The long-term effects will tend to dominate in the twenty-year forecasts developed in this study.

We begin by setting forth three general findings, on which we offer comments intended to clarify and specify the bases on which they rest. In discussing the implications of various policies, we become more specific. We then present an overview of the tools and criteria used in comparing policies and list the full spectrum of policy instruments we considered and describe the reference set of conditions against which alternative policies are compared. Finally, we submit some qualifying remarks reflecting our own assessment of the uncertainties associated with an analysis of this sort.

BROAD POLICY IMPLICATIONS

The research findings presented in this report suggest three broad implications for gasoline conservation policy.

Finding I: *Aside from limitations on gasoline supply, the only way to achieve significant gasoline savings in the near term (one to four years) is to increase the pump price of gasoline. In the* *longer term (over eight years) improvements in new car fuel economy through weight reduction and other technological improvements offer greater potential for energy conservation than do gasoline taxes (short of extremely high taxes). However, because both classes of policies generate varied social, economic, and environmental impacts, there is no clear dominance of one policy class over the other. And some combination of policies may be more effective, depending on national energy conservation objectives.*

Comment: Our analysis showed that an increase in the pump price of gasoline will reduce the amount of gasoline used for automobile trips. Higher gasoline taxes would be fully reflected in higher pump prices if the supply of gasoline for automobile travel in the United States is perfectly elastic. If the supply is limited or contains some inelasticities, part of the burden or incidence of the gasoline tax will be borne by gasoline suppliers rather than consumers, and hence the tax would not be fully reflected in higher pump prices. Therefore, if the supply is not perfectly elastic, our empirical results would apply to market price increases only, and higher taxes would be required to achieve any specified market price increase.

Under the assumption of perfectly elastic supply, we find that, for example, each cent of tax per gallon will result in close to 1 percent annual gasoline savings by 1980. By contrast, the weight reduction or technological changes that could be implemented in the near future offer only modest savings (less than 1 percent) in the first two years and only about 10 percent savings by 1980. However, by the late 1980s and thereafter, weight reduction and technological changes (implemented in the late 1970s) can achieve large annual savings—up to 40 percent. Over this longer time period, only very high gasoline taxes—over 50 cents per gallon—can achieve this level of savings.

Given the magnitude of the technological changes analyzed, maximum conservation may require the imposition of weight, technology, or fuel economy standards on automobile manufacturers. Mandated standards, imposed in 1975 and implemented over a period of years, could obtain the maximum benefits from new technology.

The use of additional fuel taxes to conserve gasoline generates a number of other impacts:

1. *User costs.* In the early years after a tax increase, total user cost of the auto stock is reduced substantially, because of reduced size of the fleet and fewer miles driven in the remaining fleet, but as scrappage rates decline and new car sales climb back to pre-tax levels, user cost reductions become relatively small.

2. *Vehicle miles traveled (VMT)*. Most of the early gasoline saving would be due to a *reduction* in automobile VMT—that is, a loss of personal mobility.

3. *Employment*. Additional gasoline taxes would cause persistent, but declining over time, *reductions* in employment in auto-related sectors, roughly proportional to the tax level. In the early years, the decline in employment is pervasive because both new car production and VMT decrease; however, in the later years, the employment decline will occur primarily in the auto parts manufacturing and service sector because of VMT reductions.

4. *Who pays*. In the near term, the impact of additional gasoline taxes on the proportion of earnings spent for auto work trips bears more heavily on commuters with earnings below $13,500 in 1975. Within this group, the impact would be roughly proportional to earnings.

5. *Emissions*. The large and persistent reduction in VMT, combined with greatly increased auto scrappage rates in the early years, result in very rapid reductions in total emissions by 1980.

Regulatory policies mandating technological, weight, or fuel economy changes in new cars will impact in ways that differ from those occasioned by higher fuel taxes:

1. *User costs*. Although user cost reductions are small in the early years, they become quite substantial by the late 1980s as older cars are scrapped and newer, less costly autos with better fuel economy dominate the auto fleet.

2. *VMT*. As new car fuel economy increases with time, due to these policies, the cost of ownership per mile driven falls and induces more *vehicle miles of travel*—but not enough to offset the large gains in gasoline conservation. As a result, urban congestion is likely to worsen.

3. *Employment*. Although the implementation of technological changes would not significantly affect auto sales or ownership per se, the increases in VMT would lead to higher levels of employment in the service and auto parts supply sectors.

4. *Emissions*. Also, because of the VMT increase, total fleetwide emissions *increase* substantially, roughly in proportion to the increase in VMT.

Finding II: *The imposition of a higher fixed tax on new car sales prices offers little promise of gasoline conservation in the near term. Moreover, if such taxes were to be graduated to* *discourage purchases of less efficient autos, the impact on the turnover rate of the automobile stock would reduce the effectiveness of such a policy.*

Comment: An increase in the average price of new cars initially shifts demand to the used car market. In addition, households will operate their autos longer (i.e., scrappage rates will fall). Because the supply of used cars is limited, their price will rise, and some buyers will return to the new car market. After these adjustment processes are completed, automobile ownership, total VMT, and gasoline consumption are virtually unchanged, while the rate at which the auto stock turns over is significantly decreased.

A graduated tax will increase the price of at least some new cars. The effectiveness of a graduated tax will thus be reduced because (1) the introduction of new, more efficient cars will be slowed, and (2) older, less efficient cars will be retained in the auto fleet for longer periods of time. A fixed or graduated ownership tax (on new *and* used cars) would tend to mitigate these adverse impacts, because used car ownership would be more costly.

Finding III: *A desired improvement in average new car fuel economy can be achieved in the longer run with several types of policies. Among those that do not sacrifice new car comfort or performance, the one that involves the lowest new car price will reduce total automobile gasoline consumption the most—because the introduction rate of new, more efficient cars will be increased and older, less efficient cars will be scrapped more rapidly.*

Comment: Fixed or graduated new car sales taxes and government mandated weight, technology, or fuel economy standards, are all primarily aimed at improving average new car fuel economy. New car sales taxes would mean some price increases and, as indicated above, imply impacts that reduce their effectiveness in conserving gasoline. The more promising approaches to government mandated weight, technology, or fuel economy standards generally turn out to involve *lower* new car prices, and to exert a *net* effect on gasoline conservation that is more salutary.

IMPLICATIONS OF SPECIFIC POLICIES

We now examine, in some detail, the implications of initiating specific policies intended to conserve fuel, and how their impact differs over time.

Implication I: *Under our assumptions, described later in this summary, price increases of 15 cents to 45 cents per gallon can achieve annual reductions in gasoline consumption by 1980 of 16 percent to 41 percent, respectively. One method, of course, of increasing prices is through gasoline taxes. Over longer periods, the impact of the tax declines due to rising incomes and inflation.*

Comment: Our analysis showed that an increase in the pump price of gasoline will reduce the amount of gasoline used for automobile trips: a one cent per gallon rise in price causes roughly a 1 percent decrease in gasoline consumption. This results because households can immediately lower the miles driven per vehicle and increase auto efficiency by driving more slowly and conservatively; in the longer run, with effects noticeable after several years, they can switch to smaller or more efficient engined cars.

Over longer periods of time, the impact of the tax steadily diminishes owing to rising household incomes and the decline in the real value of the tax due to inflation. Table S–1 presents our estimates of savings at three points in time with three levels of additional taxes, imposed in 1975.

The desirability of additional taxes must be judged in terms of their effects. Negative aspects of the tax are most severe in the near term. By 1980, annual VMT reductions could be as large as 36 percent with a 45 cent per gallon tax, and employment in auto-related sectors could decline by 19 percent for the same tax level. Moreover, additional taxes would bear initially more heavily on commuters with below average family earnings, in the absence of tax redistribution mechanisms. Each 15 cent per gallon increase in the tax results in approximately a 0.5 percent increase in the share of annual earnings devoted to auto work trips for households earning less than $13,500 in 1975. For upper income groups, the corresponding increase is only 0.1 to 0.3 percent. On the positive side, we estimate that total user costs would decline by 13 percent, and emissions by 83 percent, as a result of a 45 cent per gallon tax.

Table S–1.   Gasoline Savings Resulting from Additional Taxes
(Percent change from base case)

Additional Tax (1975 $)	1980	1985	1995
15¢	16.2	13.6	9.8
30¢	33.8	25.0	18.2
45¢	40.5	34.5	25.7

Implication II: *New technology holds great potential for improving fleetwide fuel economy by the late 1980s and thereafter. Depending upon the type of policy implemented—mandated weight reduction versus technological improvements—the annual fuel savings to be realized by 1995 range from 18 percent to 40 percent in comparison with a case where automobile technology changes only slightly.*

Comment: One may ask whether government mandated standards would be needed: would not competitive market processes achieve the same results? We did not have the resources to consider this question in detail and sought only to look at impacts *if* mandated standards are imposed. However, the most recent study of the market structure of the automobile industry argues that few incentives exist for making major technological improvements [1]. This conclusion is consistent with the results in our econometric analysis, which forecasts that large increases in real gasoline prices would lead to only small increases in average automobile efficiency. On the other hand, if automobile manufacturers would voluntarily adopt the new technologies, the savings due specifically to *mandatory* technology would be smaller, but the same real savings would occur due to the introduction (by whatever means) of superior technology.

By the late 1980s and beyond, it is possible to conserve up to 18 percent of annual gasoline consumption under our assumptions by mandating weight standards that shift production toward small cars. By mandating technology changes instead, annual savings of up to one-third can be achieved, and by mandating both types of changes, savings of up to 40 percent annually can be obtained.

Impacts vary with each type of technological policy selected. Comparing mandated weight standards with mandated technology changes—both designed to conserve as much gasoline as possible within bounds of economic and technological feasibility—we find that mandating technology changes will conserve more fuel and energy and will generally result in lower user costs in the long run. In the short run (1976 to 1985), the converse is true. In addition, a policy of mandated technology change results in greater increases in VMT after 1985 (owing to greater declines in ownership costs per mile) and this generates larger increases in both employment and emission levels. When applied in combination, rather than separately, the two policies result in more fuel and energy conservation, lower user costs, more VMT, more emissions, and higher employment over the twenty-year period.

The capital resources available to the auto manufacturing industry, either through internal reallocation (e.g., deferral of annual model changes) or from external sources (e.g., borrowing), appear adequate to finance conversion to new technology, such as an alternative type of power plant and transmission [2]. Total capital investment required is roughly the same as a single year's current capital expenditures by the motor vehicle industry.

> **Implication III:**   *If the federal government intends to subsidize automobile R&D for fuel conservation purposes, such a subsidy should include support for work on advanced versions of the internal combustion engine and on a continuously variable transmission.*

Comment: From our analysis of current engineering data, it appears that improvements in the gasoline fueled spark ignition engine, such as charge stratification, supercharging, fuel injection, and possibly rotary design, may lead to greater fuel economy than can be expected from the diesel, Rankine, gas turbine, or Stirling engines.

To illustrate the potential improvement in fuel economy possible, we analyzed a supercharged rotary engine using charge stratification, among other variants. While we cannot be certain that an engine combining all these features will perform as we predict, there are so many ways to improve the fuel economy of spark ignition engines (SIE) that we are confident substantial savings can be achieved. Thus, if the sealing problem in rotary engines prevents their use at the higher compression ratios we have assumed, a reciprocating design may be used with a moderate loss in fuel economy; if supercharging proves costly, or results in unacceptable acceleration characteristics, a higher compression ratio, stratified charge engine may lead to nearly the same performance.

Our analysis indicates that the supercharged rotary engine with charge stratification dominates all other engine types, including the diesel.[b] Compared with the conventional SIE, it yields about twice the fuel economy, requires about 40 percent less lifetime energy, and reduces initial and lifetime per-vehicle costs by over 25 percent. In terms of energy conservation potential, only one of the three advanced engines examined—the Stirling—can compete with our estimate of the advanced SIE, and we expect that the Stirling will require more time to develop and be more costly. However, Stirling

---

[b]We assumed vehicles designed for equal acceleration and passenger and trunk space. If owners of diesel powered autos are willing to accept lower acceleration and smaller space than in gasoline powered autos, the diesel engine can become more attractive.

engines offer greatly reduced emissions (less than half the weighted statutory standard) and can operate on a wide variety of fuels.

Neither the gas turbine nor the Rankine ("steam") cycle engine appear to offer as good fuel economy or cost reduction, but the Rankine offers reduced emissions comparable to the Stirling and can operate with a wider variety of fuels than the internal combustion engine. Compared with conventional engines, both the turbine and Rankine engines have operational features to which owners would be sensitive: the free turbine has poor engine braking characteristics, and the Rankine system may require longer start-up time under normal conditions and special procedures in cold weather to avoid freezing or to start after freezing.

The continuously variable transmission (CVT) can increase a conventional auto's fuel economy by about 27 to 32 percent, depending on driving cycle (urban or urban–rural driving) and auto size, all other things being equal. It does so by automatically selecting the most appropriate gear ratio between engine and wheels, thereby maximizing efficiency and fuel economy, without exceeding allowable nitrogen oxides (NO_x) emissions. Lifetime energy requirements of the auto can be reduced 18 percent; auto selling price can be reduced about 5 percent, because the more efficient CVT can attain the same performance (i.e., acceleration) with a smaller engine and lighter vehicle, although the CVT itself is heavier and more expensive than a standard automatic transmission; and lifetime cost per vehicle can be reduced by 8 percent.

Implication IV: *Our estimate that some of the technological improvements would result in lower per-vehicle initial (purchase) price and lifetime costs deserves separate mention. For some vehicles, such as an auto powered with a supercharged stratified charge rotary engine, both initial and lifetime costs are lower; for others, such as a diesel or Stirling powered auto, only lifetime costs are lower.*

Comment: These cost comparisons are made holding constant performance, interior passenger and trunk space, and unrefueled range of the auto. The initial cost, or purchase price, of the supercharged stratified charge rotary engine is reduced primarily because the smaller, lighter engine implies a smaller, lighter auto, even though the engine cost per pound may be higher than for the conventional engine. Lifetime (assumed ten years, 100,000 miles) costs are lower because both initial costs and operating costs are lower. Operating costs are lower owing both to the engine's improved fuel economy and the lighter weight of the auto. On the other hand, the initial cost of a diesel or Stirling powered auto is higher than the comparable conventional engined auto because a heavier engine results in a larger and heavier auto. Lifetime cost, however, is lower because reductions in operating costs due to improved fuel economy outweigh increases in the initial cost.

Our estimates of initial costs are based on a statistical analysis of new car sticker prices, which presumably include the amortized cost of normal capital investments needed to make annual model changes and technological improvements. Abnormally high capital investments that may be needed are not included in our estimates, because they require knowledge of auto industry pricing policies and depreciation constraints, which is information not available to us. Consequently, the purchase cost for certain technological improvements we consider may be underestimates.

Implication V: *Our automobile design analysis indicates that automobiles with new technology, but with the same acceleration and interior space characteristics as today's standard size cars, could achieve over 25 mpg, while subcompacts could achieve over 40 mpg. If a fuel economy standard is to be legislated, this finding suggests that the average range of 16 to 20 mpg standards, in recently proposed legislation [3], is perhaps unnecessarily low.*

Comment: Any fuel economy standard legislated should be written to include the improvements in efficiency attainable by equipping all new cars with radial tires and by minor aerodynamic redesign of new auto bodies, as well as improvements possible with new technology and/or a shift to small cars. Our findings suggest that an average new car fuel economy standard between 21 and 38 mpg is feasible, depending on the alternatives assumed as the bases for the standard.

It seems reasonable that the most general mandate is to be preferred among regulatory policies aimed at improving new car fuel economy, although our analysis does not lead directly to such a conclusion. A more general mandate would reduce the risk of not achieving a given level of gasoline savings and result in a more diverse product mix by offering wider consumer choices in acceleration, comfort, and roominess. In attempting to meet the fuel economy standard, one auto company may choose new technology, another may choose to shift more rapidly to small cars, and still another may choose some combination of the two. Consequently, a more general mandate is likely to result in some production of large cars with very efficient advanced engines and transmissions, and some production of small cars with relatively less efficient and more conventional engines. However, compared with a policy of mandated weight or technology change, a fuel economy standard implies greater uncertainty in *other* impacts, such as user cost, overall energy conservation, and the transportation service characteristics of new cars.

> **Implication VI:**   *If national conservation objectives are phrased in terms of constant percentage savings in gasoline consumption over time, it is possible to select combinations of declining gasoline taxes and regulatory policies (designed to improve new car fuel economy) to implement such objectives.*

Comment: For example, by imposing an additional gasoline tax of 14 cents per gallon in 1975, gradually lowering the tax to zero in 1986, and mandating an early maximum weight standard, roughly 16 to 18 percent of projected (increasing) gasoline consumption and total energy can be conserved annually over the period.

By imposing an additional gasoline tax of 41 cents per gallon in 1975, declining to zero in 1994, and mandating both a maximum weight standard and the adoption of new technology (or an equivalent fuel economy standard), roughly 39 to 43 percent of gasoline and total energy can be conserved annually over the period.

Such combined policies have differing impacts over time. In the near term, the tax impacts predominate—reduced auto ownership, a transient decline in new car sales and auto-related employment, a substantial reduction in VMT, user cost, and emissions.

In the longer term, the effects of policies that improve new car fuel economy predominate—little change in new car sales and auto ownership, substantial reductions in user cost, very large increases in VMT and, consequently, very large increases in emissions. However, by 1995, although emissions may increase by 11 to 43 percent over the reference case value for that year, depending on the policy chosen, emissions are still 60 to 70 percent *below* 1976 reference case values. Finally, although employment effects vary somewhat with the choice of regulatory policy they are generally not of large magnitude.

TOOLS AND CRITERIA FOR COMPARING POLICIES

We now describe the tools and criteria we used to compare alternative policies, enumerate and discuss the policy instruments we considered, and establish a reference point—which we call our Base Case—against which the impacts of alternative measures and policies are assessed.

Because alternative policies designed to conserve energy in private transportation may have disparate social, economic, and environmental impacts, it is useful to compare these impacts in quantitative terms whenever possible. In this study, we have developed several analytical tools that we use to compare a variety of policies over time.

One analytical tool, the Generalized Automobile Design Model, relates natural resource and energy requirements and the cost of auto ownership to the size, performance,[c] and design characteristics of the individual auto. For current technology, it predicts results within a few percent of actual values. A second analytical tool, the Auto Fleet Mix Model, relates overall auto fleet fuel consumption, total energy required, emissions, and cost of ownership to the changes in the number, nature, and mix of autos produced each year. A recursive econometric demand model (called NAV) is used to evaluate price effects at the national level; it uses annual national data for the period 1954 to 1972 to project short- and long-run effects of changes in the average price of gasoline or new cars on auto sales and total ownership, vehicle miles traveled, average fuel economy, and gasoline consumption. The model has satisfactory statistical properties. Finally, an econometric approach was developed to project employment in five auto-related sectors as a function of auto ownership, new car production and sales, aggregate vehicle miles traveled, and average new car weight.

These tools are used to compare policies over a twenty-year period in terms of the following *annual* impacts:

1. *Gasoline consumption* of the entire auto fleet.
2. Fleetwide *energy consumption,* direct plus indirect. (We include indirect energy used in the production and distribution of gasoline and in the production, distribution, sales, repair, and scrapping of autos, as well as the direct fuel energy consumed in driving.)
3. Fleetwide *user cost* of the total auto fleet. (The discounted ten-year cost stream of owning and operating the auto fleet is spread over ten equal "annual installments." It includes the amortized

---

[c]Performance is a vector including acceleration capability, unrefueled range, riding quality, and other characteristics such as noise, smoothness of operation, and so forth. We make comparisons among cars having equal acceleration and unrefueled range. Ride quality will vary somewhat with weight, and we do not attempt to hold it constant. Other performance attributes are discussed but not evaluated.

cost of purchase price, state and federal taxes and fees, gasoline and oil consumption, insurance, and repair and maintenance. In estimating fuel costs, allowances are made for the effects of inflation.)

4. Fleetwide *vehicle miles traveled* (VMT).
5. *New car sales.*
6. *Employment* in auto manufacture and related sectors. (This includes tire manufacturing, auto manufacturing, retail and wholesale trade in auto parts and accessories, auto dealers, and service stations.)
7. Fleetwide *weighted emissions.* (We use the Caretto–Sawyer weighting scheme for hydrocarbons, carbon monoxide, and nitrogen oxides emissions. It should be viewed as a proxy measure for the impact on air quality.)

POLICY INSTRUMENTS CONSIDERED

Policies for conserving energy in private transportation can act in two ways: by inducing improvements in average auto fuel economy and by reducing VMT. Average auto fuel economy improvements can be achieved through different technologies (e.g., new engine or vehicle designs) or through transportation management or control policies (e.g., speed limits or reductions in traffic congestion). Reduction in auto VMT may be achieved through policies that raise the cost of driving, reduce average auto trip length, restrict fuel availability, improve public transit service (bus, rail, and air) or reduce its fares, or through non-transportation policies such as land use restrictions that change the location of residences vis-à-vis businesses.

In this study we focus solely on two classes of policy instruments: those that *raise the price of driving* and those that aim to *improve average auto fuel economy through the use of different technology.* Included in the latter class are policies aimed at inducing shifts in new car production toward small cars with conventional technology, as well as policies that foster introduction of new technologies in both large and small cars. In addition, we examine combinations of the two policy classes.

Regulatory Instruments Affecting Costs
The *price change* policy instruments considered are:

1. *Additional gasoline taxes.* We consider three increments of 15, 30, and 45 cents per gallon (in 1975 dollars) over the 1975–1995 period. In addition, we examine the effect of dropping the incremental tax in 1980 and 1985.

2. *A tax on new car purchases.* We examine the effect of a 50 percent increase in *average* new car price.[d]
3. *A tax on auto ownership (new and used cars).* Similar to the above tax, but on ownership rather than purchase.

Regulatory Instruments Affecting Technology

Policy instruments considered that *improve average auto fuel efficiency* through use of different technology are:

1. *Mandated maximum weight standard.* We postulate a weight standard that would induce a production phase-out of full-size and intermediate-size cars at the rate of 20 percent per year (beginning in 1976 and ending in 1980), and replace them with compact and subcompact car production. In 1976 and beyond, we assume that the *relative* market shares of compacts and subcompacts would be the same as projected for 1975.[e] The market class shares in 1975 and 1980 would then be as shown in Table S-2.
2. *Mandated technology changes (a new engine and transmission).* Here we visualize a technology standard written to induce an orderly introduction of new technology. Included are radial tires, minor aerodynamic redesign of auto bodies, a more efficient transmission (the continuously variable transmission—CVT), and a new power plant. Our analysis indicates that one of the more promising is a supercharged stratified rotary spark ignition engine, although other new power plants show promise. We assume that initial introduction of the CVT and new engine begins in 1980

Table S-2.   Relative Market Shares, by Auto Size Class, 1975 and 1980

	(Base Year) 1975 (%)	1980 and Beyond (%)
Full-Size	37	0
Intermediate	18	0
Compact	17	38
Subcompact	28	62

[d]Although the analytical tools we developed in this study cannot treat explicitly graduated taxes on new car price (by weight, size, or auto fuel economy), we can and do draw preliminary inferences about the efficacy of such taxes, based on our work and the work of others.

[e]Current sales of compacts and larger size autos comprise about 70 percent of new car sales. No convincing analytical models exist for projecting market shares under such a mandated weight standard. Consequently, this alternative should be viewed as an upper bound estimate of what could be accomplished in the near term by forcing weight control upon auto manufacturers.

and, with conversion of 20 percent per year, is fully incorporated in new car production by 1985. We assume that radial tires and minor aerodynamic improvements can be fully incorporated by 1976. Of all the technological improvements examined in our study, these four together offer the greatest potential for gasoline and energy conservation.[f]

3. *Mandated average new car fuel economy standard.* We take as our fuel economy standard that implied by the mandated technology case above. Because such a mandate allows auto manufacturers considerable flexibility in *how* it is to be met, we examine three illustrative implementation alternatives: (a) by the new technology mentioned above; (b) by shifting to production of only subcompacts and two passenger, trunkless urban autos; and (c) by a mix of some new technology (radial tires, minor aerodynamic improvements, CVT) and small cars (subcompacts and trunkless subcompacts).

4. *Mandated weight standard and technology.* As an illustration of the maximum energy conservation potential possible without drastic changes in auto comfort, roominess, and luggage carrying capacity, we examine a case combining the weight and technology standards mentioned above.

In addition, we examine three alternatives designed for different, but constant (over time), percentage savings in energy consumption. All combine different declining gas taxes with mandated standards for improving fuel economy.

THE BASE CASE

All of the policy instruments considered are compared with a Base Case that reflects existing trends and market forces in the absence of new policy intervention. The Base Case includes projections of annual fleetwide gasoline and energy consumption, new car sales, total auto ownership, auto scrappage rates, VMT, user cost of the auto fleet, average fuel economy of the fleet, and fleetwide weighted emissions. The major assumptions for the Base Case are shown in Table S–3. In the last quarter of 1973 and the first quarter of 1974, the price of gasoline increased sharply. Over the entire United States,

[f]We did *not* include new fuels in considering a mandated technology. However, we did examine methanol and hydrogen, because their use could allow a large-scale shift to a non-petroleum fuel base such as coal or nuclear energy. But we found that neither of these fuels imply an *overall* reduction in energy consumption, and costs will be higher unless very high gasoline taxes are imposed.

Table S–3. Major Base Case Assumptions

Item	Assumptions
Population growth	Census Bureau *Series B and E* [a]
Income growth	Real disposable personal income per household grows at 1.9 percent average annual rate.
Gasoline price	A national average price of 59 cents per gallon for regular in 1974; a national average price of 67 cents per gallon for regular in 1975; gasoline price increases at the same rate as overall inflation after 1975. [b]
New car price	New car prices increase at the same rate as overall inflation.
New car market size classes	A slight increase in the market shares of compacts and subcompacts compared with their 1973 shares (37 percent full-size, 18 percent intermediate, 17 percent compact, and 28 percent subcompact).
Automobile equipment	All new cars are equipped with radial tires; air conditioning equipment rates, by market class (e.g., subcompact, compact, and so forth), are the same as current rates.
Speed limit	55 miles per hour.

[a]Projections under *Series E* do not differ from those under *Series B* until 1986. See U.S. Bureau of the Census, *Current Population Reports*, Series P–25, No. 394, Table A; and projections prepared for the Commission on Population Growth and the American Future, given in U.S. Commission on Population Growth and the American Future, *Population Distribution and Policy*, Sara Mills Maxie, Ed., Vol. V of Commission Research Reports (Washington, D.C.: Government Printing Office, 1972), p. 12. Census *Series E* projections assume that completed cohort fertility will be 2.11 births per woman (about what it was in 1972). The projection used in our base case is as follows:

Year	Thousands of Households
1970	63,074
1975	69,002
1980	75,442
1985	81,833
1990	87,092
1995	91,557

[b]Assumed annual inflation rates for the base case are:

Year	Inflation Rate (%)
1974	7.0
1975	6.3
1976	5.5
1977	4.8
1978	4.1
1979	3.4
1980–1995	2.6

the average pump price of a gallon of regular gasoline was 51.6 cents in April 1974. We assume that for all of 1974 the average pump price of a gallon of regular will be 59 cents and that for 1975 it will be 67 cents. *These prices mean that a large decrease in the growth of automobile gasoline consumption is already built into the Base Case.* Between 1954 and 1972, automobile gasoline consumption grew at an average annual rate of 4.9 percent; in the Base Case, automobile gasoline consumption grows at an average rate of 1.7 percent between 1972 and 1995.

We do not claim that our Base Case assumptions, and the projections based on them, are the most likely to materialize in the future. Our assumptions merely represent our best judgment at the time we began the analysis. For example, actual gasoline or new car prices may be higher or lower than we assume.

SOME QUALIFYING REMARKS

Our analysis of the interactions among gasoline consumption, auto ownership, auto travel, prices, income, and the like, uses new analytical tools not yet completely evaluated by the research community; moreover, our analysis of technological improvements must of necessity use incomplete engineering data. Accordingly, the *precision* of some of the *quantitative* differences in the impacts of alternative policies reported above may be open to question. However, for any specific impact there are strong theoretical reasons to believe that the *qualitative* differences are real and in the right direction, and that the relative differences—or, at worst, the rankings—among the alternatives reflect reality.

With regard to the precision of the econometric estimates, we see two problems that may qualify our results. One has to do with the *range* of variation of *future* value of a variable compared with its *historic range* of variation. Relative gasoline price is one example; we estimate effects of taxes that are far higher than any we have experienced. The second has to do with the *rapidity* of the adjustment process. While the statistical properties of our econometric model are satisfactory, we are concerned that its structure results in very rapid adjustments to gasoline and new car price changes—usually in two to three years. Some factors, such as VMT per auto, might be expected to adjust rapidly. But for others, such as the predicted average fuel economy and auto ownership per household, the predicted adjustment seems excessively rapid—even with large year-to-year price changes. Because some of the excessively rapid short-run adjustments damp out in the long run and other adjustments persist, we see the model as a way of predicting *long-run* impacts when large changes in gasoline and new car prices are being analyzed.

For predictions of the effects of new technology, our methods insure a *systematic* comparison among alternatives, holding all but one or a few variables constant. But because refined engineering test results using different technologies installed in autos are lacking for some technological options, our estimates should be viewed as the best attainable using current data. It may turn out, for example, that when advanced prototypes are built, the most promising new engine will be one that we rank second, but we feel confident that the *broad* policy implications we draw are valid.

NOTES TO SUMMARY OF THE STUDY

1. See Lawrence J. White, *Automobile Industry Since 1945* (Cambridge, Mass.: Harvard University Press, 1971).

2. This conclusion is presented in a recent study of the economic impact on the automotive industry of mass production of new power systems. See R. U. Ayres and Stedman Noble, *Economic Impact of Mass Production of Alternative Low Emissions Automotive Power Systems*, International Research and Technology Corporation, Report DOT–OS–200003 (Amended), prepared for the Department of Transportation, March 6, 1973. (Also summarized in *Journal of the Air Pollution Control Association*, Vol. 24, No. 3, March 1974, pp. 216–24.) Other estimates, made by DOT's Transportation Systems Center, suggest that the capital investment required for conversion to small cars plus advanced technology may be greater. (Private communication from J. K. Pollard of the Transportation Systems Center.)

3. See, for example, "Motor Vehicle Fuel Economy Act," U.S. Senate Bill S. 1903, introduced by Senator Hollings, 93rd Congress, First Session, May 30, 1973.

Part I

The Study

Chapter One

Introduction

PURPOSE AND SCOPE

This study has two purposes. One is to develop analytical tools to help evaluate national energy conservation policies for private transportation. The other is to apply the tools in a systematic analysis and comparison of several alternative measures and policy instruments.[a]

Measures and policy instruments affecting private automobile transportation have great potential for energy conservation. The ubiquitous auto accounts for over half of the direct energy consumption in transportation, or roughly 13 percent of total U.S. direct energy use, and its share has been increasing over the past decade. Consequently, policies resulting in even modest percentage savings imply large absolute savings in energy. Moreover, some measures also imply large percentage savings.

Automobile-related conservation measures may be conveniently categorized as: (1) those that improve average auto fuel economy or modal energy efficiency; and (2) those that reduce vehicle miles traveled (VMT) in autos. Improvements in average auto fuel economy can be achieved through technology changes (e.g., new engines or vehicle design, different fuels) or through transportation management or control policies (e.g., speed limits, reduction in traffic congestion, and so forth). Reductions in auto vehicle miles traveled (VMT) can be achieved by measures that raise the cost of driving, foster carpooling, reduce average auto trip length, restrict fuel availability, or improve public transit service or reduce its fares.

[a]We define a conservation measure as an action, phenomenon, or change in behavior by energy users that results in a reduction in direct energy consumption. Policy instruments are the specific means by which government can induce or implement the adoption of conservation measures.

For several reasons, this study focuses solely on measures that improve average auto fuel economy and reduce auto VMT through changes in the cost of driving. Our resources were too limited to treat all classes of measures in both the necessary breadth and depth. Moreover, previous work conducted at The Rand Corporation and elsewhere suggests that measures designed to reduce VMT by inducing modal shifts to public transit may have relatively less favorable impact (energy savings) and relatively more unfavorable impacts (e.g., higher costs, poorer transportation service) than other measures.

Also, analysis of some modal shift measures (e.g., improving urban mass transit) is more meaningful at a regional or local level, so that an evaluation on a national basis would have to begin with analyses in several regions—a task well beyond the resources devoted to this study. Finally, analysis of some modal shift measures is much more difficult, and hence less persuasive, because the available analytical tools and models have serious limitations.

This study also excludes measures and policies designed to reduce average trip length (e.g., changed land use policies), to restrict fuel availability (e.g., gasoline rationing), and to impose transportation controls.

We compare and evaluate alternative measures in terms of a number of criteria that measure energy savings, emissions, cost, transportation service, and other economic and social impacts. Building on previous work elsewhere, our approach has been to provide a consistent analytical framework for focusing on a relatively small number of measures that appear to have promise and to compare them systematically and in some depth.

PREVIOUS WORK

A number of studies of energy conservation measures and policies for private auto transportation have recently been completed. However, the field has been characterized by:

1. A rich engineering literature discussing alternative technological measures, although *systematic* and *consistent* comparisons of such measures are lacking.
2. Few broad systematic attempts to compare alternative measures in terms of their societal impacts (economic, environmental, resource use, indirect energy consumption, social and distributional implications) as well as in terms of their direct impact on energy consumption. Previous efforts usually have been characterized by

breadth (i.e., many measures considered) or depth (i.e., many impacts considered), but not both.

3. Essentially no comparisons of price-change measures with measures that improve average auto fuel economy.
4. Little or no completed work comparing and evaluating alternative policy instruments for implementing or inducing the adoption of attractive measures. Often, such work examines a single policy instrument such as a gasoline price increase.

Much of the previous work focuses solely on technological measures. One of the earlier studies, for the Office of Science and Technology (OST), by the Transportation Energy Panel (an ad hoc interagency group), assessed relevant technology for improving the usage of national energy resources by the transportation sector [1]. In the automotive field, this study focused on alternative advanced developments in heat engines, electric battery development, vehicle design improvements (such as low-loss tires, reduced aerodynamic drag, and optimized engine-transmission combinations), and new fuels. (In addition, new air and air/marine R&D efforts were identified.) Conservation assessment of each measure was made on a per-vehicle basis (i.e., change in miles per gallon). In addition, net change in the cost to the consumer and projected R&D costs over the next several years were estimated. An assessment of a few other impacts (emissions, use of strategic materials, novel fuel compatibility) was made only in qualitative terms.

A more recent study focused narrowly, but in some depth, on the economic impact of mass production of three types of low emissions automotive power systems [2]. Although the main purpose of the study was to examine the economic impacts of technological measures designed for low pollution, energy conservation implications were also examined. Several versions of low pollution conventional spark ignition, gas turbine, and Rankine cycle engines were treated. Economic impacts examined in depth under plausible sets of policy constraints and parametric variations included manufacturing costs, operating and ownership costs, consumer demand for new cars, inter-industry relationships (inputs per unit demand), industry output and employment, resource requirements, and international trade implications.

A technology assessment of the impact of fourteen advanced automobile engines was conducted for the National Science Foundation [3]. Seven scenarios of future mixes of auto production between 1976 and 2000 were constructed, and their impacts on materials resources, energy resources, emission levels, and socioeconomic variables were measured by using the conventional internal combustion engine as the baseline.

Another recent study conducted for the Environmental Protection Agency compared advanced auto engines, improvements in urban mass transit, and urban auto fuel substitution (of LPG or liquid hydrogen for gasoline) in terms of unit and total impacts on energy consumption, emissions, and cost [4]. However, the major focus was on environmental impacts.

A recent informal discussion paper prepared by DOT's Transportation Systems Center and a more recent formal paper addressed a wide variety of energy conservation measures involving all modes of freight and passenger transportation [5]. The private auto transportation measures included improving fuel efficiency (reduced auto size and engine performance, improved power train efficiencies and body design, imposition of speed limits), management measures such as carpooling for work trips, and a variety of modal shift measures (urban auto to transit, walking or bicycling, and intercity auto to bus and rail). As a basis for comparison, rough quantitative impacts on fuel savings, efficiency (Btu per passenger mile), cost (investment cost, user operating cost), and user travel time per unit of distance were estimated. Impacts on demand for non-fuel resources and safety were treated qualitatively.

Evaluation of conservation measures that increase the cost of driving requires a quantitative understanding of the determinants of demand for new cars, total auto ownership, vehicle miles traveled, and gasoline consumption. Past econometric research has sought to measure the influence of prices and income on (1) the demand for new cars and (2) the derived demand for gasoline associated with automobile ownership.[b] New car demand models have all included variables measuring new car price and personal income. None of these demand studies have included gasoline price as a variable explaining the level of new car sales; however, one study has found fuel price to be an important determinant of the distribution of sales among different weight classes of automobiles. By contrast, the econometric models of gasoline demand have included gasoline price explicitly, but generally have treated changes in automobile ownership and efficiency in only an implicit fashion, usually by the inclusion of a lagged gasoline consumption term.

Previous econometric research is not entirely adequate for the purposes of our study. To evaluate conservation measures and policy instruments, the relationships among gasoline price, automobile

[b]A more detailed discussion of previous econometric work is presented in Chapter Three and Appendix D.

ownership, fuel efficiency, and fuel consumption need to be thoroughly understood. The econometric models developed in our study represent an initial effort toward this end.

Finally, a recent study has attempted a limited evaluation of three policy instruments [6]. The effects on new car dollar sales, taxes collected, and fuel consumed over model years 1975 through 1984 (by auto market class), of various policies were examined. These included a regulation banning sales of autos not meeting a prescribed fuel economy standard; a punitive tax on fuel economy paid by consumers at time of purchase; and a less punitive tax based on an 18 mpg standard, phased in over a three-year period.

Given the nature of past relevant work in the field, it seemed clear that our resources would best be applied to devising and applying an analytical framework and tools with which *consistent* and *systematic* comparisons could be made *among* and *between* measures designed to improve average auto fuel economy and to reduce VMT. Our study uses insights gained in previous studies and seeks to evaluate promising measures in greater depth—that is, in terms of a greater variety of impacts. Moreover, considering the paucity of work on policy instrument comparisons, our study also seeks to extend its usefulness by comparing a few instruments designed to induce adoption of the measures found to be most promising.

STRUCTURE OF THE STUDY

Chapter Two describes the conservation measures and policy instruments considered and explains why certain other measures are not considered. Chapter Three provides an overview of the analytical framework and tools developed for screening[c] and evaluating the alternative measures and policy instruments. Chapter Four presents the results of a screening analysis of the technological measures considered. The measures are compared on a per-vehicle basis in terms of five criteria: (1) fuel economy, (2) lifetime energy consumption (to produce and operate an auto over ten years and 100,000 miles), (3) new car selling price, (4) average annualized lifetime cost, and (5) a weighted emissions index.

Chapter Five traces the fleetwide implications over time of the more promising technological measures. Comparisons are then made to account for differences in when measures can be introduced and when their full effects on energy conservation can be felt.

Chapter Six compares several price change measures by using three

---

[c]We define screening as the process by which the few promising measures are identified among the many; these few are then evaluated in more depth.

screening criteria: fleetwide gasoline consumption, total vehicle miles traveled, and new car sales. Finally, Chapter Seven compares alternative policy instruments, presents the results and findings of the study, and draws tentative implications for policy.

NOTES TO CHAPTER ONE

1. *Research and Development Opportunities for Improved Transportation Energy Usage*, Summary Technical Report of the Transportation Energy R&D Goals Panel, Report No. DOT–TSC–OST–73–14, Department of Transportation, September 1972.

2. Robert U. Ayres and Stedman Noble, *Economic Impact of Mass Production of Alternative Low Emissions Automotive Power Systems*, International Research and Technology Corporation, Report DOT–OS–20003 (Amended), prepared for the Department of Transportation, March 6, 1973. (Also summarized in *Journal of the Air Pollution Control Association*, Vol. 24, No. 3, March 1974, pp. 216–24.)

3. *A Technology Assessment of the Transition to Advanced Automotive Propulsion Systems*, HIT–541, Hittman Associates, Inc. (Draft), November 1972.

4. W. E. Jacobsen and J. T. Stone, *Energy/Environmental Factors in Transportation*, MTR–5391 (Draft), The MITRE Corporation, April 1973.

5. D. Rubin, J. K. Pollard et al., *Transportation Energy Conservation Options* (Discussion Paper), Report No. DP–SP–11, Department of Transportation, October 1973, and *Some Transportation Energy Options and Trade-Offs: A Federal View*, presented at California Institute of Technology Seminar on Energy Consumption in Private Transportation, January 8, 1974.

6. *A Study of Industry Response to Policy Measures Designed to Improve Automobile Fuel Economy* (Task II Draft Report), HIT–566, Hittman Associates Inc., prepared for the Council on Environmental Quality, Department of the Interior, Department of Transportation and the Environmental Protection Agency, January 1974.

Chapter Two

Conservation Measures and Policy Instruments Considered

ENERGY CONSERVATION MEASURES

Table 2–1 displays and categorizes the energy conservation measures considered in this study. The table also lists certain measures that fall within the area of interest of this study, as defined in the previous chapter but not analyzed explicitly (see footnote to Table 2–1).

We consider all of the heat engine alternatives currently under discussion or development. In addition, supercharged versions of all

Table 2–1. Auto-Related Energy Conservation Measures

Improve Auto Fuel Economy or Modal Energy Efficiency
   A. Technological
       1. Vehicle Design: Air conditioning removal, radial tires, reduced aerodynamic drag, smaller cars, lower performance (lower power engines), advanced materials, improved power train (continuously variable transmission)
       2. Engines: Emission-controlled conventional engine, rotary, stratified charge, rotary stratified charge, supercharged spark ignition engines (conventional, rotary, stratified charge, rotary stratified charge), diesel, gas turbine, Rankine, Stirling, electric[a]
       3. Fuels: Methanol and Hydrogen

   B. Transportation Management or Controls
       1. Lower speed limits
       2. Reduce congestion (improved traffic flow controls)[a]

Reduce Vehicle Miles Traveled
   A. Raise price of driving, price of gasoline, price of new cars, price of used cars
   B. Carpooling for work trips[a]
   C. Reduce average urban trip length[a]
   D. Restrict fuel availability[a]

---

[a]Not analyzed explicitly in this study.

27

spark ignition type engines are considered as ways to reduce engine and body size for the same performance. Previous applications of supercharging options by American manufacturers, such as Chevrolet's Corvair and Studebaker's Avanti, were intended to *increase* performance (acceleration and speed) while holding engine size and body constant.

We have not explicitly considered the electric auto for a number of reasons. The most recent study of electric propulsion indicates that electric cars that could be introduced in the 1980s will have no worse, or only slightly better, energy efficiency than autos with today's conventional engine, but their range and speed are quite limited; conversely, if autos with conventional engines were designed to the electric car's range and speed, they would be more energy efficient [1]. Because our study included only potential conservation measures that approximate today's auto comfort and performance standards, we have omitted electric propulsion as a measure. Moreover, even if one were to consider the electric auto its evaluation should be on a regional or urban level, because its range and speed are best fitted for urban travel. Thus, a national evaluation of electric propulsion would have to be scaled up from studies of its use in several urban areas—a task beyond the scope of this study.

Minor modifications to today's conventional engine and vehicle design, such as fuel injection (into the inlet manifold) or more economical rear-end ratios, are not considered because their impacts on fuel economy are small, and because our study emphasizes longer range measures that have greater potential for energy conservation. Also, we do not consider a system currently under investigation with a power system that generates enough hydrogen to allow operation at very lean mixtures and reduces NO_x formation [2]. Such a system shows promise as a way to reduce emissions and may offer an improvement in fuel economy. However, our present state of knowledge is inadequate to make quantitative estimates of its fuel economy. Consequently, we have not considered it in this study. If further investigation confirms that there is a potential for improved fuel economy, this system would become of interest, particularly because it may be possible to apply it to autos already in the fleet, as well as to new production.

Radial tires *are* considered, although their effect on energy conservation is modest because, as with lower speed limits, they are upon us and should be included in one of the reference cases with which other measures are compared.

We have selected methanol and hydrogen as long term fuel alternatives to gasoline for the conventional engine. These two fuels are suitable for use in autos, could be available in large quantities, and impinge on a different resource base—that is, our large resources of coal or nuclear energy—for powering the auto. (Of course, we also evaluate diesel engines with diesel fuel and the Stirling and Rankine engines with less highly refined fuels they can use.)

We do not explicitly consider carpooling or traffic flow control measures because they are best evaluated at the regional or local level. A national assessment of such measures would have to be scaled up from a series of studies in various urban areas.

We do not explicitly analyze such measures for reducing VMT as reducing average urban trip length or restricting fuel availability. The former implies changes in land use—either migration back to the central city, or relocation of industry to the suburbs—rather than a continuation of the trend toward suburban growth. Again, a national evaluation of such measures would have to be scaled up from a series of analyses in various urban areas—a task beyond this study's scope.

For each technological conservation measure, we have estimated when it could be introduced into the fleet and the change in cost associated with it. These dates represent the earliest times when the necessary research and development could be completed and plants converted. No allowance is made for delays due to a firm's desire to minimize financial risk or delays caused by unavailability of capital.

Because our estimates of introduction dates are necessarily uncertain, we have considered the measures in three groups with introduction dates of 1975, 1980, and 1985. Measures adopted in 1980 and 1985 are assumed to affect 20 percent of production per year until the entire line is converted.

The incremental cost of each measure is estimated in terms of its effect on the per-vehicle cost of ownership. These estimates assume mass production of the components and thus implicitly include an allowance for the cost of tooling and plant construction. We have not estimated these costs explicitly, because they would be of interest only if they involved such large capital investments as to prevent or slow the acceptance of a measure by the industry. Based on studies of the auto industry's ability to convert to new technology [3], the 20 percent per year rate of introduction we assume appears to be reasonable.

A brief description of each conservation measure considered follows. Appendixes B, C, D, and E describe the inputs associated with each conservation measure and used in our analytical models.

Air Conditioning

Auto air conditioning results in increased fuel consumption due both to the power required to run it and its additional weight (over 100 pounds). Air conditioning operated at its maximum may require as much as ten horsepower and may reduce fuel economy by over 20 percent. There is little information on the extent to which automobile air conditioners are operated, but EPA has suggested that their use may result in an average loss of fuel economy of 9 percent, in addition to the loss due to the weight of the unit. Air conditioning also results in an increase in the auto selling price and in the annual operating cost due to the poorer fuel economy. While it would be possible to conserve fuel by restricting or eliminating future production of air conditioners, we have assumed that public demand is so strong that cars in each size class will continue to be equipped with air conditioning in the same ratio as at present. We have, however, eliminated air conditioning from the very small "urban" cars considered.

Low Acceleration

Endowing an automobile with lower maximum acceleration by installing an engine with less power can improve fuel economy, because the smaller engine will operate at a higher mean effective pressure. The possible gain from doing this depends on the throttle settings at which the original engine is operating during normal driving. The engine in a normal full-size auto (designed to accelerate from zero to sixty mph in about eleven seconds) will be operating at less than 10 percent of its maximum power in low speed urban driving. Under these conditions, its specific fuel consumption may be 50 percent higher than its minimum specific fuel consumption, and the use of a smaller engine can result in substantial savings in fuel consumption. On the other hand, if the engine size has been reduced to a point where it is operating at 20 percent maximum power during much of its normal driving, further reduction in size will produce only modest improvements in fuel economy.

In addition to improving specific fuel consumption, a smaller engine leads to weight savings that are reflected throughout the entire design of the auto and thus results in a lighter, lower cost auto.

Radial Tires

Radial tires can effect a 20 percent reduction of rolling friction at low speeds typical of most urban driving [4]. While radials are initially more expensive than conventional tires, their longer life and savings in fuel should make them less costly overall [5]. At present, both General Motors and Ford, who account for about 80 percent of the new car output, plan to equip virtually all of their cars with radials by 1975 [6]. How fast owners of older cars will change to radial tires is less certain.

In our study we have assumed that all new cars from 1975 on will be equipped with radial tires and that owners of all cars less than five years old in 1975 will equip them with radial tires when their present tires wear out and continue to use radials thereafter.

Aerodynamic Improvements

A considerable amount of wind tunnel testing has been conducted on the aerodynamic effects on the handling characteristics of various types of auto bodies, and extensive explorations of drag reduction techniques have also been made [7]. As a result of this work it is possible to make fairly precise estimates of the drag reductions obtainable by minor and major body modifications and by changes in body size. However, the effect of these changes on fuel consumption is dependent on the driving cycle assumed and on the accuracy of our estimates of engine and transmission characteristics.

We consider three levels of drag: one that is representative of a typical present-day design (no reduction); one that could be obtained by relatively *minor* body modifications (about 24 percent less drag than a typical current design); and one that could be obtained by *major* modifications to the body. This major change results in a 50 percent reduction in drag, but also involves an increase in body weight, due primarily to a complete fairing of the underbody.

We have assumed that minor aerodynamic changes can be accomplished at no change in cost or weight and could be introduced by 1975; these changes amount to a typical body style change. No assumption as to the earliest possible introduction date for major aerodynamic improvements has been made, because we do not feel that this is a viable measure (see Chapter Four).

Trunkless Body Design

One way to improve fuel economy of autos having the seating capacity, spaciousness, and performance of a full-size car is to eliminate the conventional trunk compartment. This results in a reduction in body weight, which in turn allows the engine size required for a specified acceleration to be reduced. We examine the consequences of eliminating the trunk on all standard auto sizes (full, intermediate, compact, subcompact). In doing this, we assume that such cars could be introduced in 1980, since the changes are roughly equivalent to those involved in introducing a new smaller model.

Urban Cars

We consider also both a two-passenger and a one-passenger urban auto. These autos have the same longitudinal seat dimensions as the front seat of a standard subcompact, but the two-passenger car is slightly narrower than a subcompact, and the one-passenger car is wide enough to accommodate only one person. Neither has any trunk space, and we have designed them to have the same acceleration as a subcompact. As with the trunkless designs, we assume that these cars could be introduced as early as 1980 if desired.

Advanced Materials

The use of both glass fiber reinforced plastics and aluminum for automobile construction has been investigated [8]. Both materials offer the possibility of lighter weight and greater corrosion resistance. Both require more energy in the manufacture of the material than does steel, although aluminum offers the possibility of greater scrap recovery due to its corrosion resistance and the fact that its market value is sufficient to encourage more sophisticated scrap recovery methods.

We have investigated the use of aluminum as representative of the potential of new materials. Following the Alcoa study cited, we have restricted the likely near term use of aluminum to the hood, trunk lid, doors, front fenders, and bumpers. Conceivably, with more research and road experience, more extensive use of aluminum might be made in time. We also assumed the use of aluminum in the engine. We estimate that a 28 percent reduction in body weight and a 24 percent reduction in engine weight will result from the use of aluminum, which in turn would result in improved fuel economy. However, this gain is partially offset by the greater amount of energy required to produce aluminum (we use 107,000 Btu/lb of aluminum as opposed to 27,400 Btu/lb of sheet steel). We also assume that 70 percent of the aluminum is recovered in scrap.

Information on the cost of using aluminum in automobile body construction is sparse. Following the Cochran study, we have assumed that the cost of producing a body of given dimensions, or an engine of given power, is the same whether aluminum or steel is used.

While we find that the extensive use of aluminum can result in significant overall savings in energy and could be combined with other technical improvements, we have not pursued its use beyond this initial analysis. We made this decision because such extensive use of aluminum would require an expansion of the aluminum industry, raising uncertainties about the rate at which changes could be introduced and about other economic and social impacts. In addition, the use of new materials may raise safety questions beyond the scope of this study.

Advanced Transmissions: The CVT

Our study compares advanced technology options with a base case that includes a conventional, three-speed automatic transmission. While a manual transmission will give slightly better mileage if properly handled, it has not been considered here because it is now in the minority (93 percent of American-built cars were equipped with automatic transmission in the 1972 model year) and is probably unacceptable to many drivers.

The advanced transmission we considered is the continuously variable transmission (CVT) that allows any gear ratio between engine and wheels to be selected at any time. The selection is done automatically to maximize fuel economy, without exceeding the allowable NO_x emissions. There are two general types of continuously variable transmissions currently under serious consideration—hydromechanical and friction drive [9]. The friction type may ultimately prove simpler, but probably will be somewhat less efficient than the hydromechanical and may have problems attaining durability of the friction materials. The more complicated hydromechanical type may be more efficient and has the advantage that many of its parts are compatible with those of today's conventional, automatic transmission. Both types have demonstrated substantial savings in fuel consumption when installed in test automobiles. We have based most of our work on the hydromechanical type, but we feel that our results may be generally representative of either type. The major problems remaining in the development of the CVT are associated with the design and cost of the control mechanism, and for the friction type, the problems involve adequacy of the materials. Based on discussions with Mr. Peter Huntly of the Orshansky Corporation, we estimate the earliest possible date for introduction of the CVT to be 1980, and the cost of a CVT to be 20 percent greater than a comparable three speed automatic transmission.

Modifications to Internal Combustion Engines

We examine two ways of improving the fuel economy of the conventional internal combustion engine—charge stratification and supercharging. In addition, we examine the effects of both of these modifications on reciprocating and rotary engines. The primary advantage of charge stratification so far as fuel economy is concerned is that it is possible to use a higher compression ration without preignition. Thus, both supercharging and charge stratification result in operation at higher mean effective pressures in the cylinder. There are two possible problems in this approach—pre-ignition and excessive NO_x Generation. Pre-ignition can be eliminated completely if fuel injection directly into the cylinder is used; if not, it is usually necessary to reduce the compression ratio when supercharging is used to prevent pre-ignition. Even so, there are data indicating that gains in fuel economy can be made without using fuel injection [10]. The situation with regard to NO_x generation is less certain, but some data [11] indicate that substantial gains in fuel economy can be made by increasing mean effective pressure without an unacceptable increase in grams of NO_x per mile. It must be remembered that while an increase in mean effective pressure will result in higher temperatures in the cylinder, and presumably higher NO_x formation, it also results in an increase in power output per unit of airflow. Thus, a given power is achieved with less airflow, so that even though the NO_x generated per pound of airflow is greater, the grams of NO_x per mile may not increase.

We consider the use of supercharging without fuel injection (and with a reduction in compression ratio) in both conventional and rotary engines.

We then consider stratified charge engines using fuel injection, both with and without supercharging [12]. Again, both reciprocating and rotary engines are considered.

Rotary engines are lighter and more compact than conventional reciprocating engines of the same power [13], and these characteristics can be exploited to reduce fuel consumption. Current mass-produced rotary engines have poor fuel consumption due primarily to leakage past the seals. This situation can be expected to improve in the future: some prototype engines have demonstrated specific fuel consumption approaching that of good reciprocating engines [14]. The work by Curtiss–Wright has demonstrated that the rotary engine can be stratified successfully when fuel injection is used [15]. Stratification of carbureted rotarys may also be possible, as the NATO report indicates.

In our work, we have assumed that the specific fuel consumption of a rotary engine can match that of a reciprocating engine in either conventional or stratified engines.

We have not uncovered any data on the effect of supercharging on a rotary engine. However, we have estimated the effect of super-charging by assuming that it modifies the performance of a rotary engine in the same way it does a reciprocating engine.

While all the basic technologies considered (supercharging, charge stratification, rotary engine design, and fuel injection) have been the subject of substantial amounts of research, the combinations of these approaches that will result in the greatest fuel economy have yet to be determined. It will require a concerted research effort to do this and to demonstrate the final level of fuel economy. Considering the nature of the auto industry, it is unlikely that all manufacturers will arrive at the same technical solution at the same time. If motivated by proper policy decisions, however, they should eventually all reach comparable fuel economies. We have used our estimate of a rotary, supercharged, stratified charge engine to establish a level of fuel economy that we consider the best attainable with the internal combustion, gasoline fueled engine. We have assumed that, if pushed vigorously, this engine, or an engine having similar performance, might be first introduced in 1980.

The costs of engine modification are highly uncertain. We have estimated the effect of the major modifications on the engine cost per pound and on the cost for a given maximum horsepower as shown in Table 2–2.

Diesel Engines

Diesel autos have demonstrated better fuel economy than conventional gasoline powered autos, although they are usually designed with lower horsepower-to-weight ratios (and hence lower acceleration) than their gasoline powered counterparts. Tests of emissions of current diesel autos and calculations of emissions from diesel autos powered to give higher acceleration indicate that they can meet the ultimate statutory emission limits on hydrocarbons and carbon monoxide, but may exceed the NO_x standard. They could, however, meet the interim NO_x requirement of 2.0 grams per mile. There are still unanswered questions about the degree of acceptance of the odor, smoke, noise, and possible health hazards due to sulfates and organic compounds in the diesel exhaust.

Diesel engines are substantially heavier and more expensive than gasoline engines of the same power. In our work, we have required that the diesel meet the same acceleration requirements as comparable gasoline powered cars. We have also assumed that if diesel cars were to constitute a large fraction of the fleet, the price of diesel fuel

Table 2–2. Relative Cost of Engine Modifications

Modification	Relative Cost per Pound	Relative Cost for a Given Horsepower
Conventional Spark Ignition	1.0	1.0
Supercharging	1.1	0.8
Stratified Charge (with fuel injection)	1.3	1.24
Rotary Design	1.0	0.53

would be adjusted to the same level per Btu of energy content as gasoline. These two assumptions act to offset some of the advantages in energy consumption and cost of ownership often associated with diesel cars.

We have based our work on a turbosupercharged diesel, which appears to offer the greatest potential for fuel economy. We have estimated this diesel to weigh 36 to 40 percent more than a conventional spark ignition engine of the same power and to cost 1.5 to 2.1 times as much. (The spread is due to engine size—we estimate larger diesel engines to be relatively heavier and more expensive.) We have assumed, however, that diesel engine maintenance cost is only 60 percent that of a conventional engine.

Advanced Engine Types Other than Internal Combustion Types

We consider Rankine ("steam"), gas turbine, and Stirling engines. All these engine types are currently the subject of intensive development efforts. Consequently, it is somewhat early to estimate the levels of fuel consumption they may ultimately achieve. We have tried to picture the performance that may be achieved within the next few years by the development programs now under way. Further improvements may ultimately be possible, but cannot be estimated quantitatively at this time.

The gas turbine performance presented here is based on a free turbine design that uses regeneration and variable stator blades and operates at a maximum turbine temperature in the neighborhood of 1850°F [16]. We use data on designs developed by Chrysler [17] and General Electric [18], and a survey of gas turbine characteristics by The Aerospace Corporation [19]. We have also assumed that a continuously variable transmission is used, because the development of a new engine is a sufficiently large effort to justify the development of a transmission to match it. At present, fuel economy of the gas turbine approaches that of a conventional spark ignition engine. Emissions of hydrocarbon and carbon monoxide can meet the ultimate statutory requirements, but NO_x emissions may be higher than the ultimate requirements, although they should be less than the interim requirements. Current research on gas turbine engines is aimed at reducing specific fuel consumption at low powers by improving component efficiencies, endurance testing to evaluate the durability of the engine, investigating the use of ceramic materials in the regenerator, developing combustors that will reduce NO_x generation, and developing techniques for the mass production of turbine wheels.

Four types of Rankine engines [20] have been under research (two types of working fluids and two types of expanders). All appear capable of meeting or exceeding the program goal of one-half the ultimate statutory emissions standards. At present, all have fuel economies comparable with a conventional gasoline engine. Research has recently been narrowed to a system using water as a working substance, operating at $1000°F$ and 1000 psig pressure, and using a reciprocating expander. We have based our work on this type [21]. As with the gas turbine, we have assumed that a CVT will be developed with the Rankine engine.

At present, research on the Rankine cycle is directed toward improving fuel economy through improved component efficiencies, reducing the size of the condenser by the use of very small hydraulic diameters, and solving the freezing and lubrication problems.

As with any external burning system, the Rankine engine can use a very wide range of fuels—much wider than the spark ignition internal combustion engine, the diesel engine, or the gas turbine.

The Stirling engine is a closed cycle engine using a gaseous working fluid, usually either hydrogen or helium [22]. In principle, it combines the low emissions of an external burning system with a thermal efficiency that is superior to an internal combustion engine. Like all external burning systems, the Stirling engine can use a wide range of fuels. Other advantages include very low noise and vibration, no oil consumption, reliable starting under all conditions, and, hopefully, economy of operation due to improved fuel consumption and a lack of carbon deposits on the moving parts of the engine. The primary problems with the engine are associated with keeping its weight and bulk down to a level satisfactory for automobile use. To do this, it is necessary to design an automotive Stirling engine to operate at higher rpm's than the engines designed for stationary use or for installation in buses. As a result, the losses associated with pumping the working gas become greater and some of the potential efficiency of the Stirling engine is lost. This problem is eased somewhat if hydrogen is used instead of helium as a working fluid, but the use of hydrogen brings problems of metal embrittlement and containment that have not yet been fully explored.

We have based our work on the design currently under development by the N.V. Philips Corporation and the Ford Motor Company [23]. This design is still in an early stage and represents a very substantial improvement in weight and bulk over earlier Stirling engines [24]. If future development work leads to a somewhat heavier engine, our estimates will be correspondingly optimistic.

Ford has estimated the first production of a Stirling powered version of the Torino might occur in 1982; however, since this announcement, the engine development has been delayed. Because of this delay and because of the extreme weight saving Ford is attempting to accomplish, we have assumed that the earliest likely introduction date is 1985.

We estimate the Stirling engine to cost twice as much as a conventional spark ignition engine of the same weight, and from 2.2 to 2.4 times as much as a conventional engine of the same power. Although it is possible that Stirling engine maintenance costs may be low because no carbon deposits are formed on the moving parts, we have not assumed any reduction because these savings may be offset by the increased complexity of the engine.

Advanced Fuels

We have considered two advanced fuels—methanol and liquid hydrogen. Both of these fuels can be obtained from non-petroleum resources, methanol from coal, through a reaction with oxygen and steam, and hydrogen by the electrolysis of water. While both fuels can be obtained from other sources, these appear to be the most interesting from the point of view of broadening our energy base and making use of electrical energy that may become abundant with the widespread availability of nuclear power and with the successful development of fusion energy sources.

Minor modifications will allow both methanol and hydrogen to be burned in conventional internal combustion engines with the same efficiency as gasoline [25].

One other possibly interesting fuel is ethanol, which can be obtained from vegetable matter and thus provides a method by which solar energy could be used to power autos. Its properties as a fuel are somewhat similar to those of methanol. Before its use could be seriously considered, it would be necessary to estimate the amount that could be produced annually in the United States. We have not attempted to do this, because this involves decisions regarding the allocation of farm land for producing fuel instead of food.

Methanol can be burned in a pure form or can be blended with gasoline up to 25 or 30 percent by volume, which thus extends the petroleum energy available. We have considered only the use of pure methanol, however, because this would allow us to rely on our resources of coal rather than petroleum for auto energy.

A possibility that does not appear to have been explored thoroughly is the use of higher compression ratios with methanol than are feasible with gasoline. The auto ignition temperature in air for methanol is 870°F compared with 430°F for gasoline and the effective octane number of methanol is 106 compared with 91 for our present unleaded gasoline. This suggests that higher efficiencies might be obtained with methanol through the use of higher compression ratios. However, due to a lack of data on methanol in high compression ratio engines, we have made no allowance for this effect in our work.

Research on emissions from methanol fueled vehicles is somewhat sparse and not entirely consistant [26]. In general, the results indicate that emissions of hydrocarbons and carbon monoxide will be slightly less than those produced by gasoline. Results on NO_x are less clear, with some data indicating about the same NO_x levels as gasoline, while work at Stanford University using a Gremlin entered in the 1970 Clean Air Car Race resulted in NO_x emissions low enough to meet 1976 statutory requirements. Some work has also indicated that the use of pure methanol may result in the production of formaldehyde in the exhaust.

Methanol has only about 40 percent of the heating value of gasoline on a weight basis and about 45 percent on a volume basis. Thus, the miles per gallon of methanol are low in comparison with those we are accustomed to think of in connection with gasoline. The efficiency, however, is the same, so that the miles per Btu are the same except for the penalties associated with the need to carry a greater weight of methanol to obtain a specified range.

While the use of methanol would allow us to make use of our coal resources to power autos, it does not result in overall energy conservation. The process of converting coal to methanol is only about 60 percent efficient [27] (coal containing 100 Btu is required to produce methanol containing 60 Btu). This compares with the 90 percent efficiency of refining gasoline. In addition, the lower density of methanol may increase the energy required to distribute it.

The cost of producing methanol from coal in the large quantities considered here is very uncertain. However, it has been estimated [28] that it may ultimately approach the present cost of obtaining methanol from petroleum. We have used a cost of $2.10 per million Btu [29], which is today's cost of producing methanol from petroleum; the corresponding figure for gasoline is $1.32 per million Btu. We have also included an additional cost of distribution, obtained by increasing the distribution cost of gasoline in the ratio of the gallons/Btu of the two fuels.

The use of hydrogen as a fuel involves somewhat greater technical problems and uncertainty than the use of methanol. The storing of adequate amounts of hydrogen in the auto, and the distribution and storage of fuel, are tractable but nonetheless significant technical challenges. Three methods of storing hydrogen in the auto are presently being considered; it may be stored as a high pressure gas, a liquid, or in chemical composition with various metals, of which magnesium may be the most promising. At present, it appears that storage in the liquid form is probably lighter than either of the other methods and requires no greater volume for the same Btu content [30]. The storage of liquid hydrogen at the cryogenic temperatures required without excessive boil off requires the development of highly insulated Dewar type fuel tanks. However, the design of satisfactory tanks appears feasible [31], although much development and road testing will be required before a fully practical tank is obtained.

We have assumed that hydrogen is stored in liquid form in the auto and is produced by the electrolysis of water, distributed as a gas through pipelines to the major distribution areas, then liquified and distributed locally by truck to the service stations. The feasibility of each step in this chain appears established; however, the costs involved are highly uncertain, and it will be necessary to develop techniques for handling hydrogen safely. Hydrogen can be obtained from coal or petroleum, but we have chosen to consider the electrolysis of water because this is a way to free ourselves from dependence on either coal or petroleum. It requires a plentiful source of electricity, which may become available early from nuclear and later from fusion energy.

We have used a cost of 20 cents per gallon for liquid hydrogen distributed to the consumer. This is $3.30 per million Btu for production of hydrogen gas by electrolysis [32] plus 70 cents per million Btu for liquification and $2.60 per million Btu for distribution.

Hydrogen use does not imply overall energy conservation, because the energy of combustion must be added to the fuel (by electrolysis). Its advantage lies in that it allows us make (indirect) use of nuclear or fusion energy in autos rather than petroleum.

Price Change Measures

We consider three types of price change measures; those that increase (1) gasoline price, (2) average new car price, and (3) average (new and used car) ownership price. The econometric models developed in this study can deal with these measures only at the aggregate, national level, whether they arise from market forces, taxation, or regulation.

POLICY INSTRUMENTS

Governmental policy instruments in the automotive field may be directed at manufacturers, consumers, or middlemen. They may be regulatory in nature, impose taxation, or offer subsidies. Those directed at manufacturers provide incentives (e.g., research and development subsidies, tax credits on sales of a new product, or accelerated depreciation of new capital equipment) or impose restrictions or restraints (e.g., an outright ban on the production or sale of a product not meeting prescribed standards, imposition of production ceilings on various products, or imposition of graduated taxes on fuel efficiency, horsepower, weight, or size). Those aimed at influencing the ownership or use of autos by consumers also provide incentives (e.g., direct subsidies or tax credits), provide disincentives (e.g., taxes on fuel inefficient autos, fuel taxes, differential credit standards or rates for particular vehicles) or are of the non-price variety (e.g., rationing, restriction of autos to certain zones, or improved warranty on new products to handle transition problems). Finally, those directed at middlemen might include, for example, regulation of insurance rates—that is, cheaper for carpools and dearer for autos used by single occupants and driven long distances.

Given the nature of our analytic framework, the analytical tools developed, and the results of our evaluation of alternative conservation measures, we have selected the following classes of policy instruments for analysis:

1. Increased gasoline excise tax;
2. Mandated technological changes;
3. A mandated average fuel economy standard for new cars;
4. A mandated maximum vehicle weight standard for new cars;
5. Various combinations of the above;
6. An average increase in the new car sales tax or registration fee;
7. An average increase in the used car sales tax or registration fee.

Graduated taxes on new car fuel efficiency, weight, or horsepower are now being widely discussed. For example, one piece of legislation introduced in the Congress in 1973 combined the establishment of fuel economy standards for the aggregate of all new motor vehicles produced during a specified period with a graduated fuel conservation fee to be paid by the manufacturer, depending on the degree to which fuel economy actually exceeds the fuel economy standard [33]. However, because the econometric models we developed in this study estimate impacts only at the aggregate national level, we cannot deal quantitatively with new and used car taxes or registration fees that are graduated by fuel economy, horsepower, or weight.

NOTES TO CHAPTER TWO

1. Graham Hagey and W. F. Hamilton, "Impact of Electric Cars for the Los Angeles Intrastate Air Quality Control Region," unpublished paper. Hagey was with U.S. EPA; now his agency is part of ERDA. Hamilton is with General Research Corp. in Santa Barbara, California.

2. Harry E. Cotrill, *High Efficiency, Low Pollution Engine Development*, paper presented at the Seminar on Energy Consumption in Private Transportation, Sponsored by the Department of Transportation at the California Institute of Technology, January 1974, and *Symposium on Low Pollution Power Systems Development*, NATO Document No. 32, October 1973.

3. Robert U. Ayres and Stedman Noble, *Economic Impact of Mass Production of Alternative Low Emissions Automatic Power Systems*, International Research and Technology Corporation, Report DOT–OS–20003 (Amended), prepared for the Department of Transportation, March 6, 1973.

4. See J. D. Walter, "Energy Losses in Tires," presentation at the *Seminar on Energy Consumption in Private Transportation*, sponsored by the Department of Transportation at the California Institute of Technology, January 1974; and K. G. Peterson and R. E. Rasmussen, "What Makes a Good Radial Tire?" *Automotive Engineering*, June 1973.

5. *Consumer Reports*, August 1971.

6. Automotive News section of *Automotive Industries*, March 1973.

7. William H. Bettes, "On the Design of Automobiles for Lower Air Resistance," presentation at the *Seminar on Energy Conservation in Private Transportation*, sponsored by the Department of Transportation at the California Institute of Technology, January 1974; and Sighard F. Hoerner, *Aerodynamic Drag*, (The Obberbein Press, Dayton, Ohio, 1951.)

8. See "How Chevrolet Designed the XP–989," *Automotive Engineering*, March 1974, and C. N. Cochran, "Aluminum—Villain or Hero in the Energy Crisis," *Automotive Engineering*, June 1973.

9. See "Third Summary Report, Automotive Systems Contractors Coordination Meeting," U.S. Environmental Protection Agency, June 1972; "Hydromechanical Passenger Car Transmission—Performance Analysis," Orshansky Transmission Corporation, Report 404, May 1973; "Hydro-mechanical Passenger Car," Orshansky Transmission Corporation, Report 403, May 1973; "Effect of a Traction Drive Transmission on Fuel Economy," testimony before the Senate Commerce Committee by Marcel Gres, Vice President, Tractor, Inc., June 1973.

10. "Turbosupercharged Small Engines for Passenger Car Fuel Economy," personal communication from Mr. C. E. McInerney, AiResearch Industrial Division, Garrett Corporation, Los Angeles, California.

11. "Hydromechanical Passenger Car Transmission—Performance Analysis," Orshansky Transmission Corporation, Report 404, May 1973.

12. See E. Mitchell, A. Alperstein, J. M. Cobb, and C. H. Faist, "A Stratified Charge Multifuel Military Engine—A Progress Report," SAE Paper No. 720051,

presented at the Automotive Engineering Congress, January 1972; and A. Simko, M. A. Choma, and L. L. Repko, "Exhaust Emission Control by the Ford Programmed Combustion Process—PROCO," SAE Paper No. 720052, presented at the Automotive Engineering Congress, January 1972.

13. *Final Report, Hybrid Heat Engine/Electric Systems Study, Vol. I*, The Aerospace Corporation, June 1971.

14. See *Curtiss–Wright's Development Status of the Stratified Charge Rotating Combustion Engine*, Charles Jones and Harold Lamping, Curtiss–Wright Corporation, June 1971, and *Symposium on Low Pollution Power Systems Development*, NATO Document No. 32, October 1973.

15. According to the *Christian Science Monitor*, August 26, 1974, p. 7, Toyo Kogyo is also developing an engine of this type.

16. *Third Summary Report—Automotive Power Systems Contractors Coordination Meeting*, Division of Advanced Automotive Power System Development, U.S. Environmental Protection Agency, June 1972.

17. W. I. Carry, J. V. Gross, and C. E. Wagner, "Chrysler Corporation Progress Report, Baseline Gas Turbine Program," presented at Gas Turbine Contractors Coordination Meeting, Division of Advanced Automotive Power System Development, U.S. Environmental Protection Agency, June 7, 1973.

18. "Automobile Gas Turbine—Optimum Cycle Selection Study," presented at AAPS Development Coordination Meeting, General Electric Company, June 1972.

19. *Final Report, Hybrid Heat Engine/Electric Systems Study, Vol. I*, The Aerospace Corporation, June 1971.

20. See NATO Document No. 32; and Arthur W. Gardiner, "Automotive Steam Power, Where it Stands Today," *Automotive Engineering*, April 1973.

21. Presentation by Scientific Energy Systems Corporation, Rankine Cycle Contractors Coordination Meeting, Division of Advanced Automotive Power Systems Development, U.S. Environmental Protection Agency, June 7, 1973.

22. See NATO Document No. 32; *Present State-of-the-Art of the Philips Stirling Engine*, H. C. J. van Beukering and H. Fokker, SAE Paper No. 730646, June 1973; and *Environmental Characteristics of Stirling Engines and Their Present State of Development in Germany and Sweden*, C. B. S. Alm, S. G. Carlqvist, P. F. Kuhlmann, K. H. Silverqvist, and F. A. Zacharia, Preprint of paper presented at CIMAC Congress, April 1973.

23. Norman D. Postma, Rob Van Giessel, and Fritz Reinink, *The Stirling Engine for Passenger Car Application* SAE Paper No. 730648, June 1973.

24. *Final Report, Hybrid Heat Engine/Electric Systems Study, Vol. I*, The Aerospace Corporation, June 1971.

25. See Derek P. Gregory and Robert B. Rosenberg, "Synthetic Fuels for Transportation and National Energy Needs," Institute of Gas Technology, May 1973; and A. L. Austin, "A Survey of Hydrogen's Potential as a Vehicular Fuel," University of California, June 1972.

26. Gregory and Rosenberg, "Synthetic Fuels for Transportation and National Energy Needs."

27. Personal communication from D. Gartner of the Du Pont Corporation.

28. Gregory and Rosenberg, "Synthetic Fuels for Transportation and National Energy Needs."

29. Ibid.

30. Ibid; and Austin, "A Survey of Hydrogen's Potential as a Vehicular Fuel."

31. Joseph G. Finegold, "Liquid Hydrogen as an Automotive Fuel," University of California at Los Angeles, October 1973.

32. Derek P. Gregory, "The Hydrogen Economy," *Scientific American*, January 1973.

33. U.S. Senate Bill S. 1903, 93rd Congress, First Session, May 30, 1973, referred to the Committee on Commerce.

Chapter Three

Overview of the Analytical Framework

OVERVIEW

Figure 3-1 displays an overview of the methodological framework and the interactions among the components. The overall analytic framework and each of the major methodological tools used in the analysis will be discussed below. Subsequent chapters present the substantive results of each stage of the analysis displayed in the figure.

The two classes of measures (technological and price changes) are screened separately, although, as we explain later, the nature of the models used require some interactions among these screening efforts. The object of separate screening is to identify the few promising short-, medium-, and long-term measures in each class that need to be compared and evaluated in more depth.

The screening analysis for technological measures is done in two stages. In the first stage, a large variety of diverse measures are screened on a per-vehicle basis by using a set of five screening criteria. The major analytical tool used in this stage is a specially developed, computerized planning model that produces generalized automobile designs. The model relates natural resource and energy requirements and the cost of auto ownership to the size, performance, and design characteristics. Rapid, efficient, and accurate estimates of a wide variety of auto designs are main features of this model. Four of the screening criteria used are produced by this model. The fifth, a weighted index of emissions per mile, is produced exogenously. In this first stage of screening, we can identify among many measures the few that show the greatest promise, based on the five screening criteria. In general, we seek measures that dominate on

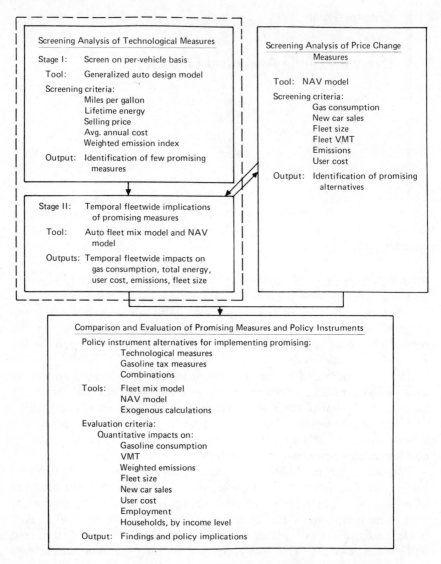

Figure 3–1. Overview of Methodological Framework: Components and Interactions.

all criteria, although where there is no clear dominance, we carry several promising measures through the subsequent stages of the analysis.

The second stage in the screening analysis of technological measures is designed to reveal the temporal fleetwide implications of introducing the promising measures identified in the previous stage. This stage also permits grouping and comparing the promising measures by when their full effects on energy conservation can be felt, because the time required to complete research and development and to convert auto plants differs among some measures. The major analytical tool is the specially developed, computerized Auto Fleet Mix Model, although certain inputs to the model are produced as outputs of the NAV Model discussed below. The Auto Fleet Mix Model relates the overall auto fleet fuel consumption, total energy required, emissions, and total cost of auto ownership to changes in the number, nature, and mix of autos produced each year. All the impacts of each measure considered in this stage of the analysis are produced by this model, but certain *inputs* to the mix model, such as annual aggregate new car sales and annual auto scrappage rate, are outputs produced by the NAV Model—the econometric demand model described below.

The major analytical tool developed in the study, to screen price change measures is called the NAV Model. It takes new car sales/auto ownership/vehicle miles traveled, and provides estimates of short and long run effects of changes in the price of gasoline, new cars, and used cars, on new car sales, total (new and used) auto ownership, used car price, vehicle miles traveled, and gasoline consumed. These impact criteria are used in screening various measures. The output of this screening stage is the identification of a few promising price change measures.

The final stage of analysis compares and evaluates policy instruments for implementing promising measures. We consider *combinations* of technological and price change measures over time as well, because the latter can be implemented in the short run, whereas many of the former will only achieve their full effects in the medium or long term. This stage of analysis compares *all* of the promising alternatives in greater depth—that is, in terms of a greater variety of impacts. For example, in addition to the criteria measured in the Auto Fleet Mix Model and the NAV Model, a variety of exogenous calculations are made to estimate other quantitative impacts such as fleet wide weighted emissions, employment in five auto-related sectors, and income distributional effects.

THE GENERALIZED AUTOMOBILE DESIGN MODEL

The major analytical tool used in screening technological measures on a per-vehicle basis is the Generalized Automobile Design model. It relates automobile resource and energy requirements and the cost of auto ownership to the auto size, performance, and design characteristics (i.e., type of engine, transmission, fuel, and so forth). The purpose of the model is to allow the effects of changes in auto size, performance, or design to be assessed when one of these variables is changed while the others are held constant.

While we assume that autos having equivalent acceleration and passenger and trunk compartments are equally attractive to owners, we recognize that the ride quality of an automobile is to some extent a function of its weight. Because many of the design changes made to improve fuel economy result in a reduction of the weight of an auto of fixed acceleration and size, there will be some reduction in ride quality. While more sophisticated suspension systems might be used to prevent this, we have not assumed that they are. It is implicit in our assumptions that autos of the same weight have the same ride quality.

Likewise, we have made no attempt to assess the effects of styling or aesthetic changes resulting from elimination of the trunk or in the design of very small autos.

The input quantities used in the model to define an automobile are of three types: (1) those defining the size of the passenger and trunk compartments and whether or not the auto is air conditioned, (2) those establishing the car's acceleration capability (from 0 to 60 mph) and its unrefueled range, and (3) those specifying the design features used.

The outputs of the model consist, first, of a description of the car. This includes its weight, overall dimensions, installed horsepower, its fuel economy over two different driving cycles, and its purchase price. Second, the outputs include a list and weights of the materials necessary to produce the car. Third, they include an itemized list of all of the energy consumed in producing, distributing, selling, and operating the auto throughout its assumed lifetime of ten years and 100,000 miles. Finally, the model provides a breakdown of the total cost of buying and operating the auto throughout its lifetime.

The design options the model can evaluate include:

1. New engine types;
2. Tire design and pressure;
3. Aerodynamic design changes;
4. New transmission types;
5. New fuels;
6. New materials;
7. Changes in the size of the passenger compartment and the trunk (including trunkless autos).

In the model, fuel economy is estimated over two standard driving cycles—the Federal Driving Cycle (FDC) (typical of urban driving) and the Environmental Protection Agency's Office of Air Programs (OAP) Driving Cycle. The latter consists of the Federal Driving Cycle plus a series of constant speed runs varying from 20 to 70 mph. It thus captures the effect of a mix of rural, freeway, and urban driving. The imposition of a speed limit (say 55 mph) can be simulated in the model by forcing all constant speed runs in the driving cycle that would normally exceed the specified speed limit to be made at the imposed limit.

Appendix A describes the model in more detail and demonstrates its validity for current auto designs. Input quantities representative of twelve actual 1973 autos, ranging from subcompact fo full-size autos were inserted in the model. The resulting estimated values of curb weight, overall length, installed horsepower, and fuel economy over the Federal Driving Cycle compare very closely (within a few percent) with actual values.

Appendix B describes the inputs used for the technological measures considered in this study. A companion report provides a full description and discussion of the Generalized Auto Design model, including a development of the mathematical relationships, the computer program used, and the inputs and outputs for all cases considered in the study [1].

Although the model does not estimate auto emissions by specie, incremental changes in weight and cost due to emission control equipment, for each engine type, are inputs to the model. The actual assumptions about the effectiveness of emission controls on all engine types considered are introduced exogenously and are discussed in Appendix C. Because this study focuses primarily on energy conservation, the impact on emissions of conservation measures is only one of several impacts considered. Therefore, this impact is framed in terms of a *weighted* emissions index, that attempts to account for the different effects of various emission species on human health and comfort. All basic comparisons are made using the weighting scheme proposed by Caretto and Sawyer [2], however, in Chapter Four, where we compare and screen technological measures, we conduct a sensitivity analysis of the results to proposed alternative weighting schemes [3].

THE AUTOMOBILE FLEET MIX MODEL

The Automobile Fleet Mix Model is a specially developed computerized model that relates the overall fleet fuel consumption, emissions, total energy required, and the total cost of auto ownership to changes in the number and nature of autos produced each year. The purpose of the model is to provide an assessment, by calendar year, of the impact on overall fleet characteristics of autos of new design or of reduced size that are introduced at specific rates.

Beginning with an existing fleet, the model increases the number of each type of vehicle by the number of new autos sold each year and reduces it by the number scrapped each year. With the new fleet mix determined, fleet emissions, fuel, energy, and operating cost are determined by summing over all types and weights of autos.

Aggregate annual new car sales is an input to the Fleet Mix Model. It is produced as one output of our NAV Model discussed below. The average aggregate rate at which autos are retired from the fleet (i.e., scrapped) is also an input. It, too, is produced as an output of the NAV Model. The variation of scrappage rate with auto age is computed in the model (using national auto registration data) to be consistent with the average aggregate scrappage rate. Because average scrappage rate is a model input, the effects of policies that change the price of new autos or gasoline and encourage longer retention or faster scrappage of used cars can be determined.

The inputs to the model are:

1. Production by year—(a) by size or market class (subcompact, compact, intermediate, full-size) and (b) by auto design type (this allows for the introduction of autos with new engines or transmission types, different vehicle design features, and so forth).
2. Number and age distribution of autos in the existing fleet.
3. Auto retirement rate as a function of age and of year (if different from that experienced in the past).

The outputs of the model are:

1. Number of autos in the fleet, by year.
2. Fleet fuel consumption, by year, and cumulated.
3. Emissions, by year, and cumulated.
4. Total user cost of auto ownership, by year.
5. Total energy consumed by the auto fleet, by year, and cumulated. This includes the energy involved in production, distribution, sales, operations, repair, and scrapping of autos (i.e., savings), as well as the fuel energy consumed in driving.

Thus, the Fleet Mix Model traces out, over time, fleetwide implications of introducing and/or phasing out one or several conservation measures. As discussed in Chapter Seven, combinations of technological and price of driving measures may be considered in the model; the former by describing the nature and number of each class of auto introduced into the fleet each year, and the latter by specifying aggregate annual sales of new cars and average annual fleetwide scrappage rate.

A more detailed description of the model, its validation, and inputs used to screen conservation measures, is given in Appendix D. A companion report develops the detailed equations used in the model [4].

ECONOMETRIC MODELS OF THE DEMAND FOR MOTOR FUEL

Measures that change the price of gasoline or autos affect gasoline consumption through four mechanisms: vehicle miles traveled (VMT), driving habits or arrangements, auto ownership (number owned and operated), and vehicle efficiency (or fuel economy). Recent research on estimating demand relationships for *gasoline* generally used flow adjustment models. These postulate that gasoline consumption is a function of gasoline price, personal income, and gasoline consumption during the last period. The inclusion of last year's consumption as an independent variable is rationalized by assuming that a fixed number of gallons of gasoline is used per vehicle every year. If this assumption is made, such models yield estimates of the scrappage rate of the vehicle stock. But this approach does not isolate other possible adjustments—that is, households or drivers can adjust to higher gasoline prices by driving less, by driving more conservatively, or by driving more efficient automobiles. Understanding the relative importance of the various modes of adjustment is important for a full evaluation of impacts. For example, whether most of the adjustment would occur through fewer vehicles of the same efficiency or through the same number of more efficient vehicle has important implications for automobile manufacturing and for the total energy consumed by the automobile sector.

Past research on demand for new cars has generally used measures of new car price and income as independent variables in an econometric model. In some models, other independent variables, such as current stock on the road, last year's new car sales, and interest rate or credit terms, were included. But, gasoline price was not used to explain new car sales in past models.

To deal with most of these adjustment mechanisms, we developed an econometric demand model that predicts the *long-run* impacts of gasoline prices or auto prices on gasoline use through changes in VMT, auto ownership, and vehicle fuel economy.

The NAV Model

The *long-run impact* model—NAV (New Car Sales/Auto Ownership/Vehicle Miles Traveled)—was developed to forecast changes in aggregate new car sales, auto ownership (new cars, used cars, cars scrapped), vehicle miles traveled, and gasoline consumption over time. A complete discussion of the NAV model, its properties, predictive power, and the data used, is contained in Appendix E. Here we present only a brief description of the model. It is a five-equation, recursive econometric model. Three equations are used to estimate auto ownership. In the first equation, the demand for new cars per household is a function of new car price, used car price, the ratio of this year's to last year's permanent income per household, and a dummy variable to account for the presence or absence of a strike in the auto industry. The second is the demand for used cars per household as a function of used car price, new car price, gasoline price, permanent income per household, and the strike dummy variable. The role of the third equation for used car price is to balance the new and used car markets. It is a function of new car price, gasoline price, permanent income per household, lagged (last year's) auto stock per household, and the strike dummy. The fourth equation estimates vehicle miles as a function of the estimated auto ownership per household, gasoline price, and a dummy variable to account for the presence or absence of significant auto safety and emission control requirements. The fifth equation estimates average fleet fuel economy (in mpg), given present auto technology, as a function of gasoline price and the auto safety/emission control dummy variable.[a] Finally, the estimates of VMT and average fleet fuel economy are used to calculate auto gasoline consumption.

NAV's input needs are modest, consisting of the following: auto ownership in an initial year, projections of the number of U.S. households and disposable personal income for each future year; estimates of average new car prices (low price, standard size), and future gasoline prices. Alternative estimates of, or assumptions about, future new car and/or gasoline prices can be used to reflect alternative policies or mixes of policies for conserving gasoline.

[a]The average automobile fuel economy equation reflects changes in new car buyers' and automobile drivers' *behavior* (i.e., buying smaller cars, driving slower). The average automobile miles per gallon estimate can be replaced with an engineering estimate when a new automobile technology is considered. The engineering estimate is made using our Generalized Automobile Design and Automobile Fleet Mix Model.

For each future year, NAV provides, as outputs, estimates of the following impacts:

1. Auto ownership (total auto stock);
2. New car sales;
3. Used car stock;
4. Automobiles retired (scrapped);
5. Automobile vehicle miles traveled (VMT);
6. Average automobile fuel economy (mpg);
7. Automobile gasoline consumption;
8. Used car price.

While the statistical properties of the NAV Model are satisfactory, we are concerned about how rapidly it adjusts to price changes; its structure results in very rapid adjustments to gasoline and new car price changes—usually in two to three years. Not only does average miles traveled per automobile adjust rapidly—as one might expect—but average fuel economy and automobile ownership per household also adjust rapidly. The speed of adjustment of the last two are surprising. During the estimating period—1954 to 1972—the year-to-year changes in many variables were small. Adjustment to the small, year-to-year changes in the independent variables seems to have taken place within a year.[b] We are not sure that adjustments to *large* year-to-year changes in the gasoline and new car prices will occur as rapidly. Consequently, for such large changes we see NAV as a way of predicting long-run, rather than short-run, impacts.

OTHER IMPACTS

In evaluating some measures and policy instruments we also estimate, in quantitative terms, employment effects in five auto-related sectors and income effects of certain policy instruments. Here we briefly describe the methodology used to estimate such impacts.

Employment Impacts

The number of jobs in certain sectors of the economy can be directly related to such factors as new cars produced, miles traveled in automobiles, and gasoline consumed by automobiles. An example is employment in automobile manufacturing, determined in part by the number and type of new cars produced. We have developed five simple regression models that relate employment to these independ-

[b]We were unsuccessful in attempting to estimate relationships between independent variables in previous years and current year dependent variables.

ent variables. These econometric relationships are used with the outputs of the NAV Model to estimate the changes in employment in auto manufacturing, auto dealerships, service stations, retail and wholesale parts firms, and tire manufacturing.

To preview our results, increased auto weight was found to have a significant positive effect on employment in the auto manufacturing sector—with other things held constant. Our model was estimated using data from the period 1958 to 1971 and thus reflects two major trends: the shift to small car production in the early 1960s and the increase in weight due to federal safety and emission controls during the late 1960s. The average new car weight during this period varied from 3,500 to 4,000 pounds, and our results suggest that in this range, increased weight leads to increased employment per vehicle and vice versa.

One explanation is that heavier cars tend to be more complex, which requires more production time per unit assembled. For long-run projections, we are not certain how a shift to small cars will affect the complexity of the vehicles produced in the future; thus, we cannot be certain that our model accurately reflects the relationship between weight and labor inputs required for the alternative production that would result from the policies considered in this study. In the analysis of Chapter Seven, we present *two* estimates of the employment impacts: the lower bound is found by assuming the full weight effect observed in the historical data (1958 to 1971), and the upper bound represents the impact with no weight effect. This range should bracket the actual impact of shifting to smaller cars.

What meaning can be attached to these employment estimates? If employment in a sector falls, most displaced workers will move into other sectors; they will produce socially useful goods and services in their new jobs. If the fall in employment is large, several years might be required for workers to find new jobs, retrain, and relocate.[c] During this period, they will not be producing socially useful goods and services and this will represent a social loss. Consequently, we feel that fewer jobs in a particular sector can be seen as a negative impact in the short run, but not in the long run.[d]

[c]A recent well-publicized example of this process is the movement of former aerospace employees to other sectors, with the reduction in government contracts during the late 1960s.

[d]A few individuals might remain unemployed for many years rather than move to new sectors. Older individuals are especially likely to remain unemployed for long periods; they might feel the cost of retraining or relocating is too large, given the time they have left to work. The classic example is that of former shoe factory workers in New England. Individuals who would remain unemployed for many years would represent a long-run negative employment impact—an impact we cannot treat within the scope of this study.

Distributional Impacts

Policy instruments intended to change the cost of driving may have significant income distribution effects. In this study, we limit our analysis to a tax on gasoline purchases. To measure the distributional impacts of this instrument, we estimate the average percentage changes in annual household earnings allocated to *work trip* gasoline expenditures.[e] Comparison of these changes across earnings groups allows us to draw preliminary conclusions regarding the relative progressiveness (or regressiveness) of the policy instrument. The conclusions must be viewed as preliminary because only the initial tax incidence is analyzed—that is, no consideration is given to the extent to which families might change their work trip behavior in response to higher gasoline taxes.

NOTES TO CHAPTER THREE

1. See T. F. Kirkwood and A. Lee, *A Generalized Model for Comparing Automobile Design Approaches to Improved Fuel Economy*, R–1562–NSF, Rand Corporation, January, 1975.

2. L. S. Caretto and R. F. Sawyer, "The Assignment of Responsibility for Air Pollution," presented at the Annual Meeting of the Society of Automotive Engineers, Detroit, Michigan, January 10–14, 1972.

3. Lyndon R. Babcock, Jr. and Niren L. Nagda, "Cost Effectiveness of Emission Control," *Journal of the Air Pollution Control Association*, March 1973.

4. See Kirkwood and Lee, *A Generalized Model for Comparing Automobile Design Approaches to Improved Fuel Economy*.

[e]Only data on work trip mileage was available for this study. We used household survey data for 1971 described in *A Panel Study of Income Dynamics: Study Design, Procedures and Available Data, 1968–1971*, Institute for Social Research, University of Michigan, Ann Arbor, Michigan, 1971. The sample size for our analysis is 4,840 of which 2,294 heads of households use private transportation for work trips. Appendix G contains a detailed description of the data and methodology used.

Chapter Four

Per-Vehicle Comparisons of Auto Design
Conservation Measures

In this chapter, we compare on a per-vehicle bases a number of automobile design changes that can conserve energy. All cases are compared with base or reference cases. The purpose of these comparisons is to screen a variety of pure and combined measures to identify the few promising ones that are carried through the subsequent analysis. For all design changes involving the conventionally powered autos with Spark Ignition Engines (SIE), we use four screening criteria: fuel economy on the Federal and OAP Driving Cycles, lifetime energy requirements, selling price, and average annual cost over the auto's lifetime. For alternative engines, a fifth criterion—the Caretto–Sawyer weighted emission index[a]—is used for both the *interim* 1975–1976 emission standards (0.41 gm/mi of hydrocarbons, 3.4 gm/mi of carbon monoxide, 2.0 gm/mi of NO_x) and the 1976 *statutory* emission standards (0.41 gm/mi of hydrocarbons, 3.4 gm/mi of carbon monoxide, 0.40 gm/mi of NO_x). Engines using external combustion (Rankine and Stirling) will have substantially lower emissions. In these per-vehicle comparisons, no distinction is drawn regarding the time when a measure will be introduced.

THE BASE CASES DEFINED

The Base Cases, against which all per-vehicle design changes are compared, reflect current Detroit design practice and buyer preferences. For each market class (i.e., subcompact, compact, intermediate, and full-size), we define a base case as follows:

---

[a]For a discussion of the merits of this index, see below in this chapter the section on Sensitivity of Engine Comparisons to Emissions Weighting Schemes.

1. Imposition of a 55 mph speed limit.
2. Weight and fuel economy reflecting 1975–1976 SIE with emission control equipment.
3. Bias-ply tires.
4. Drag representative of conventional body configuration—all market classes.
5. Full and intermediate size autos are fitted with air conditioners; compacts and subcompacts are not.
6. Engine horsepower determined by the following acceleration requirements (from 0 to 60 mph): Subcompact, 18 seconds; Compact, 16 seconds; Intermediate, 13 seconds; Full-size, 11 seconds.
7. Conventional automatic transmission—all market classes.
8. Current average overall dimensions, trunk volume, passenger compartment dimensions, and unrefueled range (i.e., gasoline tank volume) for each market class.
9. Ten-year lifetime user cost based on 38 cents per gallon of gasoline[b] (pre-1973 pump prices) and a 7.5 percent discount rate.
10. Current conventional auto scrappage process (energy recovered from scrap).
11. Conventional materials (e.g., steel bodies; no use of Fiberglas or other lightweight materials for auto bodies).
12. Current design practice for suspension systems.

BASE CASES: SIZE EFFECTS WITH CURRENT COMFORT AND PERFORMANCE CHARACTERISTICS

Table 4–1 compares the energy and cost implications among the Base Cases. Each market class reflects current design practice and buyer preferences with regard to comfort and performance. Compared with full-size autos, subcompacts are about 60 percent better in fuel economy, consume 36 percent less energy in their lifetime, and cost about half as much when new and about 35 percent less over the lifetime of the car. These figures merely illustrate the well-known fact that, on a per-vehicle basis at least, considerable energy savings are possible with new cars without *any* design changes, if buyers could be persuaded to purchase smaller cars.

Table 4–2 displays a breakdown of lifetime energy expenditures

[b]Because all of the per-vehicle cost comparisons in this section are based on pre-1973 pump prices, higher gasoline prices (used in comparisons made in later sections) would mean even *larger* cost reductions for technological alternatives that improve fuel economy.

Table 4–1. Auto Size Effects *(Base Cases)*

	Mpg		*Lifetime Energy (Million Btu)*	*Selling Price ($)*	*Average Annual Cost ($)*
	---	---	---	---	---
Size or Market Class	*FDC Cycle*	*OAP Cycle*			
Full-Size (with air conditioning)	10.7	12.8	1562	4053	1376
Intermediate (with air conditioning)	11.4	13.5	1460	3589	1264
Compact (without air conditioning)	14.5	16.9	1155	2633	1027
Subcompact (without air conditioning	17.4	20.3	960	2092	886

for the Base Case subcompact and full-size autos. *Direct* energy consumption (fuel and oil) over 100,000 miles of driving accounts for about 64 percent of the full-size auto's total and slightly more—66 percent—for the subcompact. Total *indirect* energy consumption accounts for the remainder. The two largest components of indirect energy consumption are associated with gasoline extraction, refining, transport, and sale (about 11 percent) and with auto production (about 11 percent for full-size and 9 percent for subcompact autos).

The remaining items are individually small: transport and sale of new autos, 7 to 8 percent; repair and maintenance, 4 to 5 percent; replacement tires, 2 percent; and energy recovered from scrap, less than 1 percent, given that only 15 percent of the steel recovered from scrapped autos is used in new auto construction. In the future, more refined scrapping methods may increase this saving to 2 to 3 percent. From the viewpoint of lifetime energy requirements (direct plus indirect), the auto itself accounts for only 25 percent, whereas gasoline accounts for 75 percent.

Table 4–3 displays a breakdown of lifetime costs for the Base Case full-size and subcompact autos, based on the OAP Driving Cycle. Note that given our assumptions about gasoline price and the discount rate, a new $2,100 subcompact costs the user almost $9,000 over its lifetime, and a new $4,000 full-size auto costs almost $14,000.

Lost interest accounts for 10 and 12 percent of the total for the subcompact and full-size autos, respectively. Initial costs (purchase price and state sales tax)[c] account for 24 percent for the subcompact and 30 percent for the full-size auto. There are four major items in the recurring cost category: fuel and oil, insurance, and repair and

[c]We lump the first year's state license and registration fee with the remaining nine years under the recurring cost category.

Table 4–2. Breakdown of Lifetime Energy Requirements (Base Cases: Full-size and subcompact autos)

	Full-Size		Subcompact	
	Million Btu	Percent of Total	Million Btu	Percent of Total
Direct Consumption				
Gasoline	996	63.8	630	65.6
Oil (lubricating)	8	0.5	7	0.7
Total direct	1004	64.3	637	66.3
Indirect Consumption				
Gasoline extraction and refining	89	5.7	56	5.8
Gasoline transport and sale	82	5.2	52	5.4
Total gasoline	171	10.9	108	11.2
Auto Production (includes ore extraction and processing)	174	11.1	89	9.3
Tires	33	2.2	17	1.8
Auto Transport and Sale	122	7.8	63	6.6
Auto Repair and Maintenance	69	4.4	52	5.4
Scrappage (savings)	(−11)	(−0.7)	(−6)	(−0.6)
Total auto	387	24.8	215	22.5
Total indirect	558	35.7	323	33.7
Grand total	1562	100.0	960	100.0

Table 4–3. Breakdown of Lifetime User Costs (Base Cases: Full-size and subcompact; OAP Driving Cycle; 10 years, 100,000 mi)

	Full-Size		Subcompact	
	Dollars	Percent of Total	Dollars	Percent of Total
Initial Cost				
Selling price	4,053	29.4	2,092	23.6
State sales tax	113	0.8	59	0.6
Total initial	4,166	30.2	2,151	24.2
Recurring Costs				
Fuel (at 27¢ per gallon)	2,108	15.4	1,333	15.1
Oil	120	0.9	97	1.1
Tires (replacements)	518	3.8	273	3.1
Insurance	1,386	10.0	1,273	14.4
Accessories	200	1.5	200	2.3
Engine repair and maintenance	1,375	10.0	1,033	11.7
Vehicle repair and maintenance	1,095	8.0	828	9.3
Federal taxes				
Gasoline	312	2.3	197	2.2
Oil	2	0.0	2	0.0
Tires	42	0.3	22	0.2
State taxes and fees				
Gasoline tax	502	3.6	317	3.6
License and registration fee	281	2.0	281	3.2
Total recurring	7,941	57.8	5,856	66.2
Grand total (undiscounted)	12,107	88.0	8,007	90.4
Value of Lost Interest (7.5%)	1,654	12.0	854	9.6
Lifetime Cost (7.5% discount rate)	13,761	100.0	8,861	100.0
Average Annual Cost (discounted)	1,376	—	886	—

maintenance of the engine and of the vehicle. Fuel and oil (excluding state and federal taxes) account for about 16 percent. These figures are based on gasoline at 27 cents per gallon; at higher prices, such as prevail currently, their relative contribution would be higher.[d] Current state and federal taxes on gasoline and oil add another 6 percent, so that fuel and oil, including taxes, accounts for 22 percent of the lifetime cost. Insurance accounts for 14 percent for the subcompact and 10 percent for the full-size auto. Engine repair and maintenance accounts for 10 percent (full-size autos) and 12 percent (subcompact), and vehicle repair and maintenance accounts for 8 percent for the full-size auto and 9 percent for the subcompact. Other cost categories, such as parking or toll fees, were not included in our lifetime auto cost model, because their magnitudes vary greatly among rural, suburban, and urban areas throughout the country. In terms of equivalent dollar cost impacts over the auto's lifetime, an increase of 20 cents per gallon of gasoline (i.e., a 50 percent increase) is equivalent to a 36 percent and 44 percent increase in selling prices of full-size and subcompact autos.

EFFECT OF LOWER PERFORMANCE

Current Detroit design practice is to provide larger autos with greater acceleration capability than smaller autos. This is illustrated in Figure 4-1, which displays the variation of fuel economy on the Federal Driving Cycle with required time to accelerate from zero to 60 mph, as estimated by the Generalized Automobile Design Model. Base Case designs points are denoted in the figure. Because there is some variation in performance *within* market classes, the region of current design practice is shown in the shaded area. The main point to note is that when comparing, say, a Detroit produced subcompact with a full-size auto, one is really comparing vehicles with markedly *different* performance (18 compared with 11 seconds to accelerate to 60 mph and 17.4 mpg compared with 10.7 mpg). However, if the full-size auto's engine horsepower and size were reduced to provide performance similar to a subcompact, the *difference* in fuel economy between the two cars is reduced from 6.7 mpg to 5.6 mpg. On the other hand, comparing two *full-size* cars, one with current performance and one with engine size reduced to provide the subcompact's performance, fuel economy is improved by 10 percent—from

---

[d]Because all of our per-vehicle cost comparisons in this section are based on pre-1973 pump prices, higher gasoline prices (used in comparisons made in later sections) would mean even *larger* cost reductions for technological alternatives that improve fuel economy.

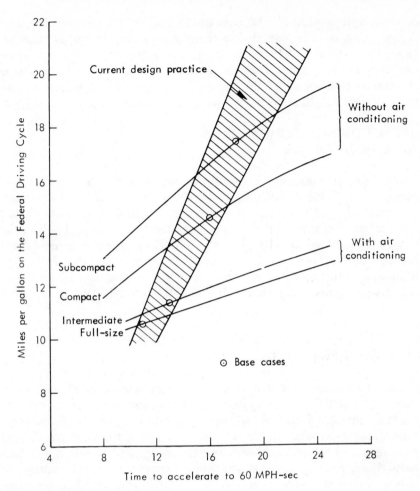

Figure 4–1. Relationship between Fuel Economy and Acceleration
Requirements.

10.7 mpg to 11.8 mpg. This results because, instead of needing a
214 hp engine (for accelerating from zero to 60 mph in 11 seconds),
the engine can be reduced to 122 hp (for accelerating in 18 seconds).
The smaller engine results in reduced overall weight, so that the low
performance, full-size auto weighs 3,953 pounds instead of 4,734
pounds for the Base Case.

Table 4–4 displays the major effects of reducing performance of
full-size autos, while holding all other parameters constant. Fuel
economy is improved by 5 to 10 percent, depending on the driving
cycle, lifetime energy is reduced by 9 percent, selling price by 15

percent, and average annual cost by 11 percent. A number of other design changes discussed below can obtain reductions as large or larger than these, but because the higher acceleration of the full-size car may be important from a marketing point of view, we have chosen to base most of the remainder of our comparisons on the present variation of acceleration with market size class.

EFFECT OF REMOVING AIR CONDITIONING

The effect of removing air conditioning from the full-size auto is displayed in Table 4-5. Compared with the Base Case, fuel economy is improved by 13 percent (9 percent is due to fuel required to run the air conditioner and 4 percent is due to its weight), lifetime energy is reduced by 10 percent, selling price by 9 percent, and average annual cost by 7 percent. Compared with the option of reduced performance, removing air conditioning is slightly more effective in conserving energy but slightly less effective in reducing cost.

EFFECTS OF VEHICLE DESIGN CHANGES WITH CURRENT ENGINES

Here we examine the effects on energy conservation of each of a number of vehicle design measures. All autos are powered by current conventional engines. Table 4-6 displays the effects of introducing each measure separately for full-size autos and subcompacts. Radial tires result in modest fuel and energy savings and small annual cost reductions. Selling price is increased, however, because radials are almost twice as costly as bias-ply tires. However, they can be introduced rapidly and widely. For the past two model years, radials have been standard equipment on certain new car models.

Minor aerodynamic improvements—rounded front corners, a squared (cut-off) rear end, and an underbody strip (dam) to cause airflow separation under the body—have somewhat more salutary impacts than radial tires, in terms of all of the impacts shown. We assume that these minor aerodynamic improvements are possible with essentially no direct increase in either weight or selling price.

Major aerodynamic improvements (rounded front corners, a reshaped rear end, and complete underbody covering), give additional gains in spite of an increase in body weight of 2.5 percent. While the major aerodynamic changes result in further improvements in fuel economy and lifetime energy consumption, particularly in small

Table 4–4.   Effect of Reduced Acceleration Requirement on Full-Size Autos *(Percent change from Base Case)*

	Mpg		Lifetime Energy (Million Btu)	Selling Price ($)	Average Annual Cost ($)
	FDC Cycle	OAP Cycle			
Full-size (Base Case)	0(10.7)	0(12.8)	0(1562)	0(4053)	0(1376)
Full-size (low acceleration—smaller engines)	+10	+5	−9	−15	−11

Table 4–5.   Effect of Removing Air Conditioning on Full-Size Autos *(Percent change from Base Case)*

	Mpg		Lifetime Energy (Million Btu)	Selling Price ($)	Average Annual Cost ($)
	FDC Cycle	OAP Cycle			
Base Case (with air conditioning)	0(10.7)	0(12.8)	0(1562)	0(4053)	0(1376)
No Air Conditioning	+13	+13	−10	−9	−7

Table 4–6.   Effect of Vehicle Design Changes *(Percent change from Base Case)*

Design Change	Mpg		Lifetime Energy (Million Btu)	Selling Price ($)	Average Annual Cost ($)
	FDC Cycle	OAP Cycle			
Full-Size Auto					
Base	0(10.7)	0(12.8)	0(1562)	0(4053)	0(1376)
Base plus radial tires	+7	+8	−6	+3	−3
Base plus minor aerodynamic changes	+6	+9	−6	−1	−3
Base plus major aerodynamic changes	+7	+13	−9	0	−3
Base plus aluminum construction	+15	+13	−13	−12	−11
Base plus CVT	+27	+28	−18	−5	−8
Base without trunk	+20	+16	−17	−29	−21
Subcompact Auto					
Base	0(17.4)	0(20.3)	0(960)	0(2092)	0(886)
Base plus radial tires	+5	+4	−3	+3	−2
Base plus minor aerodynamic changes	+7	+10	−7	−2	−3
Base plus major aerodynamic changes	+13	+22	−15	−2	−5
Base plus aluminum construction	+20	+16	−15	−12	−10
Base plus CVT	++32	+29	−18	−6	−8
Urban Auto (compared with subcompact)					
Two-passenger, trunkless design	+75	+72	−43	−58	−33
One-passenger, trunkless design	+108	+112	−53	−63	−39

cars, we have not considered them further in the study—because extreme aerodynamic refinement will require considerable compromise of passenger comfort (particularly rear seat head room) and will restrict the manufacturer's opportunity to make periodic model changes.

The use of aluminum as a structural material in bodies and engines can result in improvements in fuel consumption substantially greater than those obtained from either radial tires or minor aerodynamic changes (between 13 and 20 percent improvement over the Base Case). It also results in about 15 percent savings in lifetime energy used, 12 percent savings in selling price, and a 10 percent saving in annual cost. Although not shown in Table 4-6, the overall savings in weight due to the use of aluminum was sufficient to offset the energy required to produce aluminum, so that the total energy required to produce the aluminum automobile was the same as that required for the conventional automobile.

The introduction of CVT is the single most desirable design measure that can be introduced into autos with conventional spark ignition engines without affecting either auto comfort, drivability, or performance characteristics. Fuel economy can be increased by 27 to 32 percent, depending on driving cycle and auto size. Lifetime energy requirements are reduced 18 percent. Selling price can be reduced 5 to 6 percent, depending on auto size, because the more efficient CVT results in a smaller engine and lighter vehicle, even though the transmission itself is heavier than a standard three-speed automatic and is more expensive.[e] Finally, lifetime cost is reduced by 8 percent.

For illustrative purposes, we have also included a number of design changes that alter the auto's size and/or load-carrying capacity. Other things being equal, if the trunk in a full-size auto is eliminated, fuel economy is increased 20 percent on the Federal Driving Cycle and 16 percent on the OAP Cycle, and lifetime energy requirements are reduced by 17 percent. Cost reductions are substantial because of large reductions in auto weight (36 percent from the Base Case); selling price is reduced by 29 percent and average annual cost by 21 percent. Removing the trunk results in an auto having a passenger compartment equivalent to that of a full-size auto but a weight more nearly representative of a compact auto.

Urban one- or two-passenger trunkless autos, with leg room and seating dimensions equivalent to a subcompact, show dramatic

---

[e]These results apply to the hydromechanical type of CVT. Traction type CVTs may be less costly and lighter in weight, but less efficient than the hydromechanical type.

energy and cost savings compared with subcompacts. For the two-passenger design, fuel economy is improved by 72 to 75 percent, depending on driving cycle, and lifetime energy requirements are reduced by 43 percent. Selling price falls by 58 percent and average annual cost by a third. For the one passenger design, comparable figures are even more dramatic. Fuel economy is improved by 108 to 112 percent, depending on driving cycle, lifetime energy is reduced by 53 percent, selling price by 63 percent, and average annual cost by 39 percent.

Of course, such size and load-carrying capacity design changes imply major changes in auto *use*. A trunkless full-size auto could only be used for long trips when carrying two or three passengers, because the back seat would be used to carry luggage. The full six-passenger capacity could be used only for short trips not requiring luggage. The one- or two-passenger trunkless designs offer inherently different transportation service characteristics. These are basically autos designed for such travel as urban work trips.

COMBINED DESIGN CHANGES (WITH CURRENT ENGINES)

Thus far we have examined the effects of vehicle design changes one at a time. Here we examine the effects of *combining* such vehicle design measures; these effects are displayed in Table 4–7.

Considering first the full-size auto, we introduce all of the promising energy conservation measures that have *no* effect on comfort, drivability, or performance—that is, radial tires, minor aerodynamic improvements, and the CVT. Compared with the full-size Base Case, fuel economy is improved by 35 to 42 percent, depending on driving cycle; lifetime energy is reduced by 24 percent, selling price by 3 percent, and average annual cost by 11 percent. This combined option reflects the best that can be achieved in energy conservation with current engines and without affecting transportation service characteristics. Note also that although substantial energy savings are possible, cost impacts on the user and manufacturer are relatively small.

If, *in addition*, the consumer were willing to give up air conditioning, all luggage space, and sparkling acceleration in a full-size auto, both energy and cost savings are truly impressive. Fuel economy is improved by 121 to 136 percent, lifetime energy requirements and selling price are reduced by 54 percent, and average annual cost falls by 44 percent.

Adding radials, minor aerodynamic improvements, and the CVT to

Table 4–7. Effect of Combinations of Vehicle Design Changes (Percent change from Base Case)

	Mpg		Lifetime Energy (Million Btu)	Selling Price ($)	Average Annual Cost ($)
	FDC Cycle	OAP Cycle			
Full-Size Auto					
Base	0(10.7)	0(12.8)	0(1562)	0(4053)	0(1376)
Base plus radials plus minor aerodynamics plus CVT	+35	+42	−24	−3	−11
Above, trunkless plus low acceleration, no air conditioning	+136	+121	−54	−54	−44
Subcompact Auto					
Base	0(17.4)	0(20.3)	0(960)	0(2092)	0(886)
Base plus radials plus minor aerodynamics plus CVT	+46	+48	−27	−4	−12
Urban Auto (compared to subcompact)					
Two-passenger, trunkless plus radials plus minor aerodynamics plus CVT	+154	+156	−59	−61	−41
One passenger, trunkless plus radials plus minor aerodynamics plus CVT	+200	+216	−66	−66	−45

the Base Case subcompact results in slightly better relative improvements than introducing the same measures in full-size autos.

Adding radials, minor aerodynamic improvements, and the CVT to the one- and two-passenger, trunkless designs roughly doubles the fuel economy improvement to over 50 mpg and 60 mpg for the two- and one-passenger cars, respectively. For the two-passenger design, lifetime energy requirements and selling price are reduced about 60 percent, and average annual cost by 41 percent. Comparable figures for the one passenger design are 66 and 45 percent, respectively.

NEW ENGINES

We turn next to the possible energy conservation implications and other impacts of new engines, "new" only in relation to past U.S. auto industry practice. Some of the engines we consider have long been produced by foreign manufacturers (e.g., the diesel) or have recently been introduced by them (e.g., the rotary). Others (e.g., the gas turbine) have received serious R&D attention over some period of time by one or more U.S. auto manufacturer. Still others (e.g., the historical application of superchargers to conventional spark ignition engines, as mentioned in Chapter Two) have been in mass production in the United States, but their design philosophy differed from that used in this study.

In the medium term, say 5 to 9 years, it is technically and economically feasible to begin initial mass production of modified internal combustion engines (ICE)—the supercharged SIE, the rotary SIE, the stratified charge SIE, the stratified rotary SIE, or the diesel. More advanced engines, such as the Rankine cycle, the Stirling, and the gas turbine, are in an earlier stage of development; thus, short of an expensive crash development effort, they would probably require more time before they could be mass produced. Therefore, we first compare autos with modified internal combustion engines and select the more promising to compare with autos using more advanced engines.

Modifications to the Internal
Combustion Engine

Table 4–8 compares full-size and subcompact autos powered by ICE variants. All of the alternative autos are equipped with radial tires and have bodies with minor aerodynamic improvements, because we assume that such minor energy conservation measures would have been adopted by the time the new engines are introduced. Comparisons are made with the Base Cases and engine modifications are shown in rank order of decreasing fuel economy on the OAP cycle for the full-size auto.

Comparing these alternatives in terms of our five impact criteria, we observe that:

First, *supercharging* any specific ICE variant has modest salutary effects on fuel economy, lifetime energy requirements, lifetime cost, and the initial cost compared with the unsupercharged engine. Supercharged engines will use the same emission control equipment as unsupercharged ICEs, and we assume that they can meet the same emissions standards.

Second, *all* engine variants examined promise better fuel economy and equal or lower lifetime energy requirements than the auto equipped with the conventional 1976 emission controlled SIE.

Third, by comparing the unsupercharged *rotary* SIE with the unsupercharged *stratified charge* SIE in full-size autos, we note that the rotary engine provides somewhat poorer fuel economy, has about the same lifetime energy requirements, and is considerably cheaper (in terms of both initial and lifetime costs). For the subcompact rotary auto; fuel economy is roughly equal;[f] lifetime energy requirements are slightly lower; and costs are considerably lower. The primary reason for the cost dominance is that the rotary engine is lighter and smaller than the stratified charge engine and hence the automobile is considerably smaller and lighter.

Fourth, the *stratified rotary SIE dominates* the *pure rotary* for both size autos. Stratification provides considerably better fuel economy and requires less lifetime energy primarily because stratification enables the engine to operate at a higher compression ratio (hence, higher efficiency) without pre-ignition and without excessive NO_x emissions. Stratification implies little change in initial cost and modest reductions in lifetime costs attributable to better fuel economy.

Fifth, compared with the Base Case, the *diesel* shows considerable improvement (32 percent to 50 percent) in fuel economy, depending on auto size and driving cycle, when compared in terms of miles per gallon of gasoline having the same Btu content as the gallons of diesel fuel used.

We find that it is particularly important in comparing the fuel economy of diesel and gasoline engines to define the basis of com-

---

[f]This conclusion results from our assumption that rotary engines can obtain the same fuel consumption as comparable reciprocating engines. Currently, mass produced rotaries do not achieve this, but some experimental engines have demonstrated essential parity.

Table 4–8.   Effects of Modifications to the Internal Combustion Engine *(Percent change from Base Case)*
[55 mph speed limit; radial tires, minor aerodynamic improvements]

| | Full-Size Auto | | | | | Caretto–Sawyer Emission Index (Weighted gm/mi) | |
| | Mpg | | Lifetime Energy (Million Btu) | Selling Price ($) | Average Annual Cost ($) | | |
ICE Modification[a]	FDC Cycle	OAP Cycle				1976 Interim Standards	1976 Statutory Standards
Base (SIE with only 55 mph speed limit)	0(10.7)	0(12.8)	0(1562)	0(4053)	0(1376)	0(116.8)	0(46.4)
Stratified Rotary and Supercharging	+77	+82	−42	−26	−28	0	0
Stratified Rotary SIE	+63	+67[b]	−37	−23	−25	0	0
Diesel	+32[b]	+39[b]	−19	+21	−3	−57	+9
Stratified Charge SIE	+34	+38	−22	0	−9	0	0
Rotary SIE and Supercharging	+33	+33	−26	−26	−22	0	0
Rotary SIE	+27	+27	−22	−23	−20	0	0
SIE and Supercharging	+20	+23	−16	−6	−10	0	0
SIE (1975–1976 conventional engines)	+11	+14	−10	+2	−4	0	0

[a] Ranked in order of decreasing fuel economy (mpg) on the OAP Driving Cycle for the full-size auto.
[b] Mpg of gasoline having the same Btu content as the diesel fuel actually used.

Table 4–8.   continued

| | | | | | | Caretto–Sawyer Emission Index (Weighted gm/mi) | |
| | Mpg | | | | | | |
ICE Modification[a]	FDC Cycle	OAP Cycle	Lifetime Energy (Million Btu)	Selling Price ($)	Average Annual Cost ($)	1976 Interim Standards	1976 Statutory Standards
Subcompact Auto							
Base (SIE with only 55 mph speed limit)	0(17.4)	0(20.3)	0(960)	0(2092)	0(886)	0(116.8)	0(46.4)
Stratified Rotary and Supercharging	+73	+76	−40	−28	−25	0	0
Stratified Rotary SIE	+55	+57	−34	−24	−22	0	0
Diesel	+47[b]	+50[b]	−25	+25	−4	−57	+9
Stratified Charge SIE	+31	+36	−22	−1	−8	0	0
Rotary SIE and Supercharging	+41	+42	−29	−28	−21	0	0
Rotary SIE	+33	+33	−25	−25	−18	0	0
SIE and Supercharging	+22	+26	−18	+8	−10	0	0
SIE (1975–1976 conventional engines)	+11	+15	−11	+1	−4	0	0

[a]Ranked in order of decreasing fuel economy (mpg) on the OAP Driving Cycle for the full-size auto.
[b]Mpg of gasoline having the same Btu content as the diesel fuel actually used.

parison. Our comparison is based on equal acceleration time from zero to 60 mph for autos having the same passenger and trunk space. On this basis, the use of a diesel engine in a subcompact car on the OAP cycle shows a 31 percent improvement in equivalent gasoline consumption over the Base Case. Had we compared autos of equal weight and equal power[g] (which could not have the same size passenger and trunk compartments), we would have obtained approximately a 50 percent improvement.

Lifetime energy requirements of the diesel auto are 19 to 25 percent less than the auto fitted with the conventional 1976 emission controlled SIE, but costs are about the same because the cost savings from improved fuel economy and maintenance are roughly counterbalanced by the cost increases needed to produce the much heavier engine and body.[h] Selling price is 20 to 25 percent higher than the comparable SIE auto, depending on body size. Like the spark ignition engine, the diesel should be able to meet the interim emission standards (NO_x requirements reduced to 2 gm/mi), but may have difficulty meeting the ultimate statutory NO_x requirement of 0.4 gm/mi. In addition, diesel engines may have acceptance problems because of their odor, smoke, noise, and possible health hazards due to sulfates and organic compounds in the exhaust.

Sixth, of all the ICE variants considered, the *supercharged stratified rotary SIE dominates all others in terms of energy conservation and cost.* While its performance and emission characteristics must be demonstrated, our estimates show energy and cost savings that are truly impressive: compared with the Base Case, fuel economy is improved 73 to 82 percent depending on auto size and driving cycle; lifetime energy requirements are reduced 40 percent, selling price over 26 percent, and average annual cost over 25 percent.

Advanced Engines

Here we compare three advanced engine types *Stirling, gas turbine* and *Rankine cycle)* with the promising ICE variants; Table 4–9 displays these results. All autos (except the Base Case SIE) are equipped with advanced transmissions—the CVT, or its equivalent. In essence, these results portray the maximum improvements in energy conservation achievable with advanced engine-transmission designs.

Because the three advanced engine types are in an earlier stage of

[g]As is done in "A Study of Technological Improvements to Automobile Fuel Consumption," Southwest Research Institute, January 1974; see also the same title by A. D. Little, Inc., February 1974.

[h]This conclusion is dependent on our assumption that if diesel fuel is produced in large quantities for auto use, it will be priced and taxed at the same rate per Btu as gasoline.

development than the ICE variants, it is less certain that the predicted performance, cost, and emission characteristics will actually be achieved.

Comparing the alternatives we observe that:

First, compared with conventional engines, the stratified rotary SIE with supercharging and CVT[i] *offers the greatest savings* in energy and cost of all ICE variants—*about twice the fuel economy, about 40 percent lower lifetime energy requirements, and over 25 percent reduction in initial and lifetime costs,*[j] while meeting, but not exceeding, emissions standards. (We assume here, of course, that all ICE variants will be designed to, and in fact will meet, the emissions standards).

Second, in terms of energy conservation potential, only one of the three advanced engines—the Stirling—can compete with the supercharged stratified rotary SIE. While its equivalent gasoline fuel economy does not appear to match that of the supercharged stratified rotary (being comparable with the stratified rotary SIE) it can use a much wider range of fuels and consequently operate from a broader energy base. Because the Stirling engine is much heavier, auto size and weight are increased. For example, the full-size auto with the Stirling and stratified rotary SIE are 4,600 and 3,000 pounds, respectively; comparable figures for the subcompact are 2,250 and 1,600 pounds, respectively. Therefore, reductions (compared with the Base Case) in both initial and lifetime costs are considerably less for the Stirling auto. Compared with the ICE engines, however, Stirling engines offer greatly reduced emissions—82 percent below interim standards and 57 percent below the statutory standards.

Third, because there is no clear dominancy between the Stirling and stratified rotary engines in terms of *all* of the energy, cost, and emissions criteria, we carry both engines through the analysis in Chapter Five.

Fourth, the gas turbine engine does not offer as good fuel economy as either the Stirling or the more advanced internal combustion engines. This is due to the higher specific fuel consumption of the

---

[i]Although an engine equipped with a CVT operates at its best SFC at any specified power setting, the use of a smaller displacement, supercharged engine can result in a further improvement in fuel economy because at the low powers encountered in much of the driving cycle, it will operate at a higher mean effective pressure than an unsupercharged engine.

[j]As noted previously, these cost comparisons assume the pre–1973 gasoline pump price of 38 cents; at higher prices (which are used in succeeding sections), cost reductions would be even greater.

Table 4-9. Advanced Engines Compared with Promising Ice Modification with CVT *(Percent change from Base Case)*
[55 mph speed limit; minor aerodynamic improvement; radial tires]

	Full-Size						
	Mpg		Lifetime Energy (Million Btu)	Selling Price ($)	Average Annual Cost ($)	Caretto–Sawyer Emission Index (Weighted gm/mi)	
Engine Type	FDC Cycle	OAP Cycle				1976 Interim Standards	1976 Statutory Standards
Base (SIE with only 55 mph speed limit) ICE	0(10.7)	0(12.8)	0(1562)	0(4053)	0(1376)	0(116.8)	0(46.4)
Stratified rotary and supercharging	+109	+114	-48	-28	-31	0	0
Stratified rotary	+89	+95	+44	-25	-29	0	0
Stratified charge SIE	+68	+81	-36	-5	-15	0	0
Advanced Engines							
Stirling	+52[a]	+61[a]	-36	+8	-8	-82	-57
Gas turbine	-6[a]	+2[a]	-5	0	-9	-78	-44
Rankine cycle	+17[a]	+30[a]	-12	+15	+1	-83	-58

[a] Fuel economy converted to gasoline having the same Btu content as the fuel actually used.

Table 4–9. continued

Subcompact Auto

Engine Type	Mpg		Lifetime Energy (Million Btu)	Selling Price ($)	Average Annual Cost ($)	Caretto–Sawyer Emission Index (Weighted gm/mi)	
	FDC Cycle	OAP Cycle				1976 Interim Standards	1976 Statutory Standards
Base (SIE with only 55 mph speed limit)	0(17.4)	0(20.3)	0(960)	0(2092)	0(886)	0(116.8)	0(46.4)
ICE							
Stratified rotary and supercharging	+110	+109	−47	−30	−27	0	0
Stratified rotary	+96	+98	−44	−26	−25	0	0
Stratified charge SIE	+69	+75	−35	−6	−14	0	0
Advanced Engines							
Stirling	+87[a]	+98[a]	−46	+5	−12	−82	−57
Gas turbine	+17[a]	+20[a]	−17	0	−13	−78	−44
Rankine cycle	+21[a]	+23[a]	−12	+14	−1	−83	−58

[a]Fuel economy converted to gasoline having the same Btu content as the fuel actually used.

turbine engine that is only partially offset by its compactness and light weight. Its light weight and lower engine maintenance cost will allow it to sell for the same price as a conventional (Base Case) auto and have comparable or slightly lower cost of ownership.

Fifth, the Rankine engine appears to offer somewhat better fuel economy than the gas turbine, but because of its greater weight, it has a selling price that is higher than a conventional auto. The improvement in fuel economy is just enough to offset the high selling price, so that the overall cost of ownership is roughly the same as for a conventional SIE.

Sixth, all of the advanced engines have operational drawbacks to which owners would be sensitive. It now appears that, compared with other types of gas turbines, a free turbine system offers the greatest fuel economy, but this system has poor engine braking characteristics and may require more than normal use of brakes. The Rankine system may require a longer start-up time than drivers are used to and special procedures in cold weather, either to avoid freezing or to start after freezing. On the other hand, the Stirling engine is unusually quiet and smooth running due to the lack of intermittent combustion and the fact that piston motion in both directions is opposed by gas pressure. It should prove easy to start even under adverse weather conditions, although the equipment necessary for starting may be more sophisticated than for the ICE. However, if diesel fuel is used in the Stirling, it may face the same problems of odor, smoke, and possible health hazards of sulfates and organic compounds in the exhaust associated with the diesel engine.

Sensitivity of Engine Comparisons to Emissions Weighting Schemes

Because our study is not primarily concerned with emissions, we felt it desirable to combine the emissions of various species into one index to serve as a relative measure of total emissions. We have done this by applying the specie weighting factors proposed by Caretto and Sawyer, as discussed in detail in Appendix C. We investigated several weighting systems and found that in no case did the use of different schemes result in a significant difference in the *relative* emissions of alternative engines.

In view of the subjective nature of the weighting process, the uncertainty of much of the emissions data on new engines, and the uncertainty about actual fleet performance over time of emission control equipment for internal combustion engines, we feel that this level of agreement is adequate for the purposes of this study.

Table 4–10. Advanced Fuels *(Percent change from Base Case)*
[55 mph speed limit; minor aerodynamic improvements; radial tires]

	Mpg		Lifetime Energy (Million Btu)	Selling Price ($)	Average Annual Cost ($)
Fuel Type	*FDC Cycle*	*OAP Cycle*			
	Full Size Auto				
Gasoline					
Base (55 mph speed limit only)	0(10.7)	0(12.8)	0(1562)	0(4035)	0(1376)
Pure Methanol	−56(−2)[a]	−55(−1)[a]	+45	+13	+16
Liquid Hydrogen	−78(−10)[a]	−78(−7)[a]	+161	+35	+53
	Subcompact Auto				
Gasoline					
Base (55 mph speed limit only)	0(17.4)	0(20.3)	0(960)	0(2092)	0(886)
Pure Methanol	−55(0)[a]	−53(+4)[a]	+41	+14	+13
Liquid Hydrogen	−77(−8)[a]	−76(−2)	+150	+42	+47

[a]First figure is fuel economy in gallons of methanol or hydrogen; figure in parenthesis is in gallons of gasoline having same Btu content.

ADVANCED FUELS

The effects of using methanol and hydrogen in subcompact and full-size cars using spark ignition engines[k] is summarized in Table 4–10. By comparing these fuels, we observe that:

First, Neither methanol nor hydrogen is economical in either energy or cost compared with gasoline at the price considered here (38 cents per gallon). On a Btu basis, the costs we have used are: gasoline, $3.00 per million Btu; methanol, $5.10 per million Btu; liquid hydrogen, $9.20 per million Btu.

Second, hydrogen is substantially less economical in both energy and cost than methanol.

Third, examination of the results of the design model shows that the additional weight and bulk of the fuel and tankage result in a 9 to 12 percent loss in fuel economy for methanol and a 14 to 19 percent loss for hydrogen.

In view of these results, there is no incentive to go to methanol or hydrogen fuels *unless* either the price of gasoline increases drastically and/or there is a strong desire and effort made to switch to a non-petroleum fuel base. Hydrogen offers essentially zero emissions of carbon monoxide and hydrocarbons, and its NO_x emissions may be virtually eliminated by operating with lean mixtures. There is a possibility that methanol combustion may emit formaldehyde. If the quantities of formaldehyde involved are substantial, then this must be inhibited before methanol can be used in large quantities.

[k]While we have not evaluated these fuels in gas turbine or external combustion engines, both are suitable for use in these engines, and we would expect *qualitatively* similar comparisons with gasoline to hold for these engines.

Chapter Five

Temporal Fleetwide Implications of Promising Auto Design Conservation Measures

In this chapter, we trace the temporal fleetwide implications of the few promising auto design conservation measures that were identified in the previous chapter. To illustrate the potential range of fleetwide energy conservation between 1975 and 1995, we constructed several cases using reasonable combinations of measures for the near, medium, and long terms. All of the alternative measures are compared with a Base Case using the Auto Fleet Mix Model.

THE BASE CASE DEFINED

The Base Case, with which all auto design conservation measures are compared, is characterized by:

1. The existing auto fleet size at the beginning of 1974 is, in round figures, 100,000,000.
2. The variation with time of annual aggregate new car sales, average fleetwide scrappage rates, and average annual VMT are outputs from the Base Case projections provided by the NAV Model (see Chapter Six). The NAV Model Base Case assumptions are: (a) Census Series E, Projection 1 for population and household growth; (b) annual growth of 1.9 percent in *real* disposable household income; (c) constant *real* new car price; (d) nominal gasoline pump price per gallon of 59 cents in 1974, 67 cents in 1975, and constant in *real* terms thereafter; and (e) auto fleet size of 90,794,000 at the start of 1975 (an output of NAV).
3. The 1975 new car market class mix extends slightly the trends established over the past decade [1]. They are full-size, 37 percent; intermediate, 18 percent; compact, 17 percent; subcompact, 28 percent (small car share, 45 percent).

4. Imposition of a 55 mph speed limit (affects per-vehicle fuel economy).
5. All new cars produced from 1975 on are equipped with radial tires. Owners of cars less than five years old are assumed to switch to radials when current tires wear out (assumed to be in one year, on the average). We assume that owners of cars more than five years old do not switch to radials, but continue to replace worn-out tires with new bias-ply tires.
6. Scrappage rate, as a function of age of car, as discussed in Appendix B.
7. Auto engine and vehicle design practice and owner preference features, by market class, as described in the previous section. (Current air conditioning equippage rates for new cars: full-size, 91 percent; intermediate, 65 percent; compacts, 29 percent; subcompacts, 22 percent.)

In addition, to determine the effects of widely introducing radial tires, we compare the Base Case with one that is identical except that radials are *not* introduced; we denote this case as "Base—less Radials."

THE ALTERNATIVE CONSERVATION MEASURES DEFINED

The per-vehicle screening analysis discussed in the previous section identified a small number of promising conservation measures. Using these results, we can construct a set of cases designed to conserve energy in each of the three time periods—the near, medium, and long terms. In each time period, only technically feasible alternatives are included in the set considered.

All of these conservation measures are compared on the basis of the *same* average fleetwide scrappage rates and average annual miles traveled per auto as the Base Case. In other words, in this chapter, we ignore the induced impact of better fleetwide fuel efficiency in driving. For example, an increase in mpg would induce more driving per auto, and hence, less fuel conservation relative to the Base Case. However, in Chapter Seven, where we compare alternative policy instruments, we *do* include such induced effects.

The Near Term
In the very near term (i.e., up to five years) there are essentially three promising feasible technological options: add minor aerodynamic improvements to all new autos, continue the trend toward

small cars to the "limit," and the two combined.[a] To bound the effects on energy conservation, we have selected the first and third for examination; denoted as Cases A and B, these options are defined as follows:

Case A—Maximum Technological Change/Current Market Class Mix: The Base Case with all new car production having minor aerodynamic improvements beginning in 1975 and thereafter.
Case B—Maximum Technological Change/1976 Big Car Phase-Out: Case A with big car production (full-size and intermediates) phased out and small car production phased in over 5 years, at a rate of 20 percent per year, beginning in 1976—holding *relative* compact/subcompact shares constant at the Base Case values (i.e., 1:1.65).[b]

Case B, the big car phase-out option, is quite feasible and would not strain auto production and plant conversion capabilities, given 1974 model year experience. Given that a decision to do so is made in 1974, a 20 percent conversion rate is feasible, since it implies increasing small car (compact plus subcompact) production by roughly 1 to 1.25 million cars annually. This further implies a plant conversion rate of about 4 per year (400,000 autos/plant/year)—a rate consistent with previous DOT estimates [2].

Case B is clearly an upper bound near-term case, with regard to energy conservation, because we assume that the *relative* market shares of compacts and subcompacts remain at 1975 values. This implies that current owners or buyers of full-size and intermediate-size autos would *not* exhibit a decided preference for compacts over subcompacts, but would purchase them in the same proportions as do current small car buyers.

The Medium Term

We take as our definition of medium-term measures those that can be introduced in substantial numbers by 1980 (e.g., 20 percent of

[a]These constitute the promising set of measures, assuming no change in current comfort and owner preference features in each auto size class, such as air conditioning and luggage space. Auto air conditioners could be barred from the new car market in the near term, but we do not consider this option. Designing and introducing autos with smaller trunks, or no trunk at all, is not technologically feasible within one to two years, but is feasible within three years.

[b]Current sales of compacts and larger size autos comprise about 70 percent of new car sales. No convincing analytical models exist for projecting market shares under such a mandated weight standard. Consequently, this alternative should be viewed as an upper bound estimate of what could be accomplished in the near term by forcing weight control upon auto manufacturers.

annual new car production). This implies that medium-term cases can include some, or all, of the near-term measures.

The CVT-equipped SIE auto is clearly one candidate, given its promising nature, as identified in the previous chapter. Moreover, the CVT's developers estimate that it could be introduced by 1980 [3]. Another candidate is the substitution of the two passenger, trunkless small car for the subcompact. Still another is the introduction of the most promising ICE, the supercharged stratified rotary SIE. It appears that five to six years is adequate to do the necessary R&D, design work, and plant conversion to introduce either a new small car or a new variant of the ICE.

With this menu, we have constructed five cases for analysis that illustrate and bound the range of possibilities, depending on degree of technological change or change in owner preference features (i.e., size, comfort, luggage space). These are:

Case C—Minimum Technological Change/Current Market Class Mix: Add minor aerodynamic improvements, as in Case A; convert to CVT over five years at a rate of 20 percent per year, beginning in 1980.

Case D—New ICE Engine/Current Market Class Mix: Add minor aerodynamic improvements, as in Case C; convert to CVT, as in Case C; convert to *supercharged stratified rotary SIE* over five years, at a rate of 20 percent per year, beginning in 1980.

Case E—Minimum Technological Change/1976 Big Car Phase-Out: Add minor aerodynamic improvements and CVT, as in Case C; phase out big cars and phase in small cars, as in Case B.

Case F—Case E with 1980 Phase-In of Two-Passenger, Trunkless Auto: As Case E, but beginning in 1980, phase in uniformly, over two years, a two-passenger, trunkless auto for up to 30 percent of new car sales; assumed market class shares at the beginning of 1982 are 38 percent compact, 32 percent subcompact, 30 percent two-passenger, trunkless auto.

Case G—New ICE Engine/1976 Big Car Phase-Out: Add minor aerodynamic improvements and CVT, as in Case C; phase out big cars, as in Case B; convert to new engine, as in Case D.

In Case F, in which we begin introduction of the two-passenger, trunkless auto in 1980, we assume that their maximum market share will be 30 percent. We feel this is probably a reasonable upper bound, because such a car would attract primarily buyers from households owning two or more cars. As of 1971, about 30 percent of all households were in this category [4]. Case F continues to "limit" the near-term conversion to small cars.

We have not included a case combining a new engine, early big car phase-out, *and* the introduction of the two-passenger, trunkless auto (i.e., Case F with a new engine), although this option would show the maximum energy conservation potential. Such a case implies a continuous high rate of technological change and plant conversions in the auto industry over ten to fifteen years. Having converted to full small car production by 1980, and introduced a new engine on the heels of this conversion—which itself may be uneconomical—the auto industry is not likely to *also* introduce a new smaller car.

The Long Term
For the long term we have selected two measures involving the Stirling engine: one with the current market class mix and one with a phase-out of big cars beginning in 1976. We assume that the Stirling engine would be introduced at the rate of 20 percent per year over five years, but that introduction begins in 1985.

> *Case H—Stirling Engine/Current Market Class Mix:* Add minor aerodynamic improvements and CVT, as in Case C; phase in Stirling engine beginning in 1985.
> *Case I—Stirling Engine/1976 Big Car Phase-Out:* Add minor aerodynamic improvements and CVT, as in Case C; phase out big cars, as in Case B; phase in Stirling engine, as in Case H.

IMPACTS OF SHORT-TERM MEASURES

Figures 5-1 and 5-2 compare the impacts on fleetwide annual and cumulative gasoline consumption, annual energy consumption, and annual cost of implementing the short-term measures included in Cases A and B. These are compared with the Base Case and the Base Case—less Radials.

Annual gasoline savings due to the addition of radial tires amounts to about 4 percent, or 4 billion gallons, annually in the 1990s; cumulative gasoline savings of 70 billion gallons between 1975 and 1995 are feasible. Annual energy and cost savings are smaller in relative terms.

The implementation of minor aerodynamic improvements (Case A) has slightly larger salutary effects in the long run than the switch to radial tires; for example, annual savings in gasoline consumption are 7 percent between 1985 and 1995, and cumulative savings of some 90 billion gallons over the twenty-year period are feasible. However, because the existing fleet can be converted to radial tires quickly, whereas aerodynamic improvements are introduced into the fleet only through new car production, conversion to radial

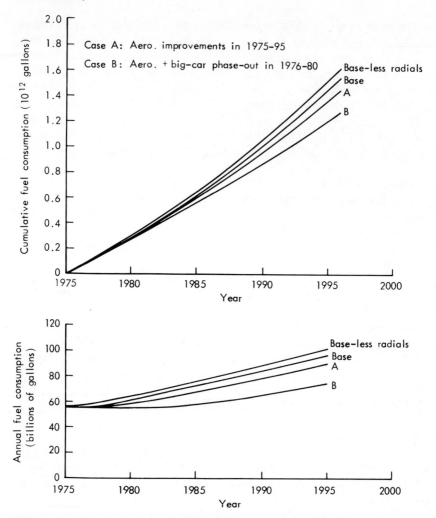

Figure 5–1. Fleetwide Annual and Cumulative Gasoline Consumption Impacts of Short-Term Technological Measures.

tires has an earlier salutary impact on annual gasoline consumption (as displayed in Figure 5–1).

Case B, the phase-out of production of large autos between 1976 and 1980 (and the substitution of compact and subcompact auto production), has much larger long-term effects. Compared with the Base Case, up to 23 percent of annual gasoline consumption (or 19 billion gallons) can be saved by 1990; however, in 1980, only about 11 percent (or 7 billion gallons) in annual savings are possible, because big cars will still comprise a large proportion of the auto stock,

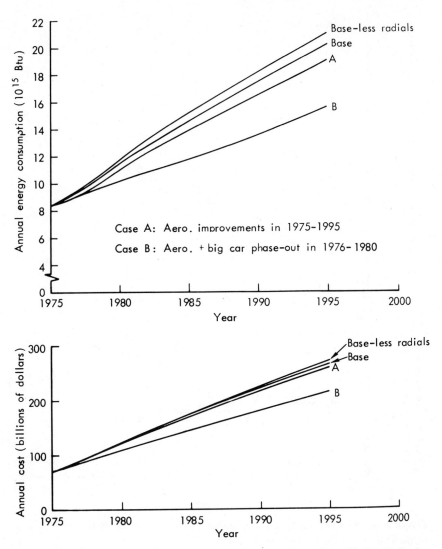

Figure 5–2. Fleetwide Energy and Cost Impacts of Short-Term Technological Measures.

even though production of new large cars has ceased. All in all, by 1995, Case B implies a cumulative savings of 270 billion gallons over the twenty-year period—or about 18 percent. By 1995, annual energy and cost savings of 23 percent and 19 percent, respectively, are also possible. Again, however, this short-term measure has small impacts in the near term.

In summary, *available short term technological measures can have*

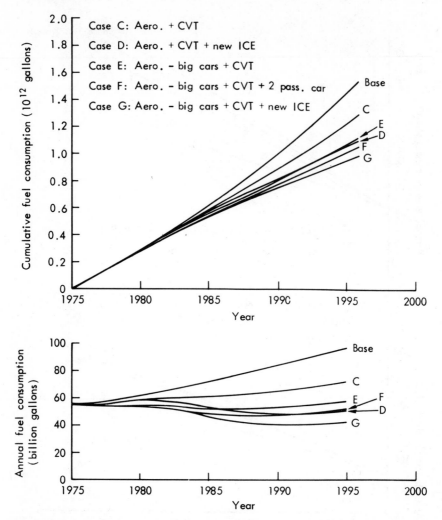

Figure 5–3. Fleetwide Annual and Cumulative Gasoline Consumption Impacts of Medium-Term Technological Measures.

only modest impact on fleetwide fuel and energy consumption in the next three to five years. And the only short term measure that can have substantial long run conservation impacts is a much more dramatic shift from large to small cars.

IMPACTS OF MEDIUM-TERM MEASURES

Figures 5–3 and 5–4 display similar impacts for medium-term measures. We turn first to a comparison of "pure" technological measures

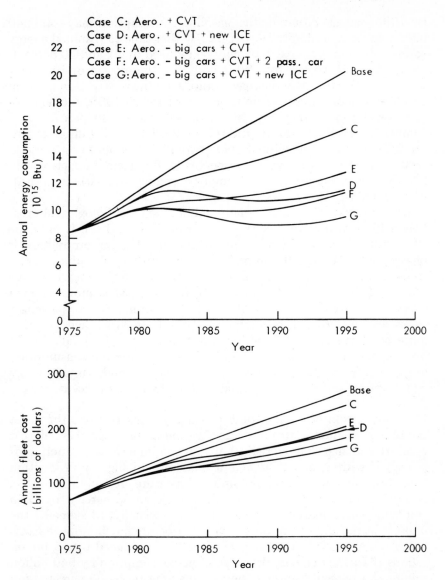

Figure 5–4. Fleetwide Energy and Cost Impacts of Medium-Term Technological Measures.

(i.e., Cases C and D) and assume that the anticipated 1975 new car market class shares are unchanged over the twenty-year period. Introducing the CVT in new cars, beginning in 1980 (Case C), can reduce annual gasoline consumption by over 15 percent (or 11 billion gallons) in 1985 and by over 25 percent (or 25 billion gallons) in 1995.

By 1995, savings in cumulative gasoline consumption may total 240 billion gallons, or almost 16 percent. By that time too, annual energy consumption and annual cost may be reduced by 21 and 10 percent, respectively. However, by *also* introducing the most promising new ICE (Case D)—the supercharged stratified rotary SIE—beginning in 1980, even more dramatic impacts eventuate. By 1995, annual gasoline consumption drops by 46 billion gallons (or 48 percent) and cumulative gasoline consumption is reduced by 430 billion gallons (or 28 percent). And annual energy consumption and cost are also reduced by 43 to 27 percent, respectively. But again, impacts within five to eight years are relatively modest and less dramatic than shifting to small cars.

We turn next to measures that combine such technological alternatives with a switch to smaller cars (Cases E, F, and G). If only the CVT, but not a new ICE, is introduced *and* big car production is phased out (Case E), the impacts are also substantial and salutary—somewhat less so than Case D (new ICE, but current market class mix) prior to the mid-to-late 1980s, and somewhat more so than Case D in the 1990s. If, in addition, a small trunkless, two-passenger car is also introduced, beginning in 1980 (Case F) impacts are even more salutary. By 1995, annual gasoline consumption falls by 45 billion gallons (or 46 percent) and cumulative gasoline consumption drops by 480 billion gallons (or 31 percent). And annual energy consumption and cost are also reduced by 44 and 32 percent, respectively.

Finally, from the viewpoint of energy conservation, the most promising medium-term measure (assuming unchanged small car comfort and size characteristics), would combine the introduction of the CVT with a new ICE *and* a phase-out of big car production (Case G). The impacts of this combined measure are truly impressive. Although annual gasoline consumption is down 36 percent by 1985 and cumulative gasoline consumption is down by 13 percent, the impacts at the end of the twenty-year period are much more substantial. Annual gasoline consumption in 1995 is reduced by 55 billion gallons (57 percent), cumulative gasoline consumption by 540 billion gallons (35 percent), annual energy consumption by 53 percent, and annual cost by 38 percent.

All of the short- and medium-term measures considered here involve the internal combustion engine and the Base Case variation of total fleet size and VMT with time. Assuming that 1976 statutory emission requirements are in fact met in all of these measures, Figure 5-5 shows the improvement with time of annual fleetwide weighted emissions. There is rapid improvement between 1975 and

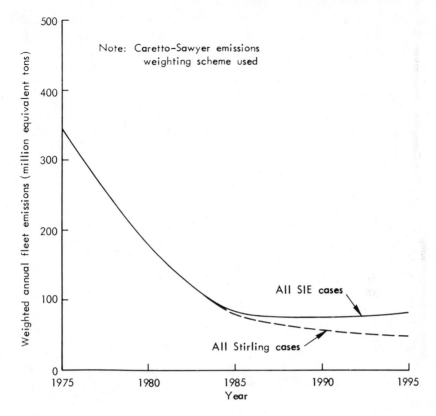

Figure 5–5. Fleetwide Weighted Emissions.

1985; emissions are reduced by 75 percent, because, by 1985, most of the fleet existing in 1975 (which is highly polluting) has been scrapped. Beyond 1985, fleetwide emissions remain essentially constant at 25 percent of the 1975 level.

IMPACTS OF LONG-TERM MEASURES

Figures 5–6 and 5–7 display the impacts of long-term measures. Cases H and I are analogous to medium term Cases D and G, respectively—that is, instead of introducing the new ICE of Cases D and G beginning in 1980, we assume that a Stirling engine is introduced beginning in 1985. Thus, Case H represents the most promising "pure" technology options involving the Stirling engine and Case I combines these technological options with an early shift to small cars.

As one would expect, gasoline and energy savings possible with the

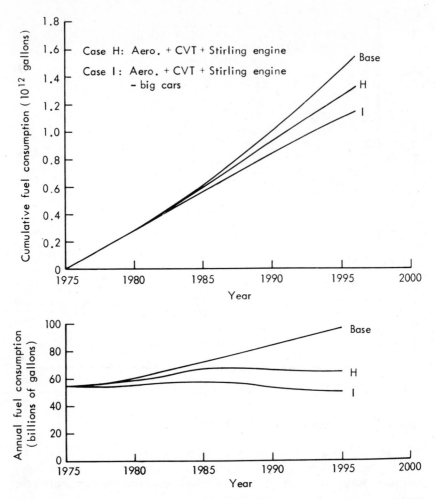

Figure 5–6. Fleetwide Annual and Cumulative Gasoline Consumption Impacts of Long-Term Technological Measures.

later introduction of the Stirling engine are considerably less than with the earlier introduction of the new ICE, over this twenty-year period. By 1995, Case H implies reductions in annual gasoline consumption of 33 percent (compared with 48 percent for the analogous new–ICE case) and in cumulative gasoline consumption of 14 percent (compared with 28 percent). Because the Stirling engine auto is heavier, more costly initially, and requires more energy to produce it, reductions in fleetwide annual energy and cost are not as impressive as in the comparable ICE case; for example, energy is reduced by 26 percent (compared with 43 percent), and cost is reduced by only 7 percent (compared with 27 percent).

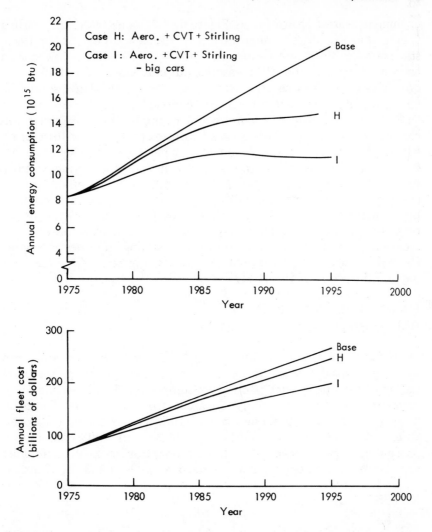

Figure 5–7. Fleetwide Energy and Cost Impacts of Long-Term Technological Measures.

Similar results obtain for Case I when compared with the analogous new–ICE case (Case G). By 1995, annual gasoline consumption falls by 48 percent (compared with 57 percent for Case G), cumulative gasoline consumption by 26 percent (compared with 35 percent), annual energy consumption by 43 percent (compared with 53 percent), and annual cost by 24 percent (compared with 38 percent).

On the basis of these four criteria, it is clear that conservation measures involving a new ICE dominate the comparable Stirling engine measures. However, as Figure 5–5 demonstrates, the Stirling engine options offer cleaner air in the 1990s and beyond. In 1995, for example, fleetwide annual emissions are 43 percent lower than those produced by the ICE measures, but compared with 1975 levels, *both* classes of options offer cleaner air. How the balance should be struck among consumer sovereignty, emissions, energy consumption, and cost, is not readily apparent. For example, these differences in emissions between the two classes of options may imply little or no adverse consequences for air quality or health, when viewed in the rural context—that is, one might well conclude that reducing emissions *below* the statutory standards has little salutary effect in rural areas and that the new ICE dominates the Stirling. In a number of urban regions, however, one may *not* be led to such a conclusion, because air quality standards may be difficult to meet without implementing a variety of clean air options, including the Stirling engine. However, analyses of regional air quality options and impacts is beyond the scope of this study.

SUMMARY COMPARISON OF ALL MEASURES

In Figure 5–8, we display all of the short-, medium-, and long-term measures considered, in terms of percent savings (from the Base Case) in fleetwide annual gasoline consumptions. How these measures compare over time is readily apparent from the figure. Opportunities for conserving gasoline prior to 1980 are limited and the overall energy conservation potential is small. Beyond 1980, combining a phase-out of large autos with the introduction of new technology promises very impressive savings indeed, as we have indicated earlier.

NOTES TO CHAPTER FIVE

1. *Passenger Car Weight Trend Analysis, Volume I: Executive Summary,* Aerospace Report No. ATR–73 (7326)–1, prepared for EPA, The Aerospace Corporation, September 30, 1973 (Rough Draft).

2. See D. Rubin, J. K. Pollard et al., *Transportation Energy Conservation Options* (Discussion Paper), Report No. DP–SP–11, Department of Transportation, October 1973.

3. Personal communication from Mr. Peter Huntley of the Orshansky Corporation.

4. *Consumer Buying Indicators, Household Ownership and Availability of Cars, Homes, etc.,* Current Population Reports, Series P–65, No. 40, Bureau of the Census, May 1972.

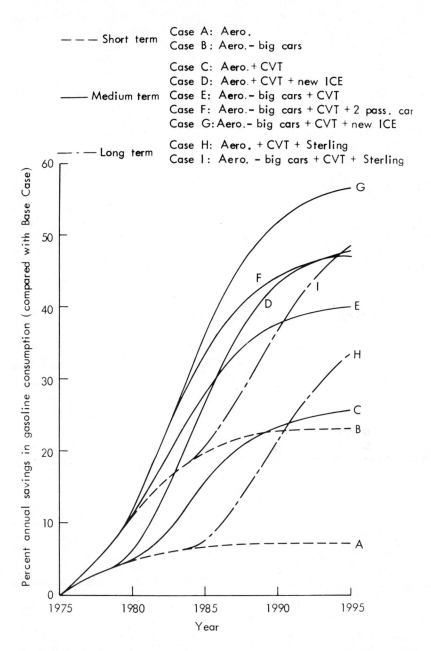

Figure 5–8. Percent Annual Savings in Fleetwide Annual Gasoline Consumption of Promising Technological Measures.

Chapter Six

Comparisons of Price Change Conservation Measures

In the last two chapters, we screened technological measures that would conserve energy in automobile transportation and identified the most promising ones. Here we turn to measures that involve changes in prices; we will deal with three types of price change measures:

1. *Gasoline price measures.* This group of measures involves a change in the price of gasoline; the change can stem from government action or market forces.
2. *New car price measures.* This group of measures involves a change in the price of new cars. Government actions could affect new car prices directly or indirectly. For example, a sales tax graduated by weight would affect new car prices directly. Mandated technological, weight, or fuel economy changes, if they alter manufacturing costs, could indirectly affect new car prices.
3. *Automobile ownership price measures.* This group of measures involves any change in the cost of owning an automobile, whether new or used.

THE BASE CASE DEFINED

From the analytical viewpoint there is a distinction between the case where the supply of gasoline is perfectly elastic at the prevailing (market) price and the case where greater supply is forthcoming only at higher prices. In the former case, variations in gasoline consumption have no effect on the market price of gasoline. This is the assumption that has been implicitly made in this study where we have assumed a constant real price of gasoline from 1975 through

1995 at every level of gasoline consumption. Clearly, this assumption is more nearly correct if the relevant supply of gasoline is based on the worldwide petroleum market. It can be argued that gasoline consumption by U.S. automobiles takes up only a small fraction of worldwide petroleum production (see Appendix E). However, under a policy of independence from (or at least, limited dependence on) foreign sources of petroleum, the supply schedule of gasoline and other petroleum products in the United States may be steeply sloped. In view of the uncertainties in connection with at least the specific details of U.S. petroleum import policy, we have concentrated on the demand side of the gasoline market. Thus, *the projections are intended to reflect the demand for gasoline if a projected future price holds*, rather than the market equilibrium projected from an analysis of supply as well as demand phenomena. The NAV Model is used to make such conditional forecasts, given assumed future real prices of gasoline (and new cars).

To use NAV, we must make assumptions concerning the number of future households, average disposable personal income per household, the inflation rate, the average price of new cars compared with other goods, and the average pump price of regular gasoline compared with other goods. Our assumptions are summarized below:

1. *Number of future households:*   Base Case forecast uses Bureau of the Census Series E and unpublished household projections [1].
2. *Real disposable personal income:*   We assume that constant dollar disposable personal income per household will increase at an average annual rate of 1.9 percent. This average annual rate is typical of the postwar period; it prevailed between 1950 and 1972.
3. *Inflation rate:*   We must consider the inflation rate because it affects the weights given to present and past incomes in the calculation of permanent income—the measure of household income used in NAV.[a] We assume a 7 percent inflation rate for 1974. The inflation rate is assumed to decline in equal annual increments to 2.6 percent in 1980 and remain at that level until 1995 (see Table S–1). This lower rate is typical of the period between 1950 and the mid-1960s. Our assumptions imply that the federal government will succeed in reducing the higher inflation rates of recent years and that price increases after 1980 will be more like those of the 1950s and early 1960s.
4. *Relative new car prices:*   The future course of new car prices in constant dollars is unclear. New car prices in constant dollars have

[a]Our permanent income measure is a weighted average of present and past incomes. A high rate of inflation gives more weight to present income.

declined since 1959 despite additional emission control and safety equipment. The New Car Component of the Consumer Price Index declined 33.5 percent between 1959 and 1973, when adjusted for the changes in non-transportation prices. On the other hand, the decline might be reversed due to more stringent requirements for emission control equipment and a higher price of energy. (Automobile manufacturing is a relatively energy-intensive activity.) Given this uncertainty, we assume average automobile prices in *real* terms to remain at their 1973 levels.

5. *Relative gasoline prices:* Between 1967 and 1972 the price of gasoline, relative to the price of non-transportation goods, declined 14.8 percent. Between 1972 and 1973, the relative price of gasoline increased 2.3 percent on an annual average basis; the large price increases in the fourth quarter of 1973 occurred so late in the year that the average price for the entire year was not much affected. The future price of gasoline remains unclear. Therefore, we will initially look at two different base cases—a High Gasoline Price Base Case and a Low Gasoline Price Base Case—used in the study.

For the High Gasoline Price Base Case, we assumed the national average pump price of regular gasoline, with taxes, to be 59 cents in 1974. This price implies a crude petroleum price of about $10.40 a barrel at the refinery.[b] Fifty-nine cents—after adjustment for overall inflation—represents a "real" increase of 41.2 percent between 1973 and 1974. We further assumed the average pump price of regular gasoline to be 67 cents in 1975. This corresponds to a further overall price increase of 13.6 percent between 1974 and 1975: 6.3 percent of this increase due to general inflation and 7.3 percent due to a further increase in the gasoline price relative to the price of non-transportation goods and services. We assumed that after 1975, the relative price of gasoline to remain constant—that is, the money price of gasoline will increase at the same rate as other prices.

In the Low Gasoline Price Base Case, we assumed the national pump price of regular gasoline to be 52 cents in 1974. This price represents a "real" price increase of 22 percent between 1973 and 1974. We further assumed the average pump price of regular gasoline to *decline* to 50 cents a gallon in 1975 as supply responds to the higher price. Fifty cents a gallon represents a decrease, in real terms, of 10 percent between 1974 and 1975, and it implies a crude petroleum price of $6.50 a barrel.[c] As in the high gasoline

[b]Based on ongoing, unpublished Rand research.
[c]Based on ongoing, unpublished Rand research.

price case, we assumed gasoline prices to remain constant in real terms after 1975—that is, they will increase at the same rate as overall inflation.

In April 1974, the national average pump price of regular gasoline with taxes was 51.6 cents. The high gasoline price case assumes further increases in 1974 and 1975. The low gasoline price case implies that nominal gasoline prices are close to a near term top and will decline in real terms.

It is important to understand what these assumptions imply for the base cases. The substantial increase in the relative price of gasoline that has taken place since the last quarter of 1973 implies decreases in gasoline consumption, vehicle miles driven in automobiles, and new car sales. The declines between 1973 and 1974 implied by the High Gasoline Price and Low Gasoline Price Base Cases are summarized in Table 6–1. As discussed in Chapter Three, we are not sure that adjustment to such large price changes will take place as rapidly as implied by the NAV Model. Whether these declines take place in one year or over several years, they represent significant reductions in gasoline consumption, vehicle miles traveled, and new car sales. All the increase assumed in the Low Gasoline Price Base Case, and about half the increase assumed in the High Gasoline Price Base Case, has already taken place. *This means that our analysis begins (in 1975) with base cases that imply a lower level of gasoline consumption, vehicle miles traveled, and new car sales, than has been the case in the recent past.*

Adjustment in the base cases to higher gasoline prices is completed rapidly; thereafter, growth in automobile gasoline consumption, miles traveled, and ownership, resumes—but at a lower rate. Annual average growth rates for the periods 1954–1972, 1972–1995, and 1980–1995 are compared in Table 6–2. The period 1972–1995 is included to show the overall impacts of higher gasoline prices on the base cases; the period 1980–1995 is included to show the impacts of the higher gasoline prices on growth rates after the initial adjustment

Table 6–1. Declines Implied by High and Low Gasoline Price Base Cases, 1973 and 1974

Base Case Changes between 1973 and 1974	*High Gasoline Price (%)*	*Low Gasoline Price (%)*
Gasoline Consumption	−22.1	−13.4
Vehicle Miles Traveled	−17.7	−10.4
New Car Sales	−20.0	−13.1

Table 6–2. Growth Rate Comparisons *(Average annual percentage rate of change)*

	Total					Per Household				
	1954–1972	*1972–1995*		*1980–1995*		*1954–1972*	*1972–1995*		*1980–1995*	
		High Price	*Low Price*	*High Price*	*Low Price*		*High Price*	*Low Price*	*High Price*	*Low Price*
Automobile Gasoline Consumption	4.9	1.7	2.7	3.3	3.1	2.9	0.3	1.3	2.0	1.8
Automobile Miles Traveled	4.4	2.0	2.8	3.3	3.1	2.4	0.6	1.4	2.0	1.8
Automobile Ownership	3.9	2.9	3.3	3.6	3.4	1.9	1.5	1.9	2.2	2.0

has passed. As a result of our assumptions, the future appears to be quite different from the recent past. Some comments are in order:

First, the growth rate of gasoline consumption falls sharply. During the years used to estimate the NAV Model—1954 to 1972—automobile gasoline consumption grew at an average annual rate of 4.9 percent. For the years 1972 to 1995, our assumptions imply growth rates of 1.7 percent in the High Gasoline Price Base Case and 2.7 percent in the low gasoline price Base Case. *In other words, we begin our analysis with base cases that have much lower growth rates than those of the recent past.*

Second, part of the decrease in growth rates is due to a decline in the growth in the number of households. Between 1954 and 1972, the number of households grew at an average annual rate of 2.0 percent. For the future periods, we are assuming 1.4 percent.

Third, the order of growth is reversed. Between 1954 and 1972, automobile gasoline consumption grew faster than VMT due to a decline in average miles per gallon. Also, VMT grew faster than automobile ownership, as VMT per automobile increased rapidly during the last five years of the period. Our assumptions cause the order to be reversed. Between 1972 and 1995, automobile gasoline consumption grows at a slower rate than VMT, because miles per gallon increases. (From 1980 to 1995, they grow at the same rate because miles per gallon is held constant.) Also, VMT grow slower than automobile ownership, because, in the NAV Model, an increase in the price of gasoline reduces VMT per automobile directly, as well as through automobile ownership.

Fourth, comparing the 1972 to 1995 period with the 1980 to 1995 period, we see that a large portion of the overall growth rate declines are due to the adjustment during the years following an increase in gasoline prices. However, after the adjustment, the change from declining real gasoline prices to high but stable (in constant dollar) prices causes a reduction in the rate of automobile gasoline consumption.

SCREENING CRITERIA

In our analysis of price change measures, we use three criteria:

1. *Total gasoline consumption.* Because the purpose of this study is to evaluate alternative ways of conserving energy in automobile travel, *the less gasoline consumed, the better.*
2. *Automobile miles traveled.* If automobile travel did not make

people better off, they would not travel. The best measure of automobile travel available for this study is vehicle miles traveled.[d] Then, *the more vehicle miles traveled, the better.*

3. *New car sales.* Fewer new car sales will result in lower earnings and less employment in automobile manufacturing. In Chapter Three, we argued that less employment, in the short run, is a negative impact. We arbitrarily define the short run as the period 1975 to 1978. *In this period, the less the fall in automobile sales, the better.*

PRICE CHANGE MEASURES COMPARED

American families and business firms can adjust to price change measures in three ways:

1. They can change the *number of automobiles* they own.
2. They can change the *miles per gallon* they get by changing their driving habits and/or the type of auto owned.
3. They can change the VMT *per automobile.*

Families and business firms will adjust to a change in price in one or more of these ways. In discussing each price change measure, we will indicate how each way of adjusting to price change measures works in the NAV Model.

Gasoline Price Measures

To illustrate the direction and magnitude of impacts within the NAV Model, we assumed a 50 percent increase in the price of gasoline in 1975. The pump price of regular gasoline increases from 67 cents to $1.00 a gallon in the high gasoline price base case and from 50 cents to 75 cents in the low gasoline price base case. After 1975, the real pump price of regular gasoline, (relative to the prices of non-transportation goods and services) is assumed constant. The impacts of this price change measure are summarized in Figure 6–1 for both the High and Low Gasoline Price Base Cases.

Adjustment Processes. A gasoline price increase will cause households to adjust in all three ways during the first year.

[d]Some might argue that a better measure of automobile travel is person miles—that is, one person traveling one mile in an automobile. Both automobile vehicle miles and person miles have drawbacks as measures. Vehicle miles ignores the fact that more than one person can travel in an automobile; person miles ignores the fact that for some trips traveling alone might be preferred to traveling with others—that is, commuting alone might be more convenient than commuting in a carpool.

1. *Automobile ownership.* In the first year, an increase in the price of gasoline will *reduce the demand for used cars.*[e] Used car prices will fall. However, the fall in used car prices will not be enough to induce families to own and operate all the used cars in the United States; *automobile scrappage will increase.* A fall in used car prices will also reduce the demand for new cars, since new cars and used cars are substitutes. *New car sales will fall.* Then, other things being equal, with new car sales down and automobile scrappage up, the number of automobiles owned will fall.

   We can indicate the size of these impacts as elasticities—that is, the percentage change in automobile ownership or new car sales divided by the percentage change in the price of gasoline. The elasticity of automobile ownership with respect to the price of gasoline is -0.34; for new car sales, it is -0.56.[f]

   At the start of the second year, total automobile ownership is less—that is, the potential supply of used cars is lower. If the price of gasoline is constant in real terms, the price of used cars begins to increase due to the lower supply. The processes described above are reversed; new car sales increase and automobile scrappage decreases.

   Within a year or two, an equilibrium growth rate in automobile ownership is reestablished. The equilibrium elasticity of automobile ownership with respect to the price of gasoline is -0.44.

2. *Miles per gallon.* A family can get more miles per gallon by changing its driving habits and by driving a different automobile. A family "produces" vehicle miles by combining its own time with an automobile, insurance, gasoline, and so forth. If the price of gasoline goes up, a family will use proportionately more of the other items, as a whole, and less gasoline to produce its vehicle miles. It can get more miles per gallon by driving slower; in effect, the family is substituting its time for gasoline. If the family owns two cars, it can increase its average miles per gallon by driving the more efficient car more often. This could also involve a substitution of the family's time for gasoline if it involved making trips at less convenient times or making more multiperson, multipurpose trips. The rate at which other items, as a whole, are substituted for gasoline is called the elasticity of substitution of gasoline in the production of automobile miles; we estimate it to be 0.17.

   While other items, as a whole, will be substituted for gasoline,

[e]The phrase "reduce the demand" means a shift of a demand curve to the left, not a movement upward along a particular demand curve.

[f]Automobile ownership and new car sales elasticities are calculated at the mean values for the period 1954–1972.

particular items might be used in either larger or smaller amounts. Above we described the automobile ownership adjustment mechanism; there, higher gasoline prices led to less automobile ownership. Higher gasoline prices might also lead to ownership of automobiles that are smaller or that have fewer power accessories.[g] This means that the miles per gallon adjustment process could include not only changes in drivers' habits, but also in owners' choice of automobile size and power accessories. In other words, *our baseline cases include some gasoline price-induced technological changes.* However, the size of our estimate of the elasticity of substitution implies that they cannot be large.

3. *Miles per automobile.* To conserve gasoline, families could drive their automobiles fewer miles. Our estimate of the elasticity of vehicle miles (given automobile ownership) with respect to gasoline is -0.37—that is, a 10 percent increase in gasoline price results in a 3.7 percent decrease in vehicle miles driven if automobile ownership remains unchanged.

Our estimate of the total price elasticity of automobile gasoline demand is -0.83 for the first year after a price change and -0.92 for the long run. In Table 6–3, we indicate the importance of each adjusting process.

Table 6–3. Adjustment to Gasoline Price Change Measures

	First Year		*Long Run*	
	Elasticity	*Percent of Total*	*Elasticity*	*Percent of Total*
Automobile ownership	-0.29	35	-0.38[a]	42
Miles per gallon	-0.17	20	-0.17	18
Miles per automobile	-0.37	45	-0.37	40
Total	-0.83	100	-0.92	100

[a]Estimated at the mean average annual growth rates of households.

[g]Note that from the viewpoint of the entire country, rather than a single family, our ability to "trade in" larger cars for smaller ones is limited at any point in time. It is limited by the available technology and market size classes in the automobile fleet and by the speed with which automobile manufacturing can shift from the production of one type of car to another. Between 1954 and 1972, year-to-year changes in new car and gasoline prices have been relatively small. Families seem to have adjusted to these small changes quickly. We are unsure whether adjustments to large changes in price measures will occur as rapidly. This is one reason why we regard our results as long term rather than short term.

Comparison with Other Estimates

Recently, several other estimates of the price elasticity of gasoline or motor fuel have appeared; these estimates are summarized in Table 6–4. These estimates use different data bases and include different adjustment processes. As might be expected, they vary greatly.

Economists have been more successful in providing good estimates of the price elasticity of *total gasoline* or *total highway motor fuel* demand than they have been at providing high confidence estimates of the price elasticity of *gasoline used by automobiles*—the focus of this study. Ramsey, Rasche, and Allen's estimates and Chamberlain's estimate use data bases closest to ours. Both lack a high level of statistical significance.

We are interested not only in comparing estimates of overall elasticities but also in comparing estimates of the elasticities associated with each way of adjusting to gasoline price change measures. We will look at individual components first; then turn to the overall comparison.

Automobile Ownership.   Economists who have provided estimates of long-run elasticities as well as estimates of first-year elasticities have used flow adjustment models. These models can be interpreted in either of two ways;[h] under one interpretation, they provide esti-

[h]It is difficult to know how to interpret the results from flow adjustment models since they can be seen in either one of two ways. One way is to view flow adjustment models as a delayed adjustment in automobile ownership. See Charlotte Chamberlain, "Models of Gasoline Demand," unpublished paper, Transportation Systems Center, DOT, Cambridge, Mass., fall 1973; and Hendrik Houthakker and Michael Kennedy, "Demand for Energy as a Function of Price," unpublished and undated paper, Harvard Univ., Boston, Mass., pp. 7–8. This view requires us to assume that average gasoline consumption per automobile and miles driven per automobile are unchanged; in other words, to assume that adjustment to gasoline price change measures can only come about through changes in the number of automobiles owned.

In the other view of flow adjustment models, one assumes that families do not completely change their consumption habits until a price change has persisted for awhile; this is the so-called adaptive expectations interpretation. On this view, all three ways of adapting to gasoline price changes are included but we have no way of knowing their relative importance.

Unfortunately, we cannot have our cake and eat it too; we cannot make both interpretations at the same time. A more complex model is required to include both adjustment processes. See Roger N. Waud, "Misspecification in the 'Partial Adjustment' and 'Adaptive Expectations' Models," *International Economic Review*, Vol. 9, No. 2, June 1968, pp. 204–17.

In most cases, it is not clear which viewpoint is being taken. Chamberlain discusses only the first. Houthakker and Kennedy and Data Resources, Inc. seem to imply—incorrectly—that both viewpoints can be maintained at the same time. See Houthakker and Kennedy, "Demand for Energy as a Function of Price," p. 8, and Data Resources, *A Study of Quarterly Demand for Gasoline and Impacts of Alternative Gasoline Taxes* (unpublished study), prepared for the Council on Environmental Quality, December 5, 1973, pp. III.2–III.3.

mates of the part of the adjustment to price change measures that results from a change in the number of automobiles owned. We estimate the part of the price elasticity of gasoline due to a change in automobile ownership to be -0.29 for the first year and -0.38 for the long run. All the other estimates of first year elasticities are lower than ours except that of Houthakker and Kennedy, which is estimated with international data. All the long-run elasticities are higher than ours except Chamberlain's, which uses U.S. data; however, it has a low level of statistical significance. However, our long-run estimate is close to the long-run estimate of Data Resources, Inc.

Miles per Gallon. We know of no other estimates of the miles per gallon adjustment process; hence, no comparisons are possible.

Miles per Vehicle. Two estimates of the miles per vehicle adjustment process are available. John Enns has estimated the price elasticity of gasoline due to the miles per vehicle adjustment process to be between -0.10 and -0.18; his estimates cover all types of highway use of motor fuel [2]. Chase Econometric Associates have estimated the elasticity of private vehicle miles due to the price of gasoline (with vehicle ownership given) at -0.32; their estimate covers vehicle miles of private passenger vehicles—automobiles and motorcycles [3]. Our estimate of -0.37, which covers only automobiles, is slightly higher.

Overall Elasticity. If we adopt the second way of looking at flow adjustment models (see footnote h), their results can be interpreted as including three ways of adjusting to gasoline price change measures. Their results then can be compared with our overall elasticity estimate.

Our overall elasticity estimate for the first year is -0.83. Clearly, all the first year elasticity estimates from the flow adjustment models are below our estimate. This is another reason why we believe that the NAV Model adjusts too quickly to gasoline price changes.

Our overall elasticity estimate for the long run is -0.92. It is slightly higher than other long-run estimates made with U.S. data. This is not surprising; the price elasticity of gasoline demand *for automobile use* could easily be higher than the price elasticity for all highway use or for all uses of gasoline. Our estimate is in the mid-range of long-run estimates made with international data.

The Impacts of a Gasoline Price Change. In Table 6–5, we summarize the estimated impacts of a 50 percent increase in the price of gasoline on our three screening criteria.

Table 6-4.   Recent Estimates of the Price Elasticity of Motor Fuel Demand

Author	Type of Data	Data Coverage	Adjustment Process	First Year Elasticity	Long Run Elasticity
J. Ramsey, A. Rasche and B. Allen	Annual U.S. data	Passenger car and motorcycles	All three	−0.77	—
Charlotte Chamberlain (D.O.T.)	Annual U.S. data	Passenger car motor fuel	Automobile and motorcycle ownership or all three	−0.06	−0.07
Data Resources, Inc.	Quarterly U.S. State data from 1963–1972	Highway motor fuel	Vehicle ownership only, or all three	−0.196[a]	−0.446
Louis Philips	Annual U.S. data for 1929–1967	Expenditures on gasoline and oil	Vehicle and equipment ownership, or all three	−0.11[a]	−0.68
Charlotte Chamberlain	Annual data for France, Germany, Netherlands, and United Kingdom	Total gasoline	Vehicle and equipment, or all three	−0.12[b]	−1.21
Hendrik Houthakker	Annual data for Austria, Belgium, Denmark, France, Germany, Italy, Netherlands, Norway, Portugal, Sweden, United Kingdom, United States	All uses	Vehicle and equipment ownership, or all three	−0.465[a]	−0.82
John Enns (The Rand Corporation)	Annual U.S. data for 1954–1969	Highway motor fuel use	Miles per vehicle	−0.10 to −0.18[a]	—

[a]Significant at or below the 1 percent level.
[b]Significant at or below the 5 percent level.

Sources: J. Ramsey, R. Rasche, and B. Allen, "An Analysis of the Private and Commercial Demand for Gasoline," unpublished paper, Michigan State Univ., Michigan, February 18, 1974.

Charlotte Chamberlain, "Models of Gasoline Demand," unpublished paper, Transportation Systems Center, DOT, Cambridge, Mass., Fall 1973.

Data Resources, Inc., Lexington, Mass., *A Study of the Quarterly Demand for Gasoline and Impacts of Alternative Gasoline Taxes* (unpublished report), prepared for the Council on Environmental Quality), December 5, 1973.

Louis Philips, "A Dynamic Version of the Linear Expenditure Model," *Review of Economics and Statistics*, Vol. LIV, November 1972, pp. 450–8.

Hendrik S. Houthakker and Michael Kennedy, "Demand for Energy as a Function of Price," unpublished and undated paper, Harvard Univ., Boston, Mass.

B. Burright and J. Enns, *Econometric Models of the Demand for Motor Fuel*, R–1561–NSF, The Rand Corporation (forthcoming).

Table 6–5. Impacts of a Fifty Percent Gasoline Price Increase
(Percent change from base case)

Year	1975	1980	1985	1990	1995
High Gasoline Price Base Case					
Automobile gasoline consumption	−34.6	−37.6	−35.3	−33.4	−32.4
Automobile miles traveled	−29.8	−32.7	−30.5	−28.4	−27.1
New car sales	−32.5	−2.3	−1.8	−1.6	−1.4
Low Gasoline Price Base Case					
Automobile gasoline consumption	−29.5	−34.4	−30.0	−29.1	−28.1
Automobile miles traveled	−24.5	−29.7	−24.9	−23.9	−22.9
New car sales	−21.8	−1.5	−1.4	−1.2	−1.1

A 50 percent increase in the price of gasoline would have a large and lasting impact on gasoline consumption and vehicle miles traveled. The difference between the two is due to an increase in average miles per gallon; we estimate that it will rise from 14.4 mpg to 15.5 mpg for the high, and from 13.7 to 14.7 mpg for the low gasoline price Base Case.

The reduction in vehicle miles traveled will be due to both a reduction in automobile ownership and fewer miles driven per automobile compared with the Base Case. In 1980, automobile ownership would be 25 percent less and miles per automobile 10 percent less in the High Gasoline Price Base Case, and 16 percent and 12 percent, respectively, in the Low Gasoline Price Base Case. In 1995, the declines would be 18 percent and 21 percent, respectively, in the High and 12 percent and 12 percent in the Low Gasoline Price Base Cases.

New car sales would fall greatly in 1975. However, as can be seen in Figure 6–1, they would recover rapidly. New car sales would be close to Base Case levels by 1978. Between 1975 and 1978, 5.3 million fewer new cars would be produced and sold than in the High Gasoline Price Base Case and 4.1 million fewer in the Low Gasoline Price Base Case.

In sum, *gasoline price change measures can lead to large and lasting savings in gasoline consumption by automobiles. However, they would be achieved through almost as large a reduction in vehicle miles driven. The impact on automobile manufacturing employment, through reduced new cars sales, would be large but transitory* (see Chapter Seven).

New Car Price Measures
Most new car price change measures have two aspects. One is to increase the price of less efficient new cars compared with the price

of more efficient ones. This type of price increase would increase the market share of more efficient new cars. The NAV Model cannot treat this effect because it is an *aggregate* model of new and used car ownership, gasoline consumption, and travel.

The other aspect is to increase the *average* price of *all* new cars. The NAV Model can deal with this directly. To illustrate the direction and magnitude of the impacts within the NAV Model, we assumed a 50 percent increase in the average price of new cars (i.e., a new car that would cost $5,000 before the tax would cost $7,500 after the tax). After 1975, the real price of new cars is assumed constant. The impacts of this price change measure are also summarized in Figure 6–1.

Adjustment Processes. In the NAV Model, an increase in the average price of new cars affects gasoline consumption only through the automobile ownership adjustment process. It does not affect the fleet fuel efficiency or the average VMT per-vehicle adjustment processes.

An increase in the average price of new cars causes the sales of new cars to fall. Our estimate of the price elasticity of new car demand (with used car prices constant) is −1.34.

But other things do change. The new car price increase shifts demand to used cars; families operate their cars longer before trading them for new ones. However, the supply of used cars is limited; it cannot exceed automobile ownership the previous year. The price of used cars must go up.

With higher used car prices, some buyers will return to the new car market. This happens not only because the price of used cars has increased but also because the used car price increase has made their owners wealthier. Our estimate of the price elasticity of new car sales, when the used car price feedback is included, falls to −0.32.

The net impact of the adjustment processes is to leave automobile and VMT essentially unchanged.[i] With fewer new car sales, the automobile scrappage rate must fall. The average age of scrapped automobiles increases. *In short, an increase in the average price of new cars will reduce the turnover rate of the U.S. automobile stock.*

[i]Automobile ownership and VMT actually increase slightly. However, the increase is not significantly different from no change. When new car prices increase, automobile ownership is affected in two ways that could offset each other. One is a *wealth effect.* Used cars are owned by families and business firms; an increase in used car prices would increase their wealth. One way that families could use their increased wealth would be to own more automobiles.

The other effect is an *ownership cost effect.* Here ownership cost means the value now of an automobile less its value next year. Ownership cost is a function

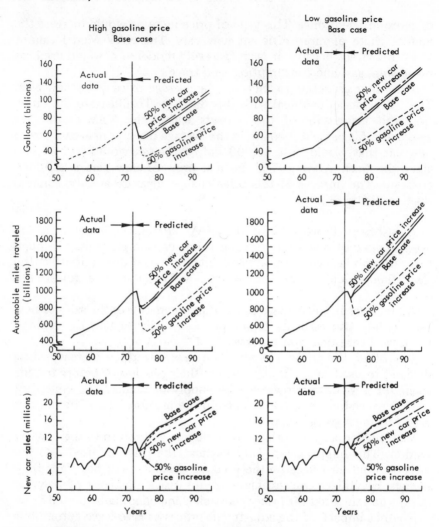

Figure 6-1. Base Cases and Price Increase Measures.

of the new price and of the depreciation rate. New car prices are increased by assumption; this would increase ownership costs. However, an increase in new car prices causes average car age at scrappage to increase; the depreciation rate falls. The fall in depreciation rates acts to offset the effect of an increase of new car prices on ownership costs. Ownership costs do not increase as much as new car prices. Conceivably, they could decrease. In the NAV model, an increase in new car price results in a less than proportional increase in ownership costs when reasonable assumptions about new car price and scrap value are made.

In sum, our empirical results indicate that the wealth effect is slightly more important than the ownership cost effect. However, the increase in automobile ownership is so slight that it could be due to statistical error.

Comparison with Other Estimates. Economists have been estimating the price elasticity of new car sales since the late 1930s [4]. With one recent exception, these estimates have ignored the feedback through the used car market. They can best be compared with our estimate of the price elasticity of new car sales, holding used car prices constant. Most of the estimates are between −1.0 and −1.5. Our estimate is −1.34.

The exception is work by Frank Wykoff [5]. He has estimated a demand relationship for new cars that includes measures of both new car and used car prices. He estimates the cross-elasticity of used car price on new car sales to be between 2.06 and 2.16. The elasticity in the NAV Model is 0.68. Our measure of price and Wykoff's differ; except for this difference, we cannot account for our divergent results. More work is required to settle the question.

Impacts of a New Car Price Change. In Table 6–6, we summarize the estimated impacts of a 50 percent increase in the average price of

Table 6–6. Impact of Fifty Percent Average New Car Price Increase
(Percent change from base case)

Year	1975	1980	1985	1990	1995
High Gasoline Price Base Case					
Automobile gasoline consumption	+3.0	+3.5	+3.1	+2.8	+2.5
Automobile miles traveled	+3.0	+3.5	+3.1	+2.8	+2.5
New car sales	−10.5	−12.5	−11.7	−11.0	−10.3
Low Gasoline Price Base Case					
Automobile gasoline consumption	+2.7	+3.1	+2.8	+2.5	+2.3
Automobile miles traveled	+2.7	+3.1	+2.8	+2.5	+2.3
New car sales	−9.7	−12.2	−11.7	−10.9	−10.1

Also note that a positive elasticity of automobile ownership with respect to new car price can only last until the automobile scrappage rate reaches zero, if the price elasticity of new car sales is negative. When the scrappage rate reaches zero, the elasticity of automobile ownership with respect to new car price must become negative, because automobile ownership can be increased further only with new car purchases.

Finally, even if an increase in new car prices results in a slight increase in total automobile ownership, it might not result in an increase in total VMT. In the NAV model, all automobiles—regardless of age—are treated alike. An increase in the number of seven year old automobiles would have the same impact on total VMT as an equal increase in the number of one year old cars. However, older automobiles are driven fewer miles per year than newer ones; see the Highway Safety Research Institute's National Exposure Survey. An impact of an increase in average new car prices is to increase the average age of automobiles on the road. One would expect annual miles per vehicle to fall. Because of the aggregate nature of the NAV model, we could not include this effect.

new cars on our three screening criteria: gasoline consumption, vehicle miles traveled, and new car sales.

A 50 percent increase in the average price of new cars would not conserve gasoline. Vehicle miles traveled and gasoline consumption would be virtually unchanged. New car sales would fall and remain below their Base Case levels. Between 1975 and 1978, 6.1 million fewer new cars would be sold than in the High Gasoline Price Base Case, and 4.0 million fewer than in the Low Gasoline Price Base Case. Not only new car sales but also automobile retirements would fall. In the High Gasoline Price Base Case, automobile retirements would fall from 9.4 million to 7.5 million in 1980; in the Low Gasoline Price Base Case, from 9.3 million to 7.4 million. With both new car sales and automobile retirements down, the turnover rate of the U.S. automobile stock would fall.

The fall in the turnover rate would reduce the effectiveness of a graduated tax that also increased overall new car prices. The purpose of a graduated tax is to improve average automobile fleet efficiency over time. How large an improvement in average automobile fleet efficiency would result from an increase in the price of inefficient vehicles, relative to the price of efficient vehicles, will depend on two things: the size of the shift in market shares[j] and the rate of turnover of the automobile fleet. An increase in the average price of new cars would reduce the turnover of the automobile fleet and, thus, lessen the effectiveness of a graduated tax.

[j]We are aware of two econometric studies that are trying to assess the impact on new car market shares of a tax graduated by weight class. Their results may be considered preliminary; work appears to be continuing on both.

The studies take different approaches. One is being done by Chase Econometric Associates; see "Report No. 2" (unpublished report), prepared for the Council on Environmental Quality), January 9, 1974. It uses standard regression analysis and national time series data. The other is being done at the Transportation Systems Center of the Department of Transportation; see Charlotte Chamberlain, "A Preliminary Model of Auto Choice by Class of Car: Aggregate State Data," unpublished paper, Transportation Systems Center, DOT, Cambridge, Mass., January 31, 1974. This analysis uses logic analysis and state cross-section data for 1972.

Their tentative findings indicate that a graduated tax could lead to a significant decline in the market shares of new full-size and luxury cars. However, both also indicate that there is a stable component of demand in each size class that is not influenced by cyclical, demographic, or price factors.

Even if a graduated tax is shown to have a large impact on market shares, this result would not imply that it should be the preferred policy. The same increase in average new car efficiency associated with any graduated tax could be achieved by some mandated weight or efficiency standard without the negative impacts of VMT and automobile turnover rate. Our technical analysis in Chapter Four showed that new automobile technologies would not have large adverse impacts on new car prices.

Automobile Ownership Price Change Measures

Like new car price change measures, automobile ownership (i.e., of new *and* used cars) price change measures can be characterized in two ways: increases in the relative prices of less efficient automobiles and an increase in the average price of automobile ownership. We can treat only the latter with the NAV Model.

In the NAV Model, the impacts stemming from this aspect of automobile ownership price change measures will approximate the impacts stemming from the parallel aspect of new car price change measures. Another forecast is not required. The reason for this result is explained below.

Automobile ownership price change measures are really two measures combined; the *new* car price change measure, discussed above, plus an additional tax or registration fee on used car ownership. The impacts of a new car price increase will be the same as those described above.

What about the additional tax on used car ownership? In the NAV Model, the price of used cars is demand determined because the supply of used cars cannot be expanded. The total price of a used car—market price plus present and future tax payment—will be the same as the new car price change measure case discussed above. The market price at which used cars are bought and sold will be reduced by present and discounted future tax payments. In other words, the additional taxes on used cars will be capitalized into the value of used cars. In the NAV Model, the net impact of the additional tax on used car ownership would be to transfer wealth from used car owners to the government.

In fact, complete capitalization of a tax on used cars would not occur (unless the scrappage rate was zero). Used cars always have some value as scrap. For any given price of scrap, the lower the *market* price of used cars, the more used cars would be scrapped. Compared with a measure that increases only new car prices, a measure that increased the cost of owning all automobiles in the same proportion would result in lower market prices for used cars and higher scrappage rates. Older, less efficient used cars would not be kept in the fleet as long. This means that adding a used car tax to a new car price increase measure would reduce the negative impacts of a new car price increase.

A SUMMARY EVALUATION OF PRICE CHANGE MEASURES

Earlier in this chapter, we offered three screening criteria—gasoline consumption, VMT, and new car sales in the years 1975 to 1978. (As discussed before, lower values of the first criterion are considered desirable, while lower values of the last two criteria are considered undesirable.)

We used the NAV Model to screen each price change measure with regard to these criteria. We were able to screen gasoline price change measures fully, but we were only able to partially screen new car price change measures and automobile ownership price change measures. We dealt with the last two insofar as they involved an increase in the *average* price of new cars.

We find that gasoline price change measures could reduce automobile gasoline consumption but also would mean reductions in vehicle miles traveled in automobiles over the entire time period considered. New car sales would decline sharply but recover quickly; the loss in unit output would range between slightly less to about the same for a 50 percent increase in the price of gasoline than for a 50 percent increase in car prices between 1975 and 1978.

To the extent that they involve an increase in *average* new car prices, *new car price change measures are counterproductive.*

How large an improvement in average automobile fleet efficiency would result from an increase in the prices of inefficient, relative to the prices of efficient vehicles, will depend on two things: the size of the shift in market shares and the rate of turnover of the automobile fleet. *We point out that an increase in the average price of new cars would reduce the turnover of the automobile fleet and, thus, lessen the effectiveness of the measures.*

Automobile ownership price change measures have two parts: a new car price change and a used car price change. We argued that, as a first approximation, ownership price change measures could be treated like new car price change measures because most of the used car price change would probably be capitalized into used car prices. The NAV Model treats automobile ownership price change measures in this way.

In fact, the negative impacts of an automobile ownership price increase would be less than those of just the new car price increase; the automobile scrappage rate will be higher for an automobile ownership price increase than for only the new car price increase. A higher automobile scrappage rate means lower total automobile ownership and a more rapid turnover of the automobile fleet. In other words, *if* a policy that involves an *average* increase in new car prices is contemplated, strong consideration should be given to a policy that would also increase the total cost of used car ownership.

While we have evaluated new car price change measures and automobile price change measures only partially, we showed that automobile price change measures have impacts that will reduce their effectiveness as gasoline conservation measures. On this basis, we will not consider them further. *In the next chapter we consider only policies involving gasoline price changes.*

FROM PRICE CHANGE MEASURES TO TAX POLICIES

We are moving from a broad consideration of many measures to a more detailed consideration of a few policies. Above we dropped new car and automobile ownership price change measures. From here on, we will compare policies using only one Base Case—the High Gasoline Price Base Case. We chose the High Gasoline Price Base Case because it is the one from which it would be most difficult to get extra savings.

The measures we considered above were expressed as percentage increases to Base Case prices. Their dollar value increased with inflation. In the past, gasoline taxes have been levied as a specific number of cents per gallon. We feel that it is realistic to assume that this kind of tax will be used in the future. In the next chapter, we will consider policies of increasing the gasoline tax by 15 cents, by 30 cents, and by 45 cents in 1975 and later years.

In considering government policies with respect to the price of gasoline, we have not explicitly analyzed the *incidence*[k] of a specific tax on gasoline. We have assumed that a 30 cent per gallon tax on gasoline results in a 30 cent increase in the retail price of a gallon of gasoline. In addition, we have not analyzed the effects that policies to limit the supply of gasoline (through import quotas, for instance) may have on gasoline prices and hence on consumption; rather the analysis here is limited to the case of a perfectly elastic supply of gasoline at the prevailing (market) price. If the supply is not perfectly elastic, the imposition of a tax on gasoline will result in a higher price for consumers but also a lower price for retailers and lower earnings for retailers, distributors, oil refiners, and eventually owners of oil producing lands. If the supply is perfectly elastic or near-perfectly elastic, the incidence will be primarily on consumers and retail prices will rise by the full amount or nearly the full amount of the tax. If the supply is perfectly inelastic or near-perfectly inelastic, the incidence will be primarily on the suppliers of

[k]*Tax incidence* is defined as the change in the distribution of income available for private use as the result of a tax. R. A. Musgrave; *Theory of Public Finance: A Study in Public Economy*; 1959; New York, McGraw–Hill, pp. 207–8.

gasoline and the retail price of gasoline will rise little if at all as the result of a tax. The question of the elasticity of supply is both an empirical question and a question of future government policy toward imports. Given the existence of marginal oil-producing lands, of unexplored areas, and of untapped petroleum sources such as shale oil, it seems reasonable to conclude, however, that there is at least some degree of elasticity even in domestic production. Therefore, a given increase in price can probably be achieved through a tax increase, although the tax increase may need to be somewhat larger than the desired price increase to account for the part of the tax borne by suppliers rather than consumers.

The lack of consideration of oil import policies and its effects on gasoline prices and consumption is due to this study's focus on the demand side of the gasoline market. Equivalently, we have not considered tax policies aimed at the production, refining, or importation of petroleum or petroleum-based products. Presumably some combination of "severance" (production) and import taxes could result in a price increase similar to that achievable through retail taxes on gasoline sales. Again, the emphasis in this study has been on policies *directly* affecting the demand for gasoline by private automobiles in the United States.

If inflation continues, the real cost and effectiveness of these taxes will fall. Our assumptions imply that the average price level will be 60 percent higher in 1995 than in 1975; an additional tax of 30 cents a gallon in 1995 would equal an additional tax of 18.7 cents in 1975. This means that *after* the taxes are imposed in 1975, the real price of gasoline *declines* for the rest of the period. Consequently, the growth rates of gasoline consumption and VMT, *after* the adjustment to the initial price increase, are higher than for the cases considered above. The impacts of each tax on gasoline consumption, VMT, and new car sales are shown in Figure 6-2.

In Chapter Seven, we will also look at gasoline taxes that decline through time and that are eventually removed. They will be assessed in combination with new automobile technologies and weight standards. Before moving to the next section, we want to show the impacts (in the NAV Model) of removing a gasoline tax. In Figure 6-3, we show the impacts of removing a 30 cents tax in 1986. Gasoline consumption and VMT return to Base Case levels in three years. New car sales jump for a year or two, as families increase their automobile ownership, and then return to their normal growth path.

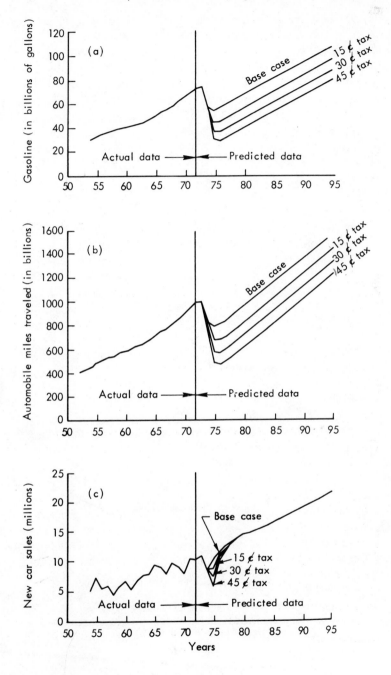

Figure 6–2. Impacts of Gasoline Tax Policies.

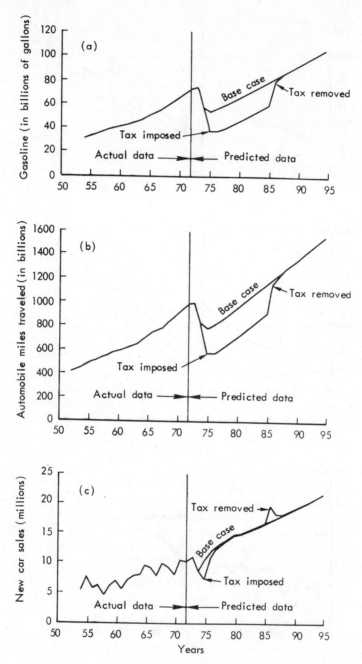

Figure 6-3. Impacts of Removing a Gasoline Tax.

NOTES TO CHAPTER SIX

1. See U.S. Bureau of the Census, *Current Population Reports*, Series P–15, No. 394, Table A; and projections prepared for the Commission on Population Growth and the American Future, given in U.S. Commission on Population Growth and the American Future, *Population Distribution and Policy*, Sara Mills Maxie, Ed., Vol. V of Commission Research Reports (Washington, D.C.: Government Printing Office, 1972), p. 12. Census *Series E* projections assume that completed cohort fertility will be 2.11 births per woman (about what it was in 1972).

2. Burright and Enns, *Econometric Models of the Demand for Motor Fuel*, R–1561–NSF, The Rand Corporation (forthcoming).

3. Chase Econometric Associates, "Report No. 2" (unpublished report), prepared for the Council on Environmental Quality, January 9, 1974.

4. For a summary of these estimates, see Lawrence J. White, *The Automobile Industry Since 1945*, pp. 94–95. More recent estimates include: M. K. Evans, *Macroeconomic Activity: Theory, Forecast, and Control: An Econometric Approach* (New York: Harper and Row, 1969); F. T. Juster and P. Wachtel, "Anticipatory and Objective Methods of Durable Goods Demand," *American Economic Review*, Vol. LXII, No. 4, September 1972, pp. 564–79; Richard B. Westin, "An Echo Theory of Automobile Demand," Ph.D. thesis, University of Minnesota, 1971; and S. Hymans, "Consumer Durable Spending: Explanation and Prediction," *Brookings Papers on Economic Activity*. Arthur M. Okum and George L. Perry, eds., Vol. 2, 1970, p. 196.

5. Frank C. Wykoff, "A User Cost Approach to New Automobile Purchases," *Review of Economics Studies*, Vol. 40, No. 3, July 1973, pp. 877–89.

Chapter Seven

An Exploratory Comparison
of Alternative Policy Instruments

To this point, we have examined *some* of the consequences and *impacts* of a number of energy conservation *measures*, on the assumption that such measures are indeed implemented. In this chapter, we view energy conservation options from the vantage point of the *federal policymaker*. We examine and compare the application of a number of *policy instruments* (singly and in various combinations) for achieving various levels of gasoline conservation. We consider different levels, but in some cases they vary with time; in others, they are relatively constant over time.

Guided by our previous analyses and screening of technological and price change conservation measures, we have constructed a number of alternative policy instruments for implementing the promising measures over time. These alternatives are compared in each of several years, in terms of the full array of impacts we mentioned in Chapter Three. They are the annual percentage change (compared with a Base Case) in:

1. Fleetwide *gasoline consumption.*
2. Fleetwide *energy consumption.*
3. Fleetwide *user cost.*
4. Fleetwide *VMT.*
5. *New car sales.*
6. *Employment* in five auto-related sectors.
7. Fleetwide *weighted emissions.*
8. Total *auto fleet size.*
9. A measure of *income distributional effects.*

Estimating these impacts (except for distributional and employment effects) required integration of the NAV, Auto Fleet Mix, and generalized Auto Design Models. Only in this way could we fully reflect all of the interactions and adjustment processes.[a] For example, in Chapter Five, we compared technological measures—assuming the same profile over time of auto fleet size, new car sales, and VMT. By integrating the models, we can reflect the induced effect on VMT of a change in the auto fleet fuel efficiency, as well as the induced effects of gasoline price changes on the VMT, total auto ownership, and new car sales of auto fleets with differing technological characteristics.

THE BASE CASE DEFINED

The Base Case, against which all the alternatives are compared, is the same as that used in Chapters Five and Six—that is, market class shares, owner preference features, imposition of a speed limit, and technological characteristics of the new cars, are as defined in Chapter Five. Assumptions regarding projections of population, real disposal household income, gasoline price, and auto fleet size are identical with those used in Chapter Six; these led to the Base Case projections of new car sales, used car demand, used car price, total auto ownership, VMT, and gasoline consumption shown in that chapter.

ALTERNATIVE POLICY
INSTRUMENTS DEFINED

In the screening analyses displayed in Chapters Five and Six, we were able to identify several promising measures, as well as some that show little promise. Guided by these results, we have constructed a series of cases for comparison, characterized as follows.

First, we define a series of cases representative of "pure" technological and "pure" economic policy instruments. Within each case we attempt to design the *level* and *speed* of application to maximize annual gasoline conservation, subject to reasonable technological feasibility constraints and reasonable rates at which new technology can be introduced or auto production plants converted. In other words, for these "pure" policy instruments, we adopt the view that the "energy crisis" requires the most vigorous efforts to conserve gasoline.

Because, as we shall see below, economic policies promise immedi-

[a]Estimates of income distributional and employment effects are made exogenously, but they depend on impacts (such as new car sales and VMT) that *are* estimated in the integrated set of models.

ate conservation payoffs, while technological policies require more time before payoffs are substantial, *combinations* of the two offer a reasonable solution to *both* shorter- and longer-term problems. We therefore construct a set of cases using combinations of technological and economic policies, with each case designed to offer a different, but relatively constant, level of conservation over time. Thus, for these combined policies, we ask and attempt to address the following question: Assuming alternative national objectives requiring that, between 1975 and 1995, projected annual gasoline consumption be reduced by x percent (where x is constant over time), can we design policies and estimate their impacts for several values of x? In this series of comparisons we make no attempt to "optimize" policies, because given the variety of impacts such policies can have, in both the public and private sectors, it is not clear how optimality should be defined.

With these considerations in mind, we turn now to a definition of the alternative policies. Throughout, we assume that, beginning in 1976, auto manufacturers will voluntarily equip all new cars with radial tires and redesign all auto bodies to include minor aerodynamic improvements.

Technological Policy Instruments

In Chapters Four and Five, we dealt with technological measures; there we did not consider *how* they might come about. We did not have to ask whether government action would be needed. Here we deal with potential government policies. First, however, we must ask whether government action would be needed.

We showed in Chapter Four that an automobile with interior and trunk space and performance characteristics similar to today's standard size car, but with much better fuel efficiency, could be produced at a cost no higher than today's cars. If the conclusion is right, and if the U.S. automobile industry is competitive, economic theory predicts that U.S. auto makers would build such a car without government action. Only if U.S. automobile manufacturing is not competitive in some way, would government action be needed to carry out the measures.

This question would have required a detailed study of the market structure of the U.S. automobile industry and the effects of foreign competition on this industry. We did not have the resources to do such a study. *Therefore, we cannot be sure that what could be achieved by mandating weight, technology, or fuel efficiency standards might not also be achieved through competitive market processes.*

However, others have studied technological innovation in automobile manufacturing and some evidence is available. Lawrence J. White recently studied the industrial organization and market structure of U.S. automobile manufacturing [1]. A major theme of White's book is that since the Second World War, U.S. automobile manufacturers have been slow to introduce major technological advances. White argues that this slowness is due to (1) the market structure of U.S. automobile manufacturing and (2) risk avoidance behavior.

Market Structure. In a competitive market with many auto makers, a particular auto maker would expect a technical innovation to increase his sales at the same price. The sales increase would come from (1) households that previously would not have bought a car and (2) households that would have bought a car from another auto maker. The innovator would expect to take a few sales from each of his many competitors. Consequently, he would not expect any other auto maker to react by bringing out a similar car. In U.S. automobile manufacturing, there are only four major auto makers. In this situation, each can take into account the possible reactions of the others before bringing out a new type of automobile. If an American auto maker believes that other makers would attempt to match his new type of automobile, he would also expect a smaller increase in his sales than would the auto maker in the competitive environment. He would expect to win fewer customers from his competitors. His incentive to bring out a new type of automobile is lessened. To support his argument, White compares U.S. automobile manufacturing today with U.S. automobile manufacturing before the Second World War, with U.S. truck manufacturing, and with European automobile manufacturing today. The pace of technological innovation in each of the comparison cases seems to have been faster than in today's U.S. automobile manufacturing industry. He attributes the faster pace to the larger number of firms in the three comparison cases.

Risk Avoidance. The demand for new automobiles is largely a demand to replace older automobiles. If U.S. automobile makers could get Americans to replace older automobiles sooner, their annual sales would increase. If U.S. automobile manufacturers provided more desirable cars, some Americans would replace their older cars sooner; a replacement demand means that auto makers have an incentive to provide new cars that buyers feel are more desirable than the ones they are driving. White argues that U.S. automobile manufacturers have chosen to provide more desirable automobiles through annual model changes and moderate incremental technological advances rather than through major technological advances. Annual model changes and moderate technological advances are less risky for U.S. auto makers. Developing a new car involving a major technological advance would mean greater costs, longer lead times, and less ability to adapt to a change in customer preference.

White brings together and summarizes his argument as follows:

> More generally, this author would argue that in cases in which the product variation is expensive and carries high risks and in which the mutual interdependence among the oligopolists is strong and is recognized as such, there will be a tendency for product competition to be limited. This is *not* to say that all product competition will cease and that the industry will become a virtual cartel. Rather, we should expect to see competition channeled into areas in which the oligopolists feel themselves more in control of the risks that are present and feel safe from the risks of breakthroughs by rivals. It seems likely that this is one of the reasons why the auto industry has chosen styling, rather than fundamental technological change, as the basic area of competition and why the free exchange of information has been so great in the industry.

If Lawrence White's analysis of the U.S. automobile industry is correct, a government policy action would be needed to carry out the technological measures. However, White's case is not completely airtight. One could make several counterarguments:

First, White offers his analysis as a way of explaining the behavior of American automobile manufacturers during the postwar period. Some factors that could affect the behavior of the automobile industry did not change much from year to year; gasoline prices are an example. Consequently, it is risky to rely on White's analysis to predict auto manufacturers' future behavior when there are large year-to-year changes in these factors.

Second, one must consider the role of imported cars in the American market. Innovations by foreign car manufacturers might force American automobile manufacturers to act; imports' increased share of the total market is often said to have caused American automobile manufacturers to introduce more efficient cars in the late 1950s and again in the late 1960s.

Third, our study covers a period of twenty years. Even if small efficiency improvements were introduced slowly, they could have a large impact by the end of the period.

To the extent that these counterarguments are valid, they would have little effect on the outcomes of cases involving government mandated technology, since presumably the government mandate overrides any natural tendency to innovate. However, in the Base Case and cases involving tax policies, consumption of gasoline may be overstated if the possibility of the independent adoption of new technology by the industry is ignored. Hence, the projected gasoline consumption under government mandated technology may be correct although the incremental effects of the policy of mandating technology may be overstated. The difference between the Base Case, say, and the case involving a specific government mandate is attributable to the difference in technology but not necessarily to the government policy *per se*, since some innovation may have occurred without government policy.

Finally, there is a whole range of possible government actions to influence automotive technology, ranging from jawboning to limitations on fuel economy, to specific technology. The analysis here has focused on "hard" measures that would result in clearly definable industry responses and not on "soft" measures based on persuasion, where response of industry is more difficult to predict. Of course, policies of either type that lead to the same actions by industry are equivalent.

We define four basic policy instrument alternatives: (1) a mandated maximum vehicle weight standard for new car production, (2) mandated technological change for new cars, (3) a mandated average annual fuel efficiency (mpg) standard for new car production, and (4) a case *combining* mandated weight standards and mandated technology—that is, (1) and (2) combined. All of the cases defined imply some variation of average new car fuel efficiency over time. For Case 3, below, we design three alternatives; for the others, we consider only one.

Case 1—Mandated Maximum Weight Standard

In this case, we postulate a regulatory standard that would implement Case B discussed in Chapter Five. The weight standard would be written to force auto manufacturers to phase out production of full-size and intermediate cars at the rate of 20 percent per year (beginning in 1976 and ending in 1980), and replace them with compact and subcompact car production. In 1976 and beyond, we assume that the *relative* market shares of compacts and subcompacts would be the same as in 1975. The market class mixes of new car production in 1975 and 1980 would then be as follows: Full-Size, 37 percent (1975) and 0 percent (1980 and beyond); Intermediate, 18 percent (1975) and 0 percent (after 1980); Compact, 17 percent (1975) and 38 per cent (after 1980); and Subcompact, 28 percent (1975) and 62 percent (after 1980). (See also Table S-2.)

This case is designed to illustrate the best that could be accomplished in the near term by forcing weight control upon the manufacturers. As our previous screening analysis indicated, *other* technological measures imply less conservation in the first eight years.

Case 2—Mandated Technology (CVT Plus New ICE)

In this case, we postulate that the most promising combination of new technological alternatives (but not auto weight control) is mandated. As our previous screening analysis showed, conversion to the CVT and the supercharged stratified rotary SIE, at a rate of 20 percent per year, beginning in 1980, holds the greatest promise in terms of gasoline and energy savings. The technological characteristics of this case corresponds to Case D of Chapter Five.

Case 3—Mandated Average New Car Production Fuel Efficiency (mpg) Standard

Mandating a new car fuel efficiency standard allows the auto industry more flexibility in meeting a standard designed to achieve specified conservation levels over time. Within such constraints, the auto industry presumably would seek to maximize profits or return on investment, although it is by no means clear how they would value profits in the short, as against the long, term. It is conceivable that one auto company might choose to emphasize one and another company the other. Even if there was a consensus, and its character was publicly known, there is insufficient knowledge and data with which to translate maximization of profit or return on investment into practical decisions about the mix of new technological and weight control measures that will achieve a given mpg standard. Therefore, to bound the range of possible impacts, we have constructed three cases that meet the *same* specified standard: one using only new technology, one using only auto weight (or size) control, and one using both.

We take as our fuel efficiency standard that implied by Case 2—the introduction of the CVT and the new ICE. Figure 7-1 displays the fuel efficiency standard profile over time. (For comparative purposes, we also display the average new car fuel efficiency profiles that result by implementing a mandated weight standard (Case 1) as well as combining the Case 1 mandated weight standard with the

Case 2 mandated technology—see Case 4, below). The fuel efficiency of the Base Case new car fleet remains constant at 16 mpg. In Case 1, the new car fleet average mpg is 17.2 in 1975, which reflects the addition of minor aerodynamic improvements; as large cars are phased out, in accordance with the mandated weight standard, and replaced by small cars, fuel efficiency rises to 21 mpg in 1984 and remains constant thereafter. The Case 3 fuel efficiency standard is constant at 17.2 mpg between 1975 and 1979 and then rises steeply to 32 mpg in 1984 when both the CVT and the new ICE are fully introduced into new car production. After 1985, the standard remains constant at this value.

As we noted above, one polar alternative is to attempt to meet the standard solely by the introduction of new technology. We denote this alternative as Case 3a; in terms of impacts, it is identical with Case 2.

Another polar alternative is to try to meet the standard by only producing very small cars; we denote this alternative as Case 3b. One way to do this is to phase out full-size and intermediate production in 1980, then increase modestly the share of compacts produced in 1980–1981, followed by a halt in their production, with a rapid buildup of subcompact production between 1980 and 1982 until they account for 90 percent of all new car production. Finally, with a gradual introduction of the urban two-passenger trunkless auto beginning in 1980, followed by a decline in the subcompact share and conversion to the urban auto, in 1984 and thereafter, the subcompact/urban auto shares are 35 to 65 percent, respectively. This case is summarized in Table 7–1.

We see that, in attempting to meet such a stringent fuel efficiency standard purely by auto weight control, we are led to a very different world in 1985—a world in which auto comfort, roominess, and trunk space is reduced to subcompact levels in 35 percent of new cars and to urban runabout levels in the remaining 65 percent of new cars. This case implies that there would have to be substantial modal shifts to bus, rail, and air for long trips. Moreover, such a plant conversion schedule may also strain the auto manufacturers' capabilities. Although we do not consider such a case to be very realistic, we have included it in our analysis to bound the range of impacts that may result from the imposition of a stringent fuel efficiency standard.

Finally, we consider a third alternative (Case 3c) in which some limited new technology—that is, a CVT—is introduced in combination with a phase-out of big cars. In this case, new car production consists of roughly half subcompacts and half trunkless subcompacts. The market class share profiles are summarized in Table 7–2. Compared with Case 3b, Case 3c implies less substantial modal shifts to

Table 7–1. Market Class Shares, by Policy Option: Case 3b—Mandated Size Control

	Market Class Shares (%)					
	1975–1979	*1980*	*1981*	*1982*	*1983*	*1984–1995*
Full-Size	37	23	0	0	0	0
Intermediate	18	11	0	0	0	0
Compact	17	22	32	0	0	0
Subcompact	28	44	68	90	62	35
Urban, Two-Passenger, Trunkless	0	0	0	10	38	65

Table 7–2. Market Class Shares, by Policy Option: Case 3c—New Technology plus Size Control

	Market Class Shares (%)					
	1975–1979	*1980*	*1981*	*1982*	*1983*	*1984–1995*
Full-Size	37	26	14	0	0	0
Intermediate	18	13	7	0	0	0
Compact	17	20	26	18	25	0
Subcompact	28	41	53	72	75	51
Trunkless Subcompact	0	0	0	0	0	49

bus, rail, and air for long trips. But such modal shifts would still be significant, because in half of the new cars, long trips requiring luggage to be carried are only possible with two occupants.

Of course, had we selected a less stringent fuel efficiency standard for analysis, auto weight control measures needed would imply less change in auto transportation service characteristics. But our purpose here is to illustrate the range of possible impacts (given alternative approaches by the auto industry) of setting standards aimed at maximizing fuel conservation.

Case 4—Mandated Weight Standard and Technology (Cases 1 and 2 Combined)

This case combines Cases 1 and 2. The average new car fleet fuel efficiency that would result is included in Figure 7—1. Note that until

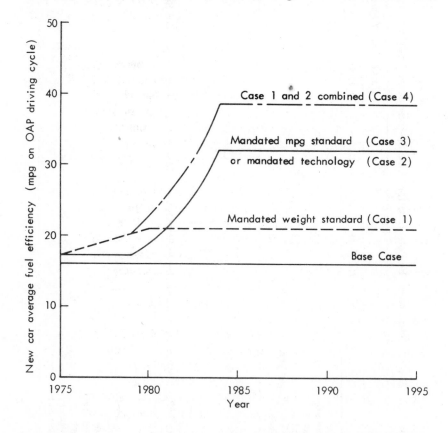

Figure 7—1. Predicted or Mandated Average Fuel Efficiency of the New Car Fleet (mpg).

1978 it is identical with Case 1, but thereafter increases rapidly, and reaches an impressive value of 38.5 mpg in 1984.

Case 5—Additional (Constant) Gasoline Taxes

We explore the effects of three levels of additional gasoline taxation (to the Base Case); 15, 30 and 45 cents (in 1975 dollars)—all held constant over the twenty years.

Case 6—Variable Additional Gasoline Tax
and a Mandated Weight Standard

In Cases 6, 7 and 8 we combine variable (with time) gasoline tax schedules with Cases 1, 2, and 4, respectively. In Case 6, we add a variable additional tax on gasoline (in 1975 dollars) to the mandated weight standard (Case 1), so that annual fleetwide reduction in gasoline consumption remains relatively constant at 16 to 18 percent over the twenty year period. Figure 7–2 displays the variable additional tax needed to achieve such a conservation level—from 14 cents

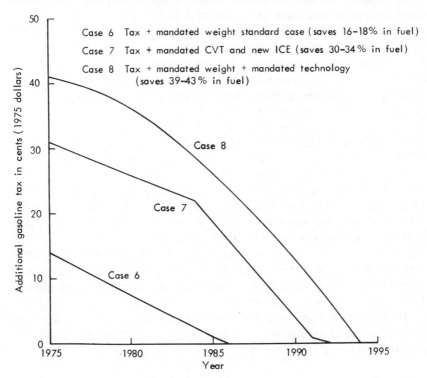

Figure 7–2. Variable Additional Gasoline Taxes Needed to Achieve Specified Conservation Levels.

in 1975 declining to zero in 1986. In essence, Case 6 is designed to illustrate the impacts of near term policy instruments aimed at relatively modest, constant (in relative terms) fuel conservation over time.

Case 7—Variable Additional Gasoline Tax and Mandated Technology

In Case 7 we add a variable additional tax (declining from 31 cents in 1975 to zero in 1992) to the mandated technology of Case 2. This case illustrates the impacts of combining a tax with promising medium term technology—the CVT and a new ICE—all designed to conserve 30 to 32 percent of the annual fuel consumed over the twenty year period.

Case 8—Variable Additional Gasoline Tax Plus Mandated Weight Standards and Technology

In Case 8 we illustrate the impacts by combining a tax with Case 4—a mandated weight standard and mandated technology—all designed to conserve 39 to 43 percent of the annual fuel consumed over the twenty year period. The tax declines from 41 cents in 1975 to zero in 1994. In essence, this case is designed to conserve the maximum constant fraction of fuel consumption that is possible with additional gasoline taxation, new technology, and a shift to small cars.

FINDINGS: TECHNOLOGICAL VERSUS TAX POLICIES

Here we discuss the findings resulting from the application of "pure" technological and "pure" pricing policies (Cases 1 to 5). Tables 7–3 through 7–6 compare the estimated impacts resulting from implementation of these policies in each of four years: 1976, 1980, 1985, and 1995. In addition to showing the Base Case impacts, we display the percentage change in each impact compared with its Base Case value in that year. Income distributional effects are discussed in the text, but not shown in the tables.

We leave it to the reader to make detailed quantitative comparisons of impacts among the policies; here we present the broad findings in largely qualitative terms:

First, in the *near term*, a constant (in 1975 dollars) *gasoline tax is much more effective in reducing gasoline and energy consumption*, whereas policies aimed at improving fuel economy, by changing technology and/or inducing a dramatic shift to small cars, do not have substantial energy conservation impacts until after 1980. However, *by the 1980s and early 1990s*, the impacts are reversed; *regulatory policies* aimed at improving fuel economy *show more promise* (short of additional gasoline taxes greater than 50 cents per gallon) *than a gasoline tax.* In the near term, it can be expected that annual fleetwide gasoline consumption can be reduced by roughly 1 percent for every additional cent of gasoline tax imposed; by the 1990s, gasoline conservation per additional 1975 cent of tax is reduced to roughly 0.6 percent, assuming constant real pump price (before taxes) of gasoline over the twenty-year period.

Second, imposition of additional *gasoline taxes* have a number of other impacts. There is a small, but *significant reduction in new car sales in the early years*, but the effect does not persist, and sales climb back to roughly the same value as in the Base Case. However, *auto ownership is reduced significantly* over the entire time period, but particularly in the early years, as owners retire their used cars rapidly. This leads to a *large reduction in VMT*, which is roughly proportional to the relative savings in gasoline consumption. A reduction in VMT presumably would lead also to reduced urban congestion. The combined effects of much higher auto scrappage rates (of older cars with high emission rates) in the early years and a persistent reduction in VMT, results in *very rapid reductions in total emissions by 1980.* For example, by 1980, a 45 cent additional tax leads to an 83 percent reduction in fleetwide emissions. Although fuel cost per mile rises because of the tax, the *reduction in total annual user cost of the auto stock is substantial in the early years*, because of off-setting effects of reduced ownership and VMT. But as scrappage rates decline and new car sales climb back to their Base Case values, the cost reductions become relatively small.

Additional gasoline taxes cause persistent, but declining, reductions in employment roughly proportional to the tax level. In the early years the decline in employment is felt in all five sectors because both new car production and VMT decrease, but in the later years the employment decline is only felt in the sales and service sectors, because new car production is largely unaffected.

In the near term, the impact of additional gasoline taxes on the proportion of earnings spent for auto work trips bears more heavily on commuters from families with below average earnings. Each 15 cent increase in the tax per gallon results in approximately a 0.5 percent increase in the share of earnings devoted to auto work trips for households earning less than $13,500 in 1975. For upper earnings groups the percentage increase is only 0.1 to 0.3 percent.

Table 7-3. Comparative Impacts of Alternative Policy Instruments: 1976

		Impact Category	
Case No.	Policy Instrument(s)	Annual Fleetwide Gasoline Consumption (% change)	Annual Fleetwide Energy (% change)
—	Base Case	(55.8 billion gal)	(9.00 x 10^15 Btu)
	Technological		
1	Maximum weight standard	−1.5	−4.3
2	Mandate technology (aerodynamics plus CVT plus new ICE)	−1.1	−3.0
3	Average new car fleet mpg standard		
	a. By new technology (Case 2)	−1.1	−3.0
	b. By small cars only	−1.1	−3.0
	c. By small cars plus CVT	−1.0	−3.0
4	Case 1 and Case 2 combined	−1.5	−3.2
	Price		
5	Additional gasoline tax		
	a. 15¢; 1975–1995[b]		
	b. 30¢; 1975–1995[b]		
	c. 45¢; 1975–1995[b]		

[a]Employment changes are denoted as a range; the lefthand entry is calculated including a weight effect on auto production, while the righthand entry assumes no weight effect on employment.

[b]As discussed in Chapter Six, the NAV Model predicts very rapid adjustments of

Third, *by 1980* it is possible to *conserve up to 10 percent* of annual fleetwide gasoline consumption by implementing regulatory policies that will induce a dramatic shift to small cars. Policies that only affect the introduction of new technology—such as CVT and a new ICE (the supercharged stratified rotary SIE)—have less influence on conservation in the near term. However, by 1995, mandating technology conserves much more gasoline than mandating weight standards.[b] And *mandating both can conserve up to 40 percent of gasoline consumption.*

[b]We might be underestimating the gasoline savings for the cases with a mandated shift to smaller cars, (i.e., in Cases 1, 3b, 3c, and 4.) With a constant real price of gasoline and a mandated increase in average new car fuel economy, the real cost of driving *per mile* falls. In the version of the NAV Model used here, the fall in the real cost of driving per mile induces more driving; the added driving acts to partially offset the gasoline savings due to the initial increase in miles per gallon. This process is valid when automobile comfort and performance is un-

Table 7–3. continued

			Impact Category		
Annual Fleetwide User Cost (% change)	Annual Fleetwide VMT (% change)	Annual New Car Sales (% change)	Employment[a] (% change)	Annual Fleetwide Weighted Emission (% change)	Total Auto Fleet Size (% change)
($78.2 billion)	(805 billion mi)	(11.8 million)	(2.98 million)	(309 million equivalent tons)	(90.9 million)
−1.8	+1	0	−4 to −2	~ 0	0
−1.6	+0.7	0	−2 to −2	~ 0	0
−1.6	+0.7	0	−2 to −2	~ 0	0
−1.7	+0.7	0	−2 to −2	~ 0	0
−1.6	+0.7	0	−2 to −2	~ 0	0
−2.0	+1	0	−4 to −2	~ 0	0

auto ownership, VMT, and gasoline consumption to gasoline price changes; consequently, we feel that its predictions of these impacts (and fleetwide energy, user cost, employment, and emissions that depend on these impacts) are unrealistic for the years immediately following a gasoline price change.

Fourth, technological policies and gasoline tax policies have differing impacts. In general, we predict *no change in new car sales and auto ownership*, because in our models, these are dependent on new and used car prices, gasoline prices, and income—none of them different from the Base Case values. However, as new car fuel economy increases with time due to these policies, the cost of driving per mile falls and *more vehicle miles are driven*. We estimate the VMT increase roughly in proportion to gasoline savings. VMT increases also are

changed, as in cases where technology is mandated (Case 1) or where mandated fuel economy standards are implemented by introducing new technology. It might *not* give correct results when new car weight and size are decreased due to government mandates. If individuals enjoy riding in a smaller automobile less than in a larger one, the mandated weight and size reductions might lead to *less* driving. The NAV Model does not account for this effect. If this effect exists, conditional forecasts of VMT are too high and our conditional forecasts of gasoline savings are too low in Cases 1, 3b, 3c, and 4.

Table 7–4.   Comparative Impacts of Alternative Policy Instruments: 1980

Case No.	Policy Instrument(s)	*Annual Fleetwide Gasoline Consumption (% change)*	*Annual Fleetwide Energy (% change)*
		Impact Category	
—	Base Case	(66.1 billion gal)	$(11.80 \times 10^{15}$ Btu)
	Technological		
1	Maximum weight standard	−9.5	−7.6
2	Mandate technology (aerodynamics plus CVT plus new ICE)	−7.0	−3.4
3	Average new car fleet mpg standard		
	a. By new technology (Case 2)	−7.0	−3.4
	b. By small cars only	−7.0	−3.4
	c. By small cars plus CVT	−7.0	−3.4
4	Case 1 and Case 2 combined	−10.3	−8.5
	Price		
5	Additional gasoline tax		
	a. 15¢; 1975–1995	−16.2	−11.8
	b. 30¢; 1975–1995	−29.2	−21.9
	c. 45¢; 1975–1995	−40.5	−31.2

[a]Employment changes are denoted as a range; the lefthand entry is calculated including a weight effect on auto production, while the righthand entry assumes no weight effect on employment.

likely to lead to increased urban congestion. Also, because VMT increase, (but scrappage rates do not change from Base Case values), *total fleetwide emissions increase substantially*, being roughly proportional to the increase in VMT. For example, by 1995, a policy of mandating new technology results in about a 39 percent increase in VMT and emissions, but a decrease in gasoline consumption of 34 percent. *Although user cost reductions are small in the early years, they become quite substantial in later years.* For example, by 1995, depending on the policy, user cost is reduced by 13 to 29 percent.

Although new car sales and auto ownership are unchanged, the increase in VMT and auto weight changes have varied effects on employment. Auto weight reductions lead to reduction in manufacturing employment, but improved fuel economy, which results in more VMT, leads to increased employment in all sectors. If the weight effect on employment holds for large decreases in new car weight, it dominates in all years, resulting in up to an 11 percent

Table 7–4. continued

double counting

			Impact Category		
Annual Fleetwide User Cost (% change)	Annual Fleetwide VMT (% change)	Annual New Car Sales (% change)	Employment[a] (% change)	Annual Fleetwide Weighted Emission (% change)	Total Auto Fleet Size (% change)
($124 billion)	(953.5 billion mi)	(14.7 million)	(3.37 million)	(181 million equivalent tons)	(109.3 million)
−6.5	+8.5	0	−8 to +1	+4.3	0
−1.7	+5.9	0	−3 to 0	+2.2	0
−1.7	+5.9	0	−3 to 0	+2.2	0
−1.7	+5.9	0	−4 to 0	+2.2	0
−1.7	+5.9	0	0 to 0	+2.2	0
−7.3	+8.9	0	−10 to +1	+5.0	0
−4.1	−13.6	−0.6	−8 to −8	−29.8	−9.2
−8.9	−25.2	−0.9	−14 to −14	−61.7	−18.5
−13.0	−35.7	−1.4	−19 to −19	−82.7	−27.8

decline (depending on the policy); if only the VMT effect is considered, there is only a small decrease in employment in the early years, but there is up to a 16 percent *increase* in employment by 1995 (depending on the policy).

Capital resources available to the auto manufacturing industry—either through internal reallocation (e.g., deferral of annual model changes) or through external sources (e.g. borrowing)—appear adequate to finance conversion to an alternative type of power plant and transmission, according to a recent study of the economic impact on the industry of mass production of new power systems [2]. Total capital investment required is roughly the same as a single year's current capital expenditures by the motor vehicle industry. (And the industry's price leader, General Motors, currently makes no use of borrowed funds).

Fifth, a number of observations may be made regarding the comparative impacts of technological policies. Comparing mandated weight standards with mandated technology, both designed to conserve as much gasoline as possible within bounds of economic and

Table 7–5.   Comparative Impacts of Alternative Policy Instruments: 1985

Case No.	Policy Instrument(s)	Annual Fleetwide Gasoline Consumption (%) change)	Annual Fleetwide Energy (% change)
		Impact Category	
—	Base Case	(79.6 billion gal)	(15.2 x 10^{15} Btu)
	Technological		
1	Maximum weight standard	−16.2	−13.8
2	Mandate technology (aerodynamics plus CVT plus new ICE)	−20.2	−13.8
3	Average new car fleet mpg standard		
	a. By new technology (Case 2)	−20.2	−15.8
	b. By small cars only	−20.2	−18.4
	c. By small cars plus CVT	−20.2	−17.1
4	Case 1 and Case 2 combined	−26.2	−23.7
	Price		
5	Additional gasoline tax		
	a. 15¢; 1975–1995	−13.6	−9.9
	b. 30¢; 1975–1995	−25.0	−17.7
	c. 45¢; 1975–1995	−34.5	−25.7

[a]Employment changes are denoted as a range; the lefthand entry is calculated including a weight effect on auto production, while the righthand entry assumes no weight effect on employment.

technological feasibility, we see that *mandating a CVT and new ICE* will *conserve more fuel and energy* and will generally result in *lower user cost*, but *increased VMT, emissions, and employment* in the *latter decade*. In the 1976 to 1985 time period the converse is true. Compared with either alone, *combining the two policies* results in *more fuel and energy conservation, lower user cost*, and *more VMT and emissions* over the twenty-year period. Through 1985, *employment is lower*; thereafter, it is comparable to or higher than with either policy alone.

Sixth, *mandating an average new car fuel economy standard* (equivalent to one that would result from mandating a CVT and a new ICE) can result in *different impacts on user cost and energy conservation, as well as on transportation service characteristics*, depending on the approach taken by the auto industry. An attempt to meet the standard by new technology alone produces the least relative reductions in user cost and total energy consumption, but

Table 7–5. continued

			Impact Category		
Annual Fleetwide User Cost (% change)	Annual Fleetwide VMT (% change)	Annual New Car Sales (% change)	Employment[a] (% change)	Annual Fleetwide Weighted Emission (% change)	Total Auto Fleet Size (% change)
($177 billion)	(1149 billion mi)	(16.7 million)	(3.78 million)	(88.3 million equivalent tons)	(134 million)
−11.6	+15.3	0	−6 to +4	+12.2	0
−8.0	+19.7	0	−8 to +6	+16.7	0
−8.0	+19.7	0	−8 to +6	+16.7	0
−15.2	+19.7	0	−15 to +6	+16.7	0
−11.3	+19.7	0	−12 to +6	+16.7	0
−17.0	+27.4	0	−11 to +8	+23.6	0
−2.9	−11.3	−0.4	−8 to −8	−41.1	−7.0
−5.1	−21.0	−0.8	−14 to −14	−48.7	−14.3
−8.0	−29.8	−1.2	−18 to −18	−53.4	−21.4

consumers would still be able to purchase larger, more comfortable autos with substantial trunk space.

If the industry attempts to meet the standard solely by converting to the production of subcompacts and two-passenger trunkless urban autos, user cost savings are more than twice as great in 1995 (29 compared with 13 percent) and total energy savings are 7 percent greater (36 compared with 29 percent). But transportation service characteristics are much poorer; long trips involving several passengers with luggage would either be forgone or switched to other travel modes.

If the industry chooses to use both approaches, (e.g., by introducing a CVT *and* switching to subcompact and trunkless subcompact production), the cost, transportation service, and energy impacts would lie between these two polar extremes.

If the effect on employment of changing auto weight is real, a choice of implementing the mpg standard by a shift to small cars would result in a greater decline in employment than would result from adopting new technology.

Table 7–6.   Comparative Impacts of Alternative Policy Instruments: 1995

Case No.	Policy Instrument(s)	Impact Category	
		Annual Fleetwide Gasoline Consumption (% change)	Annual Fleetwide Energy (% change)
—	Base Case	(108 billion gal)	(21.1 x 10^{15} (Btu)
	Technological		
1	Maximum weight standard	−18.4	−16.6
2	Mandate technology (aerodynamics plus CVT plus new ICE)	−34.1	−29.4
3	Average new car fleet mpg standard		
	a. By new technology (Case 2)	−34.1	−29.4
	b. By small cars only	−34.1	−35.5
	c. By small cars plus CVT	−34.1	−32.7
4	Case 1 and Case 2 combined	−40.3	−38.0
	Price		
5	Additional gasoline tax		
	a. 15¢; 1975–1995	−9.8	−7.7
	b. 30¢; 1975–1995	−18.2	−14.2
	c. 45¢; 1975–1995	−25.7	−20.9

[a]Employment changes are denoted as a range; the lefthand entry is calculated including a weight effect on auto production, while the righthand entry assumes no weight effect on employment.

Seventh, thus, mandating a fuel economy standard would produce roughly the same impacts as mandating weight and/or technology changes but the effects on user cost, total energy consumption, transportation service, and auto industry employment and profits are uncertain. However, such a general mandate would give the auto industry the most flexibility in improving fuel economy compared with the other regulatory policies. It is not at all clear which policy would reduce uncertainties more. Mandating technology hangs fuel conservation on the success of specific technology programs. Mandating a fuel economy standard implies more cost and transportation service uncertainties, but less uncertainty in fuel conservation. Mandating weight standards reduces uncertainties about fuel conservation and cost, but implies considerable uncertainty regarding the demand for small cars (with large car production phased out) and, hence, employment in auto-related industries.

Table 7–6. continued

			Impact Category		
Annual Fleetwide User Cost (% change)	*Annual Fleetwide VMT (% change)*	*Annual New Car Sales (% change)*	*Employment[a] (% change)*	*Annual Fleetwide Weighted Emission (% change)*	*Total Auto Fleet Size (% change)*
($273 billion)	(1553 billion mi)	(21.7 million)	(4.6 million)	(83.7 million equivalent tons)	(186 million)
−13.2	+17.4	0	−5 to +6	+16.6	0
−13.2	+39.3	0	−6 to +9	+38.5	0
−13.2	+39.3	0	−6 to +9	+38.5	0
−28.5	+39.3	0	−13 to +9	+38.5	0
−22.0	+39.3	0	−10 to +9	+38.5	0
−22.3	+51.0	0	−5 to +16	+49.3	0
−2.2	−8.0	−0.3	−3 to −3	−12.9	−4.4
−4.4	−15.2	−0.4	−7 to −7	−19.7	−9.0
−7.3	−21.6	−0.6	−10 to −10	−25.7	−13.5

In summary, additional gasoline taxes[c] hold the only hope for considerable fuel and energy conservation in the near term, whereas regulatory policies aimed at improving technology and at shifting production to small cars hold the best hope for the longer term. Tax policies have salutary effects on user cost, emissions, and urban congestion (due to less VMT), adverse effects on auto ownership, VMT, and new car sales (only in the first few years after imposition), and imply a decline in employment. Moreover, in the near term they bear more heavily on commuters with below average family earnings. In contrast, regulatory policies mandating technology, weight, or fuel economy standards would have little income distributional effects, little effect on new car sales (except for extreme policies affecting auto size) and ownership, a more salutary effect on user cost, VMT, and employment, but as adverse effect on emissions and urban congestion.

[c]Or supply restrictions or other restrictions that raise gasoline prices.

Table 7–7. Impacts of Combined Policy Instruments for Alternative Conservation Levels

Case No.	Policy Instrument(s)	Annual Fleetwide Gasoline Consumption (% reduction)	Annual Fleetwide Energy (% change)
		Impact Category	
	1976		
	Base Case	(55.8 billion gal)	(9.0 x 10^{15} Btu)
6	Declining gas tax plus Case 1[b]		
7	Declining gas tax plus Case 2[b]		
8	Declining gas tax plus Case 4[b]		
	1980		
	Base Case	(66.1 billion gal)	(11.8 x 10^{15} Btu)
6	Declining gas tax plus Case 1	16 to 18	−15.2
7	Declining gas tax plus Case 2	30 to 34	−25.4
8	Declining gas tax plus Case 4	39 to 43	−38.7
	1985		
	Base Case	(77.6 billion gal)	(15.2 x 10^{15} Btu)
6	Declining gas tax plus Case 1	16 to 18	−15.2
7	Declining gas tax plus Case 2	30 to 34	−29.0
8	Declining gas tax plus Case 4	39 to 43	−40.3
	1995		
	Base Case	(108 billion gal)	(21.1 x 10^{15} Btu)
6	Declining gas tax plus Case 1	16 to 18	−16.1
7	Declining gas tax plus Case 2	30 to 34	−28.9
8	Declining gas tax plus Case 4	39 to 43	−38.4

[a]Employment changes are denoted as a range; the lefthand entry is calculated including a weight effect on auto production, while the righthand entry assumes no weight effect on employment.

[b]As discussed in Chapter Six, the NAV Model predicts very rapid adjustments of

These findings suggest that if it is necessary to conserve gasoline in both the short and long term, it would be useful to examine *combinations* of taxing policies and regulatory policies affecting technology. We now turn to an analysis of the effect of these combined policies.

Table 7–7. continued

		Impact Category			
Annual Fleetwide User Cost (% change)	*Annual Fleetwide VMT (% change)*	*Annual New Car Sales (% change)*	*Employment*[a] *(% change)*	*Annual Fleetwide Weighted Emission (% change)*	*Total Auto Fleet Size (% change)*
($78.2 billion)	(805 billion mi)	(11.8 million)	(2.98 million)	(309 million equivalent tons)	(90.9 million)
($124 billion)	(955.5 billion mi)	(14.7 million)	(3.37 million)	(181 million equivalent tons)	(109.3 million)
−8.8	0	−0.7	−17 to −7	−13.3	−4.6
−10.6	−20.0	0	−14 to −12	−55.1	−16.3
−21.4	−26.0	0	−24 to −16	−79.4	−22.5
($177 billion)	(1149 billion mi)	(16.7 million)	(3.78 million)	(88.3 million equivalent tons)	(134 million)
−11.8	+13.8	+1.0	−7 to +4	−18.3	−0.8
−11.9	+0.4	+1.1	−15 to −3	−33.3	−10.0
−22.6	+0.6	+0.8	−21 to −3	−33.2	−13.3
($273 billion)	(1553 billion mi)	(21.7 million)	(4.6 million)	(83.7 million equivalent tons)	(186 million)
−12.4	+17.5	0	−5 to +6	+11.2	0
−12.4	+40.0	0	−1 to +15	+32.6	0
−22.3	+51.0	0	−3 to +19	+43.5	0

auto ownership, VMT and gasoline consumption to gasoline price changes; consequently, we feel that its predictions of these impacts (and fleetwide energy, user cost, employment and emissions which depend on these impacts) are unrealistic for the years immediately following a gasoline price change.

FINDINGS: TAX AND TECHNOLOGICAL POLICIES COMBINED

Table 7–7 compares the estimated impacts resulting from implementation of the *combined* policies in 1980, 1985 and 1995. Figure 7–3 shows the estimated level of gasoline conservation achieved

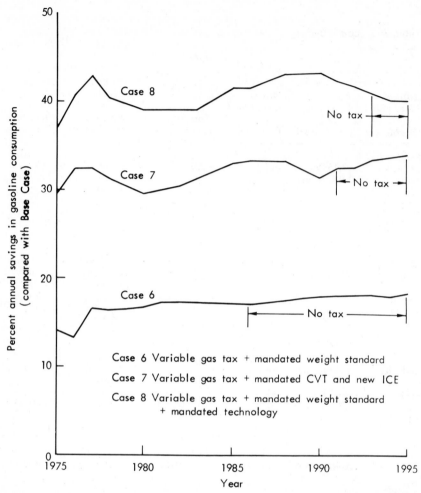

Figure 7–3. Annual Fleetwide Gasoline Conservation Levels Achievable with Combined Gas Tax and Regulatory Policies.

with the combination of a variable gasoline tax and each of the three technological policy alternatives. Note that Case 7, which uses a tax and a mandated CVT and new ICE can also be interpreted as a tax and a mandated fuel economy standard, if the auto industry meets the mpg standard by introducing these new technologies.

Figure 7–4 displays the variation with time of fleetwide VMT and weighted emissions under the combined policies. The figure is useful for understanding some of the interactions that occur due to the separate and opposing effects of declining gasoline taxation and rising new car fleet fuel economy.

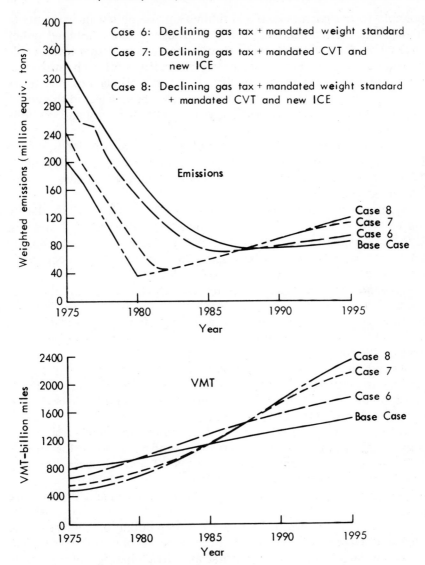

Figure 7–4. Fleetwide Emissions and VMT under Combined Policies.

Again, we leave it to the reader to make detailed quantitative comparisons among the policies over time; here we present the broad findings in largely qualitative terms:

First, if national energy conservation objectives are phrased in terms of constant relative gasoline or energy savings over time, it is possible to design reasonable combinations of policy instruments to implement such objectives. We have designed one combined policy alternative for each of three levels of conservation. Other levels could be examined, as well as other policy alternatives for each level, since we make no claims of optimality. But for each class of regulatory policy for improving auto fuel economy, we have selected the policy that maximizes fuel conservation, yet is technologically and economically feasible.

By imposing an additional gasoline tax of 14 cents in 1975, declining to zero in 1986, and mandating an early weight standard, roughly 16 to 18 percent of gasoline consumption and total energy can be conserved annually over the period.

By imposing an additional gasoline tax of 31 cents in 1975, declining to zero in 1992, and mandating new technology (a CVT and new ICE)—or mandating an equivalent fuel economy standard—roughly 26 to 34 percent of gasoline and total energy can be conserved annually over the twenty year period.

By imposing an additional gasoline tax of 41 cents in 1975, declining to zero in 1994, and mandating both a weight standard and new technology (or an equivalent fuel economy standard), roughly 39 to 43 percent of gasoline and total energy can be conserved annually over the period.

Second, in general, combining a declining gasoline tax with the gradual introduction through regulatory policies of more efficient automobiles (by reducing size, improving technology, or both), results in *differing* impacts over time.

In the near term, the tax impacts predominate, which results in a substantial decline in auto ownership, a modest transient loss in new car sales, and a substantial reduction in VMT and user cost. Reduced VMT, coupled with the rapid scrappage of older "dirtier" cars, leads to very large reduction in emissions. Also, employment declines are most severe.

In the medium term (1980 to 1985, depending on the case), the opposing effects of taxes and improved fuel economy on VMT and emissions largely cancel each other and little change from the Base Case is experienced. However, employment declines remain large.

In the longer term, the improved new car fleet fuel economy impacts of the regulatory policies predominate, resulting in only small changes in new car sales and auto ownership, substantial reductions in user cost, very large increases in VMT and, consequently, very large relative increases in emissions. However, by 1995, although emissions are increased by 11 to 43 percent (depending on the case) over the Base Case value in that year, emissions are still 60 to 70 percent *below* 1976 Base Case values. Urban congestion is likely to worsen. Finally, employment effects vary somewhat with the particular regulatory policy; the size of the effects vary from substantial declines to substantial increases, depending on the presumed strength of the auto weight reduction effect as opposed to the VMT effect.

TENTATIVE POLICY IMPLICATIONS

We see several tentative policy implications emerging from our analysis:

First, although all of the policy instruments examined offer some potential for energy conservation, because of their varied social, economic, and environmental impacts, *there is no clear dominance of one policy over others in the medium and long term.*

Second, if there is a need for substantial conservation of gasoline in the short run, the only hope (among the alternatives we examined) is to impose additional gasoline taxes.[d] We estimate that for every additional cent of tax imposed, gasoline consumption can be reduced one percent. However, such taxes have some adverse impacts. They have the largest impact on commuters with below average family earnings, they imply small transient declines in new car sales, and persistent but declining reductions in auto-related employment.

Third, in the longer term, regulatory policies aimed at improving new car fuel economy offer greater potential for gasoline and energy conservation than do gasoline taxes (short of extremely high taxes). But regulatory policies have adverse impacts too—on emissions (because lower costs per mile produce more driving), on urban congestion, and on employment, if auto weight declines play a significant role.

Fourth, new auto technology holds great potential for improving fuel economy. If the federal government intends to subsidize automobile R&D for fuel economy purposes *such a subsidy should include work on advanced versions of the internal combustion engine and on a continuously variable transmission.* Our analysis shows that some combination of supercharging and charge stratification of a rotary *spark ignition engine* is most promising in terms of both cost and energy conservation.[e] Moreover, its ability to meet statutory

[d]We ignore the conservation potential of policies aimed at small effects, such as modest mandatory fuel economy standards or technology that would induce manufacturers to introduce small improvements, such as radial tires or minor aerodynamic redesign of auto bodies. Our analysis here *assumes* that such minor improvements will be voluntarily implemented.

[e]We do not mean that R&D on *other* engines should be halted, only that it not be neglected for this engine.

emissions standards may be no worse than other internal combustion engine variants.

Fifth, although not a direct result of our analysis, it would seem that among regulatory policies aimed at improving new car fuel economy, *the most general mandate is probably to be preferred. Mandating an average new car fuel economy standard* is more general than mandating a weight standard or a technology standard. The more general mandate is more likely to reduce the risks of not achieving a specified conservation level and is more likely to result in a diverse product mix of new autos that provide a greater choice of performance, comfort, and roominess—since one auto company may choose new technology, another may choose to shift more rapidly to small cars, and still another may choose some combination of the two. Thus, a more general mandate is likely to result in some production of new large cars with very efficient advanced engines and transmissions, and some production of small cars with relatively less efficient and more conventional engines. However, compared with mandatory weight limits or new technology, a fuel economy standard implies greater uncertainty in *other* impacts such as cost and transportation service characteristics. By our analysis, it is also clear that a mandated new car fuel economy standard *much higher than the 16 to 20 mpg* standard currently discussed *is feasible.*

Sixth, if a new car fuel economy standard is implemented, it should be written to *include* the improvements made possible by equipping all new cars with radial tires and by minor aerodynamic redesign of all new auto bodies.

Seventh, if national energy conservation objectives are phrased in terms of *constant relative* savings of gasoline or energy over time, it is possible to design reasonable combinations of gasoline tax policies and regulatory instruments (for improving new car fuel economy) to implement such objectives.

Eighth, the imposition of a fixed tax on new car sales price offers little promise for gasoline conservation in the near term. Moreover, if such taxes were to be graduated to discourage purchases of less efficient autos, the impact on the turnover rate of the automobile stock would reduce the effectiveness of such a policy. A fixed or graduated ownership tax (on new *and* used cars) would mitigate this adverse impact; because used cars would be more costly, and the turnover rate of the stock would rise compared with the effect of a new car tax alone.

Ninth, a desired improvement in average new car fuel economy in the longer run can be achieved with several types of policies. Of these policies, the one that involves the lowest new car price (while maintaining· the comfort and performance of today's automobiles) will reduce total automobile gasoline consumption the most.

NOTES TO CHAPTER SEVEN

1. Lawrence J. White, *The Automobile Industry Since 1945* (Cambridge, Mass.: Harvard University Press, 1971).

2. R. U. Ayres and Stedman Noble, *Economic Impact of Mass Production of Alternative Low Emissions Automotive Power Systems*, International Research and Technology Corporation, Report DOT–OS–20003 (Amended), Prepared for the Department of Transportation, March 1973. (Also summarized in *Journal of the Air Pollution Control Association*, Vol. 24, No. 3, March 1974, pp. 216–24.)

Part II

The Ensuing Public Dialogue

Chapter Eight

Testimony: A Comparison of Some Public Policies for Conserving Gasoline Used by the Personal Automobile

Sorrel Wildhorn

During the past fiscal year I led a team of economists, engineers and policy analysts, in a study comparing alternative public policies for conserving gasoline used by the personal automobile. The work, conducted at The Rand Corporation, was sponsored by the National Science Foundation, Office of Research Applied to National Needs. The study that I will discuss is part of a larger research program at Rand that analyzes a wide range of energy policy issues that arise from the conflict between rapid increases in demand for energy in all sectors of the U.S. economy and the national goal of reducing our dependence on foreign energy supplies. The findings, views, and conclusions expressed in this testimony are those of the author and should not be interpreted as representing those of The Rand Corporation or any of the agencies sponsoring its research.

The purpose of this testimony is to expose the different layers of the problem, to outline the difficulties of choosing among public policies for conserving gasoline, and to discuss how our study bears on that choice.

The necessity or desirability of adopting specific new energy conservation policies rests on the answers to four questions:

1. Should we conserve gasoline?
2. If so, how much should we conserve and by when?
3. Can we rely on existing private incentives to accomplish specific conservation goals?

This chapter contains the written statement of testimony submitted to the U.S. Senate Committee on Commerce Hearings, 93rd Congress, 2nd Session, November 26, December 10 and 11, 1974. See the Committee's *Energy Conservation Working Paper*, pp. 330–40.

4. If government conservation policies are needed, how do *all* of the alternatives compare?

In our work we did not address the first three questions. With respect to the fourth, we compared *some*, not all, of the alternative public policies on the *assumptions* that conservation was needed and that the private sector would respond to future gasoline prices consistent with their past responses.

The purposes of the study were twofold: to develop analytical tools, then to apply the tools in a systematic comparison of the impacts of several alternative conservation measures and policy instruments. Previous studies of auto conservation policies, conducted over the past couple of years, have generally focused on either technology or on economic policy, but usually not on both. In this study, therefore, we designed an approach in which both aspects of policy could be evaluated on a comparable basis.

Although our charter was transportation in general, we decided early on to focus on national policies directly affecting the personal automobile, because that is where the large payoffs seem to be. The auto accounts for more than half of the direct transportation energy use, or about 13 percent of total direct energy used in the United States.

SCOPE

A fairly comprehensive list of public policies for conserving gasoline, either by inducing a reduction in total auto travel or by improving the fuel economy of the auto fleet, would surely include:

1. Regulatory:
   Mandated maximum weight standards;
   Mandated technology standards; and
   Mandated average fuel economy standards for new car production.
2. Additional taxes:
   On gasoline;
   Fixed or flat excise taxes on new cars; and
   Graduated (by weight, horsepower, or fuel economy) excise taxes on new cars.
3. Encourage or limit supply of gasoline (e.g., rationing, import limitations).
4. Alternative tax treatment of oil companies (e.g., different depletion allowance).

5. Transportation management or control policies (e.g., carpooling, congestion relief).
6. Public transit improvement or fare reduction.
7. Land use policies.

Given limited study resources and the study's national focus, we decided to limit our analysis to two kinds of policies: regulatory policies aimed at improving the fuel economy of the auto fleet, and price-change policies on gasoline and new cars. Of course, these are not independent or mutually exclusive policies, since price increases in gasoline or new cars may induce technological change, and technological changes in autos may affect new car prices.

The three types of regulatory policies we analyzed were: maximum weight standards, that are introduced in the latter half of the 1970s; mandated technology changes, which assume that, among other things, a new engine and a new transmission are introduced into the fleet in the early 1980s, and finally, average fuel economy standards for new car production.

One way to change prices is through additional taxes. We analyzed different levels of additional gasoline taxes and *average* or flat new car excise taxes, both applied over the twenty-year period between 1975 and 1995. We did *not* analyze new car excise taxes that are graduated with respect to either weight, horsepower or fuel economy, for methodological reasons I will touch on later.

We also did not analyze other national policies, such as those which limit the supply of gasoline or alter the tax treatment of oil companies. Because of the study's national scope, we also did not study three other policy categories that are best analyzed at a regional or local level. These were: transportation management or control policies; policies aimed at improving public transit, or reducing its fares; and long run land use policies aimed at reducing the average distance between where people live and work.

Our basic approach was to compare various economic, social and environmental impacts of alternative policies over the next twenty years with the impacts projected for a Base Case. In the Base Case projection we made specific assumptions about future gasoline and new car price levels in the absence of additional governmental intervention.

The fleetwide impacts we considered are shown in Figure 1. [See Table 8-1 of this volume.] They include: gasoline consumption; total energy consumption (in the production, distribution and use of gasoline and in the production, distribution, sales, repair and scrappage of automobiles); user costs (assuming auto lifetimes of ten years

Table 8–1.   Policy Impacts Compared for Total Auto Fleet

- GASOLINE CONSUMPTION
- TOTAL ENERGY CONSUMPTION (DIRECT + INDIRECT)
- USER COST (10 years AND 100,000 miles OF DRIVING)
- VEHICLE MILES TRAVELLED
- WEIGHTED EMISSIONS
- NEW CAR SALES
- AUTO OWNERSHIP
- EMPLOYMENT IN FIVE AUTO RELATED SECTORS ONLY
- WHO PAYS? (IMPACT OF NEAR TERM GASOLINE TAX POLICIES ON WORK TRIPS ONLY)

Source: Figure 1 of the testimony, *Energy Conservation Working Paper,* p. 332.

and 100,000 miles of driving); vehicle miles traveled; weighted emissions (which is a proxy for air quality); new car sales; and total auto ownership. Finally, we made only partial and initial estimates of employment and income distributional effects. We made estimates of initial employment changes in only five auto-related sectors of the economy, which in 1971 employed close to 3 million workers, or about 4.5 percent of the total non-agricultural work force. Fewer jobs in a particular sector may be a negative impact in the short run, but not necessarily in the long run, because most displaced workers will move into other sectors.

As to income distributional effects, we have estimated the initial impact on different earnings groups of additional expenditures for gasoline used only for work trips. We emphasize strongly here, that although we did not study alternative uses to which the additional tax revenues could be put for alleviating distributional inequities or auto sector unemployment resulting from increased prices, there are many ways to do this.

Other potential policy impacts, such as auto safety, auto damageability, or balance of trade implications were not considered at all.

A QUALITATIVE SUMMARY OF THE STUDY'S FINDINGS

Let me summarize here our major findings in qualitative terms. Following that, I will discuss briefly the methodological approach used in the study, and lastly, I will compare the impacts of the several alternative policies in quantitative terms.

The major findings are shown in Figure 2. [See Table 8–2 of this volume.] In the short term, apart from rationing, only higher gaso-

Table 8-2. Major Findings

- IN SHORT TERM—HIGHER GASOLINE PRICES ONLY ALTERNATIVE
- IN LONG TERM—REGULATORY POLICIES WHICH IMPROVE FUEL ECONOMY
- NO CLEAR DOMINANCE OVER TWENTY-YEAR PERIOD
  - —Different Social, Economic, Environmental Impacts
  - —Combination of Gas Taxes and Regulatory Policies More Effective
- FIXED AVERAGE EXCISE TAX ON NEW CARS OFFERS LITTLE PROMISE FOR CONSERVATION
  - —Reduced Effectiveness of *Graduated* Excise Tax
- NEW TECHNOLOGY OFFERS GREAT PROMISE
  - —New ICE and CVT
  - —Over 25 mpg for Full Size: Over 40 mpg for Subcompact
  - —May Mean Lower New Car Prices and Lifetime Costs
  - —Any Federally Supported R&D Should Not Neglect New ICE and CVT
- IF NEW CAR mpg STANDARDS MANDATED
  - —Technology and Small Cars Offer Up to 38 mpg Average in Long Term
  - —Recently Proposed Standard of 20 mpg Could be Higher

Source: Figure 2 of the testimony, *Energy Conservation Working Paper*, p. 333.

line prices will achieve significant conservation of gasoline. Later on, I will discuss the quantitative implications of higher gasoline pump prices if the policy instrument used is the gasoline tax, assuming that such a tax is passed along to the consumer.

In the longer term, apart from extremely high gasoline taxes, we find that policies that improve fuel economy without raising new car prices—preferably lowering them—offer the best promise for conservation. Under such policies new car sales will rise, and people will scrap their older gas hogs more quickly. A number of alternative policies might have such an effect. Regulatory standards are one example, providing that they do not diminish the consumer appeal of the resulting product line. Subject to the same qualification, a graduated excise tax, perhaps with subsidies for the most efficient models, might be another. A combination of a graduated excise tax on new cars and a gasoline tax might be yet another. In our study, we made quantitative comparisons only among regulatory standards, a flat excise tax on new cars, a gasoline tax, and combinations of regulatory standards and a gasoline tax.

Because each of the policies considered in this study has different social, economic and environmental impacts, combinations of policies, such as gasoline taxes and regulatory standards may be more effective *if* a national objective is to achieve significant levels of gasoline conservation over the *entire* twenty-year period we examined.

Under a flat excise tax on new cars, new car prices will rise, sales will fall, people will retain their older gas hogs longer, and as a result, total auto ownership and the amount of driving will be virtually unchanged—with little or no reduction in gasoline consumption. A graduated excise tax, without subsidies for most efficient cars, will also increase average new car prices.

New technology offers great promise. In addition to relatively minor improvements like radial tires and better aerodynamic design for new cars, we find that if a new internal combustion engine and a new transmission, such as the continuously variable type, are introduced, full size cars may achieve over 25 miles per gallon and subcompacts may achieve over 40 miles per gallon on a combined urban–rural driving cycle. Then, too, depending on the technological option pursued, this can mean lower new car prices and lower lifetime costs. These results suggest that if federal R&D support is necessary, a new internal combustion engine and transmission should not be neglected. (Under EPA sponsorship, the federal government already is sponsoring R&D on more unconventional engine types such as the gas turbine, steam engine, and the Stirling engine—but no R&D on advanced internal combustion engines is currently being undertaken. Private R&D activities include work on some variants of the internal combustion engine.)

If new car fuel economy standards are to be mandated, our analysis indicates that, with a combination of new technology and a shift to small cars, an average of up to 38 miles per gallon for new car production is possible in the longer term. This suggests that standards between 17 and 24 miles per gallon between 1976 and 1980 recently considered by various agencies of the executive branch and by Congress in a variety of proposed legislation could be set higher in the long term.

Mandated fuel economy standards are probably preferable to specific mandated weight or technology standards, for several reasons. An important consideration is the uncertainty about the performance of specific new technologies, resulting in the risk that highly specific technological standards would not be achieved, or would lead to high costs. Under mandated miles per gallon standards, a greater variety of technological and weight limiting approaches could be pursued by manufacturers, which would improve conservation possibilities and offer the consumer a greater variety of choices in automobile characteristics.

An alternative policy to mandated fuel economy standards is the graduated (by weight, horsepower or fuel economy) excise tax on new car price, perhaps with subsidies for the most efficient, lightest or smaller-engined autos. When subjected to close analysis, it may prove to be more attractive than mandated fuel economy standards. But the methodology for analyzing the impacts of such a policy is only now being developed.

METHODOLOGY AND SOME RESULTS OF THEIR USE

We turn next to a brief discussion of our study's methodology. To forecast gasoline consumption and other impacts over the twenty-year period, we developed and linked together four analytical models: a generalized automobile design model, an econometric consumption and sales model, an auto fleet mix model, and an econometric employment model. Our discussion will focus on the first two, because they are the major analytical tools developed in this study.

The generalized auto design model is an application of an approach pioneered twenty years ago at Rand and originally applied to the design of aircraft and gas turbines. Essentially, such an approach applied to autos provides a rapid and efficient way of assessing the effects of auto size, comfort, performance and design features, when one or more of these variables is changed, while the others are held constant (see Figure 3). [See Table 8–3 of this volume.] The outputs of the computerized model are a description of the automobile, its fuel economy on an urban and urban–rural driving cycle, weights of materials used, and breakdowns of costs and energy consumption. For current technology, the model predicts values within a few percent of actual values.

Figure 4 [See Table 8–4 of this volume.] illustrates what new technology offers, as predicted by our generalized design model. All of the results shown are for individual standard size autos, each having the same passenger and trunk space, acceleration capabilities, and each meeting the ultimate statutory emission controls. All entries for the Base Case are in absolute terms, whereas entries for cases employing new technology show percentage differences from the comparable Base Case figures.

Compared to a Base Case auto with 1975 technology, we find that adding radial tires, improved aerodynamics, and a new continuously variable transmission (Case 2), can result in a quite sizable increase in fuel economy and reductions in lifetime energy consumption, initial cost and lifetime cost. Cases 3 and 4 are examples of what can be

Table 8–3.   The Generalized Auto Design Model

INPUTS:

- COMFORT (PASSENGER AND TRUNK SPACE, AIR CONDITIONING)
- PERFORMANCE (ACCELERATION CAPABILITY) AND UNREFUELED RANGE
- DESIGN FEATURES
  —Engine and Transmission Types
  —Aerodynamic Design
  —New Fuels or Materials

OUTPUTS:

- AUTO WEIGHT, DIMENSIONS, HP
- FUEL ECONOMY ON URBAN AND URBAN–RURAL DRIVING CYCLE
- MATERIALS
- COSTS
- ENERGY CONSUMPTION

VALIDATION:

- FOR CURRENT TECHNOLOGY, PREDICTED CLOSE TO ACTUAL VALUES

Source: Figure 3 of the testimony, *Energy Conservation Working Paper*, p. 334.

achieved by introducing different advanced internal combustion engines in addition to the new technology included in Case 2. By combining charge stratification and supercharging in a rotary design, the greatest improvement is possible—a doubling in fuel economy—because the power plant is lighter and more efficient, resulting in a much lighter and smaller auto. Such an auto is also less expensive initially and over its lifetime. However, if further research and development indicates that the rotary engine's sealing problems are too intractable, Case 4 illustrates that another alternative requiring less development, such as the stratified charge piston engine, still offers a sizeable increase in miles per gallon. Of the advanced, or unconventional engine types, such as the gas turbine, steam or Stirling engines (two of these are shown as Cases 5 and 6), we find that the Stirling is the only one which offers real promise in terms of fuel economy. However, it is much heavier and more costly initially.

Turning next to our demand methodology, its notable feature is that, unlike the simpler econometric demand models developed previously, ours attempts to account for many of the important interactions among the variables and to estimate the separate effect of each of the adjustment processes to price changes in gasoline or

Table 8–4. What New Technology Offers (Standard Size Auto With Air Conditioning) (Emission Controls to Meet Statutory Standards)

| Case | Description | HP | Curb Weight (lb) | Miles Per Gallon | | | Lifetime Energy Consumption (Million Btu) | Sticker Price (1973$) | Average Annual Cost ($) | Weighted Emission Index (gm/m.) |
				Urban Cycle	Urban-Rural Cycle					
1	Base (W/55 mph)	214	4730	10.7	12.8		1560	5200	1376	46.4
2	Base + Radials + Aero + New Transmission	−27%	−6%	+35%	+42%		−24%	−3%	+11%	0%
3	Case 2 + Super-Charged Stratified Rotary	−41	−37	+109	+114		−48	−28	−31	0
4	Case 2 + Stratified-Charge Piston Engine	−19	−8	+68	+81		−36	−5	−15	0
5	Case 2 + Stirling	−15	−2	+52	+61		−36	+8	−8	−57
6	Case 2 + Rankine	+11	+40	+17	+30		−12	+15	+1	−58

Source: Figure 4 of the testimony, Energy Conservation Working Paper, p. 335.

new cars. Even so, our approach is still a partial one. Figure 5 outlines the structure of the model. [See Table 8–5 of this volume.] It is a five-equation recursive model in which separate estimating relationships were developed for new car sales, used car demand, used car price, vehicle miles traveled, and average fleet fuel economy. All price variables are defined in relative terms—relative to the price of other things—an important consideration during periods of high inflation. It is an aggregate model, however, and new car sales are not broken down by market size class (which would be necessary to analyze a graduated excise tax on new cars). This consumption and sales model was developed using annual time series data (from standard sources) over the 1954–1972 period. In our model, we assumed a perfectly elastic supply of gasoline and new cars.

In the Base Case forecast, an important point to notice is that the assumed price of gasoline in 1975 is 67¢, probably higher than will, in fact, materialize. This means that the Base Case forecast already has built into it much lower growth rate in annual gasoline consumption that occurred over the past two decades—an average of only 1.7 percent annual growth projected over the 1972–1995 period, compared with almost 5 percent experienced historically. Auto travel and ownership grow at lower than historical rates in the Base Case forecast and there is only a small increase in average fuel economy in the auto stock in response to the assumed higher prices of gasoline.

Figure 6 displays the *long-run* gasoline price elasticities of demand, as predicted by our model. [See Table 8–6 of this volume.] The price elasticity of demand is the ratio of the percent change in gasoline consumption to the percent change in gasoline price. American families can adjust gasoline consumption to gasoline price increases in three ways: by owning fewer cars, by driving more conservatively and/or shifting to cars with better fuel economy, or by driving less miles per auto. Our model predicts an overall elasticity of about—0.9 at prices corresponding to the average price of the last two decades. This is somewhat higher than other analysts' previous estimates based on U.S. data and somewhat lower than other estimates based on international data. Interestingly enough, our results indicate that the auto ownership and the miles per auto adjustment mechanisms each accounts for about 40 percent of the overall price elasticity, whereas the shift to more efficient cars account for only about 20 percent.

Figure 7 briefly describes the other two models developed in this study. [See Table 8–7 of this volume.] The fleet mix model is simply a way of keeping track of the number and types of autos in the fleet as new cars are added and old ones scrapped, and of the annual changes in other characteristics of the fleet. In the econometric

Table 8–5. Econometric Demand Model

STRUCTURE:

DEPENDENT VARIABLE	*INDEPENDENT VARIABLES*
NEW CAR SALES	NEW AND USED CAR PRICES, INCOME
USED CAR DEMAND	NEW AND USED CAR PRICES, INCOME, GASOLINE PRICE
USED CAR PRICE	NEW CAR PRICE, INCOME, GASOLINE PRICE, LAST YEAR'S AUTO STOCK
VEHICLE MILES TRAVELED	AUTO OWNERSHIP, GASOLINE PRICE
AVERAGE FLEET MPG	GASOLINE PRICE

BASE CASE INPUT ASSUMPTIONS:

CENSUS BUREAU POPULATION PROJECTIONS
REAL DISPOSABLE INCOME GROWS AT 1.9% ANNUALLY
GASOLINE PRICE: 59¢ IN 1974
                67¢ IN 1975
                AFTER 1975, REAL PRICE CONSTANT
NEW CAR PRICE GROWS AT SAME RATE AS INFLATION
INFLATION RATE: 6.3% IN 1975 DECLINING TO 2.6% IN 1980, CONSTANT THEREAFTER

BASE CASE FORECAST:

1.7% ANNUAL GROWTH IN GASOLINE CONSUMPTION, 1972–1995
(4.9% HISTORICALLY, 1954–1972)
TRAVEL AND OWNERSHIP DOWN
SMALL INCREASE IN AVERAGE MPG

Source: Figure 5 of the testimony, *Energy Conservation Working Paper*, p. 336.

Table 8–6.   Long-Run Adjustment to Gasoline Price Change

	RAND MODEL ELASTICITY	*OTHER ELASTICITY ESTIMATES*
AUTO OWNERSHIP	−0.38	NO ESTIMATES
GALLONS PER MILE	−0.17	NO ESTIMATES
MILES PER AUTO	−0.37	−.2 TO −.3
TOTAL	−0.92	$\left\{\begin{array}{l} -.4 \text{ TO } -.8 \text{ (U.S.)} \\ -.8 \text{ TO } -1.21 \text{ (INTERNATIONAL)} \end{array}\right.$

Source: Figure 6 of the testimony, *Energy Conservation Working Paper*, p. 336

Table 8–7.   Fleet Mix and Employment Models

FLEET MIX MODEL:
- A BOOKKEEPING MODEL FOR 1975–1995 PERIOD
- INPUTS (BY YEAR AND AUTO TYPE)
  - —New Car Sales (Total and Breakdown by Size and Design Type)
  - —Number and Age in Existing Fleet
  - —Scrappage Rate by Year and Type
  - —Emissions and User Costs per Auto by Year and Type
- ANNUAL OUTPUTS (FLEETWIDE)
  - —Size and Composition
  - —Gasoline Consumption, Emissions, Total Energy, User Cost

EMPLOYMENT MODEL:
- IN FIVE SECTORS
- INDEPENDENT VARIABLES
  - —New Car Sales
  - —Vehicle Miles Traveled
  - —Average New Car Production Weight
  - —Auto Ownership

Source: Figure 7 of the testimony, *Energy Conservation Working Paper*, p. 337.

employment model, we estimate initial and partial employment impacts only in each of five auto-related sectors; employment levels depend on some of the independent variables shown on the chart. These five sectors are: auto manufacturing, auto dealerships, retail and wholesale parts, service stations and tire production.

A QUANTITATIVE COMPARISON
OF THE IMPACTS OF ALTERNATIVE
CONSERVATION POLICIES

Turning finally to a quantitative comparison of the national impacts of these alternative policies, as predicted by our methodology, Figure 8 indicates the impact, in 1980, of policies implemented in the mid-1970s. The subsequent figure displays long-term effects, circa 1995. Both figures show percent change in each impact criterion from the Base Case projection. So we are comparing estimates of impacts of alternative policies with a Base Case projection in each year.

Confining our attention to the left-hand column of Figure 8 for the moment, the gasoline and new car price-change policies shown are self-explanatory. [See Table 8-8 of this volume.] The mandated weight standard analyzed visualizes a production phase-out of full and intermediate size autos at the rate of 20 percent per year, beginning in 1976 and ending in 1980, and replacing them with compacts and subcompacts. Since no convincing analytical models exist for projecting market shares under such a weight mandate, we simply assumed that the 55 percent market shares projected for the two larger size autos in 1975 would be apportioned to the two smaller size autos in the same ratio as in the current market. If, under such mandated weight standards, there is a much greater demand for compacts rather than subcompacts, our figure of gasoline consumption would overestimate the level of conservation achievable.

The mandated technology standard visualizes the introduction of radial tires and aerodynamic improvements in all 1976 model auto production. In addition, a new internal combustion engine, such as a stratified charge, supercharged rotary design, and a new continuously variable transmission is introduced in 1980. With an assumed conversion rate of 20 percent per year, it is fully incorporated in new car production by 1985. Market shares by size class are held constant at current values.

The combined weight and technology standards case simply combines the two previous cases. Now, one could also think of each of these weight and/or technology standards as one way auto companies might implement more general fuel economy or mile per gallon standards.

Turning now to some quantitative comparisons of the impacts of different policies by 1980, we see that an additional tax of 45¢ per gallon on top of 67¢ per gallon of gasoline in '75 (or $1.12 per gallon total, if the tax is fully reflected in the pump price) will reduce gas

Table 8–8.   National Impacts of Alternative Energy Conservation Policies: 1980

Policy	Gasoline Consumption	Total Energy	User Cost	Auto Ownership	Vehicle Miles Traveled	Emissions	New Car Sales	Auto Sectors Employment
Base Case	66.1 (Billion Gal)	11.8 x 10^{15} (Btu)	$124 Billion	109 Million	954 (Billion Mi)	181 (Mil Equiv Tons)	14.7 Million	3.4 (Million)
Taxes								
Additional 45¢ Gas Tax 1975–1995	–40%	–31%	–13%	–28%	–36%	–33%	–1.5%	–19%
50% Increase in New Car Price 1975–1995	~0	—	—	~0	~0	—	–12	–4
Regulation								
Weight Standards (or 21 mpg Std by 1980)	–9	–8	–6	~0	+8	+4	~0	–8 to +1
Technology Stds—New Engine and Transmission (or 33 mpg Std by 1985)	–7	–3	–2	~0	+6	+2	~0	–3 to 0
Weight and Technology Stds (or 33 mpg Std by 1985)	–10	–9	–7	~0	+9	+5	~0	–10 to +1

Source: Figure 8 of the testimony, *Energy Conservation Working Paper*, p. 338.

consumption by 40 percent of the gasoline consumed in the Base Case. Estimates based on other models would be slightly lower. However, estimates of short-run, say by 1976, adjustments are only one-third of the 1980 savings, or 13 percent of the Base Case, and mainly due to reduction in miles driven per auto. None of the existing models, including our own, is able to predict with any accuracy the trajectory of gasoline consumption over time in response to gasoline price changes.

Similar percentage (i.e., 40 percent) gasoline conservation levels could also be achieved with a 33¢ additional tax on 50¢/gallon gasoline—a base price closer to actual prices today.

To return to our 45¢ per gallon tax case—such a tax implies *very* large reductions in vehicle miles driven, in auto ownership and in smog. Effects on 1980 new car sales are minor, after an earlier drop, but the large reduction in auto travel would mean a sizeable initial drop in auto sector employment, mainly in the auto parts, repair and service station sectors. This drop may or may not be reflected in overall employment, depending on general economic conditions and government economic policies. In particular, if gas tax revenues lead to at least an equal increase in government spending the effect may be expansionary, depending on the type of spending. Moreover, such spending could be targeted to ease the transition for those adversely affected by the tax.

We have made a rough preliminary estimate of the impact of the gasoline tax on the cost of driving autos to work for different income groups. In contrast to the primary analysis of this study, for this purpose we have had to make the simplifying assumption that families do not change their patterns of gasoline consumption from those in 1970 in response to sharp increases in gasoline prices. We find that for households earning *under* $13,500 in 1975, the percentage increase in the cost of work trips relative to earnings is constant over all groups. For households earning *above* $13,500, the impact is less than proportional to earnings. Other Rand work, however, shows that, with the exception of the very lowest and very highest income groups, household gasoline expenditure for *all* uses appear to be constant, as a percent of total expenditures. The very lowest (i.e., below about $6000 annually in 1973) and very highest (i.e., above about $25,000 annually in 1973) appear to spend relatively less than the middle groups.

Turning next to new car price policies, we see that even with a flat 50 percent increase in new car price, gasoline consumption, auto ownership and auto travel are virtually unchanged, but there is a

significant drop in new car sales, and only a small drop in employment. Again, I should note that we were unable to make quantitative
impact estimates for graduated taxes because of methodological and
study resources limitations.

In general, regulatory policies which aim to improve new car fuel
economy, whether by imposing weight and/or technology standards
or by imposing fuel economy standards, will have modest impact on
total auto gasoline consumption by 1980, primarily because of the
lead time required to introduce new technology or to shift production to small cars and the fact that annual new car sales are only
about 10 percent of the total auto fleet. Other fleetwide impacts of
regulatory policies are modest too in 1980.

Turning next to long-term impacts of these policies (Figure 9), we
see a very different picture by 1995. [See Table 8–9 of this volume.]
The effects of the 45¢ tax decline over time due to rising incomes
and inflation. Instead of the gasoline tax-induced 40 percent reduction in gasoline consumption estimated for 1980, the comparable
figure is only 26 percent by 1995, and other impacts are similarly
affected.

However, by 1995, after the technological changes and/or shift to
small cars have had their full effect on the total auto fleet, we find
that, depending on the specific regulatory policy, gasoline consumption is down between 18 and 40 percent. This level of gasoline
conservation is possible even though improved technology will
induce *more* driving because the cost of driving per mile is reduced.
(Our analysis shows between 17 and 50 percent more travel.) Thus,
urban congestion will worsen. With more travel will come a comparable increase in emissions, unless there is an offsetting reduction in
emissions per vehicle mile. Initial auto sector employment effects
may vary greatly, depending on whether the reduced weight of new
cars, which is implied by the introduction of smaller cars or certain
new technology, has a real effect on employment. The strong statistical relationship we found between weight and employment, particularly during the late 1960s and early 1970s, may reflect changes in
complexity as well as weight, as safety and emission controls were
adopted. Because we are uncertain of the relative roles played by
these two factors, we estimated employment effects two ways. The
lefthand number in the employment impact column includes this
weight effect, whereas the righthand number does not. If the weight
effect is correct there will be a small net drop in employment. Without the weight effect, there will be an *increase* in employment,
primarily due to the increase in the number of miles driven, occasion-
ing more employment in the repair and auto parts sectors.

Table 8–9. National Impacts of Alternative Energy Conservation Policies: 1995

Policy	Gasoline Consumption (Billion Gal)	Total Energy (Btu)	User Cost (Billion)	Auto Owner- ship (Million)	Vehicle Miles Traveled (Billion mi)	Emissions (Mil Equiv Tons)	New Car Sales (Million)	Auto Sectors Employ- ment (Million)
Base Case	108	21.1×10^{15}	$273	186	1550	84	21.7	4.6
Taxes								
Additional 45¢ Gas Tax 1975–1995	−26%	−21%	−7%	−14%	−22%	−26%	−1%	−10%
50% Increase in New Car Price 1975–1995	~0	—	—	~0	~0	—	−10	−3
Regulation								
Mandated Weight Stds (or 21 mpg Std by 1980)	−18	−17	−13	~0	+17	+17	~0	−5 to +6
Technology Stds—New Engine and Trans- mission (or 33 mpg Std by 1985)	−34	−29	−13	~0	+39	+39	~0	−6 to +9
Weight + Technology Stds (or 38 mpg Std by 1985)	−40	−38	−22	~0	+50	+50	~0	−5 to +16

Source: Figure 9 of the testimony, *Energy Conservation Working Paper*, p. 340.

Lifetime cost can drop significantly too, especially if the technological options pursued result in much smaller and lighter cars, but with the same interior space, range and acceleration characteristics as today's cars.

In summary, the relevance of our work to the specific provisions of Title I of the Senate Commerce Committee's Energy Conservation Working Paper is as follows:

1. Our work indicates that a 50 percent improvement in average new car fuel economy by 1980, over the 1974 figure of 14 miles per gallon, appears feasible.
2. After 1980, much higher average new car fuel economy appears feasible, if new technology is pursued vigorously, and R&D is successful. For example, fuel economy standards over 30 miles per gallon might be possible by 1985.
3. Among the limited number of policy alternatives we compared, new car fuel economy standards appears to be an attractive *long-term* policy. Such standards will not have much impact on total gasoline consumption before the mid–1980s. In the short run, apart from rationing, only higher gasoline prices promise substantial gasoline conservation.
4. Policies that improve new car fuel economy without raising new car prices—preferably lowering them—offer the best promise for long-term gasoline conservation. Under such policies new car sales will rise and people will scrap their older gas hogs more quickly.
5. Because our work (and the work of others) only considered *some* relevant policies, others should be analyzed too, using similar techniques. In particular, a graduated excise tax on new cars, with and without subsidies for more efficient cars, should be analyzed—and other researchers have begun to do so. When such work is completed, the basis of selecting energy conservation policies for the auto should be much clearer.

Chapter Nine

Auto Manufacturers' Comments

QUESTIONS POSED TO AUTO MANUFACTURERS

The following excerpts are from a letter by Senator Warren G. Magnuson, Chairman, U.S. Senate Committee on Commerce, sent to Mr. Henry L. Duncombe, Jr., Vice President and Chief Economist, General Motors Corporation. Identical questions were posed to other auto manufacturers by Senator Magnuson.

December 23, 1974.

Mr. Henry L. Duncombe, Jr.,
Vice President and Chief Economist
General Motors Corp.
General Motors Building
Detroit, Mich.

Dear Mr. Duncombe:

During the December 10th hearing on the Commerce Committee's Energy Conservation Working Paper, at which you testified, Senator Inouye instructed the staff to provide copies of a recent Rand Corporation Report to automobile industry witnesses, with a request for comment. That report, entitled "How to Save Gasoline: Public Policy Alternatives for the Automobile," is enclosed with this letter, along with a separate executive summary of the report and a copy of Dr. Sorrel Wildhorn's written statement of testimony

This chapter contains correspondence between Senator Warren G. Magnuson, Chairman, U.S. Senate Committee on Commerce, and the four major U.S. auto manufacturers regarding the auto makers' comments on the original study published by The Rand Corporation. All the letters can be found in U.S. Senate Committee on Commerce, *Energy Conservation Working Paper,* pp. 285–301.

submitted to the Committee. In accord with Senator Inouye's request, I would appreciate receiving, by January 6, 1975, your written comments on the following enumerated sections of these documents, as well as any other comments you wish to submit for inclusion in the hearing record. Please be as specific as possible in your responses.

(a) Chapter IV of the full report, entitled "Per-Vehicle Comparisons of Auto Design Conservation Measures." (We are especially interested in your comments on Rand's conclusions with regard to feasible technological improvements and the associated time scales for implementation, as well as their conclusions with regard to possible fuel savings.)

(b) The following two statements on page 22 of Dr. Wildhorn's written statement:

"Our work indicates that a 50 percent improvement in average new car fuel economy by 1980, over the 1974 figure of 14 miles per gallon, appears feasible."

"After 1980, much higher average new car fuel economy appears feasible, if new technology is pursued vigorously, and R&D is successful. For example, fuel economy standards over 30 miles per gallon might be possible by 1985."

(c) The following statements from the executive summary:

"However, the most recent study of the market structure of the automobile industry argues that few incentives exist for making technological improvements. This conclusion is consistent with the results of our econometric analysis, which forecasts that large increases in real gasoline prices would lead to only small increases in average automobile efficiency." (Page 5)

"The capital resources available to the auto manufacturing industry, either through internal reallocation (e.g., deferral of annual model changes) or from external sources (e.g., borrowing), appear adequate to finance conversion to new technology, such as an alternative type of power plant and transmission. Total capital investment required is roughly the same as a single year's current capital expenditures by the motor vehicle industry." (Page 6)

"Our analysis indicates that the supercharged rotary engine with charge stratification dominates all other engine types, including the diesel. Compared with the conventional SIE, it yields about twice the fuel economy, requires about 40 percent less lifetime energy, and reduces initial and lifetime per-vehicle costs by over 25 percent." (Page 7)

"The continuously variable transmission (CVT) can increase a conventional auto's fuel economy by about 27 to 32 percent, depending on driving cycle (urban or urban–rural driving) and auto size, all other things being equal. It does so by automatically selecting the most appropriate gear ratio between engine and wheels, thereby maximizing efficiency and fuel economy, without exceeding allowable nitrogen oxides (NO_x) emissions. Lifetime energy requirements of the auto can be reduced 10 percent; auto selling price can be reduced about 5 percent because the more efficient CVT can attain the same performance (i.e., acceleration) with a smaller engine and lighter vehicle, although the CVT itself is heavier and more expensive than a standard automatic transmission; and lifetime cost per vehicle can be reduced by 8 percent." (Page 7)

"Our automotive design analysis indicates that automobiles with new technology, but with the same acceleration and interior space characteristics as today's standard size cars, could achieve over 25 mpg, while subcompacts could achieve over 40 mpg. If a fuel economy standard is to be legislated, this finding suggests that the average range of 16 to 20 mpg standards, in recently proposed legislation, is perhaps unnecessarily low." (Page 8)

In addition, I would also appreciate receiving your written answers to the enclosed questions not necessarily relating to the Rand report . . .

Sincerely yours,

Warren G. Magnuson, *Chairman.*

COMMENTS BY AMERICAN MOTORS CORPORATION

The following letter was written in response to quotations in Senator Warren G. Magnuson's letter of December 23, 1974, to R. A. Petersen, Director, Powertrain Engineering, American Motors Corporation.

American Motors Corp.,
Detroit, Mich., February 12, 1975.

Hon. Warrern G. Magnuson,
Chairman, Committee on Commerce,
U.S. Senate, Washington, D.C.

Dear Senator Magnuson:

Your December 23, 1974 letter requested that American Motors comment on the Rand Report entitled, "How to Save Gasoline: Public Policy Alternatives for the Automobile." You also asked other specific questions relating to vehicles and fuel economy. We have reviewed the Rand Report and have compared various statements against data and judgments that we have obtained over many years of engineering and developing vehicles for optimum fuel economy. We cannot subscribe to the conclusions voiced in the Rand study although we do agree that most of its suggested areas for improvement are directionally correct in terms of fuel economy improvement.

(*a*) We find that the Rand Report contains conclusions which are often based on erroneous or argumentative assumptions. There is essentially no documentation to justify or clarify those assumptions and therefore it is very difficult for us to indicate the specific corrections that are required in their analysis. However, the following areas of difference can be addressed:

1. AIR CONDITIONING

The Rand Report indicates that air conditioning increases fuel consumption by 13%. This is exaggerated and completely unsupported by any facts in our possession. There are several types of systems popular in modern vehicles and these have varying impact on fuel use rate. American Motors uses the cycling type in which the compressor is operating only when cooler air is demanded. Our system imposes a 5%–7% additional fuel penalty when operating at full load. Obviously, when analyzing the impact of this feature on an annualized average basis, the effect of time in which full load operation is required must be a major portion of the equation. We do not have valid statistics to indicate the exact percentage of time the air conditioning compressor is operating in each climatic segment of the United States. However, we believe that it is obvious that full load operation occurs far less than 25% of total vehicle operating time and, therefore, the actual Nationwide effect of air conditioning on fuel economy would be at the most a 2% figure and, more probably, less than 1%. Therefore, the Rand suggestion that an "average" gain of 9% be assigned to elimination of air conditioning is not correct.

2. RADIAL PLY TIRES

American Motors has voluminous test histories, predominantly on the SAE track-type test cycle, that show that radial ply tires, when operated at recommended pressures, offer a 4% fuel economy improvement when compared to bias ply tires. This differs from the 7% quoted by the Rand Report. The Table on Page 114, Appendix B, shows values for the rolling resistance coefficients used in the Rand analysis that are nearly 25% higher than those which available literature generally suggests as representative for standard type tires.

3. AERODYNAMIC CHANGES

The Rand study indicates that three specific types of body changes would offer increased fuel economy by minimizing vehicle air resistance and they suggest that these changes are feasible in the "near term." We do agree that a front underbody spoiler, rounding of frontal corners and a total spoiler treatment will improve fuel economy. At the lower driving speeds simulated during the EPA dynamometer fuel economy test, the front underbody spoiler would have the most potential. We do not know if a coefficient of drag reduction as great as 25% is realistic or attainable through these types of changes; we doubt, however, that any significant drag reduction can be obtained while simultaneously meeting mandated safety standards and while providing for all the practical and necessary elements of customer operation such as ground clearance, etc. However, even if a 25% drag reduction is attainable, the presently used combined EPA test cycle would show a zero percent fuel economy improvement using current dynamometer loading procedures and only a 2.3% improvement if some practical way could be established to accurately adjust the dynamometer load to compensate for the drag reduction. The Rand Report over-emphasizes the effect aerodynamics would have at the relatively low speeds used to measure fuel economy with the EPA procedure.

Any substantial drag reduction would require a large front spoiler which is not practical since it would severely limit ground clearance. Spoiler provisions at the rear of the vehicle are not very beneficial because of their small impact on overall drag at low speeds. We believe a 10% drag coefficient reduction is probably the limit of practicality for any "minor" type of body revision.

The Rand Report goes on to state that use of "major" aerodynamic changes that could be made, in conjunction with the theoretical "minor" changes, would result in a combined 13% reduction in fuel economy. Our analysis of combined EPA city-highway cycles shows that the *total affect of air resistance represents only 8% to 10% of the fuel used* during those cycles. Thus, if as much as a 50% drag reduction could be somehow achieved, only a 4% to 5% improvement in fuel economy would be obtained using this test procedure.

A complete body under-pan would be very effective in reducing air drag losses. However, this would create tremendous problems in controlling heat from the underhood or from the exhaust systems and we assume would require very substantial upgrading of materials, along with system redesigns. Even with these types of corrections, incorporation of large amounts of insulation would be needed. The net effect would be to increase both the cost and weight of the vehicle thus negating any fuel economy gains achieved from the drag reduction.

4. WEIGHT REDUCTION

We agree that lesser weight is a meritorious objective and a requirement for superior fuel economy. Reduced weight provides some fuel improvement in steady state high-speed operating economy. It is of even greater benefit in low speed, stop-start, operations common in urban traffic. However, we cannot agree that reducing vehicle weight by either 20% or by 36% (per Rand's two examples) will achieve fuel gains of 15% or 20% respectively. Our tests and calculations both indicate that weight reductions of 20% on a 3,500-lb. base car would show a net fuel economy reduction of 5%. A weight reduction of 36% on this 3,500-lb. car would give a net fuel savings of 9%. If reductions of these magnitudes were accompanied by representative reductions in engine sizes, a larger benefit would be realized without any performance detriment. However, time and resource constraints do not allow us to completely redesign all vehicles, while simultaneously engineering, tooling and producing new engines for such vehicles by the 1980 model year.

5. CVT: (CONSTANTLY VARIABLE TRANSMISSION)

We agree that a constantly variable transmission has the theoretical potential for providing better fuel economy but we have no reason to believe that the attributes are sufficient to justify the claim that a 27% fuel economy improvement is available on all production vehicles. We have made analytical simulations of theoretically perfect transmissions and these indicate that a potential improvement of more than 20% is possible for certain types of cars if present performance objectives are maintained. These calculations assume total efficiencies greater than any efficiencies that we have been documented, and we have no reason to believe that this optimum unit is actually producible. More important, for the purpose of this reply, we see no near term availability of such a transmission and are very doubtful that the research, design, development, certification and tooling times needed for such a unit would allow its production before the 1985 model year, even if a completely viable concept were available as a starting point today. We are not certain that such a concept can ever be fully proven and brought to production although we are carefully following some configurations that may have long-term merit.

6. NEW ENGINES

We feel that the conclusions regarding fuel economy gains and midterm availability of the stratified, super-charged rotary engine are inadequately documented by the Rand study. This is not to infer that some economy gains could not be achieved through the route referenced, however, we have seen absolutely no technical or scientific backing for the inter-related conclusion that stringent emission control can be achieved and economy losses can be prevented with this type of approach. Conversely, we believe that ample data exists both within our own laboratories as well as in the public domain indicating that, at the present stage of development of the rotary engine, a backward step in fuel economy is to be expected when controls needed to achieve substantial HC reductions are employed. It must also be realized that no known method exists for reaching the .4 NO_x level mandated for 1978. Therefore, the assumptions made for this powerplant do not bear any resemblance to the facts available to us. The claims are completely inconsistent with our data base and totally without formal documentation in the Report. We thus are unable to be more specific on detail areas of difference; we can only state that we consider the conclusions that a stratified, super-charged rotary engine would provide a 73%–82% gain in fuel economy to be non-supportable by either known laboratory tests or by comprehensive engineering analysis. Even if some gains could be achieved, it should be recognized that our 1980 models must be completely engineered and operational on the official emission certification schedule by the fall of 1978. The time span available for any major change in 1980 model year powerplants is totally inadequate for the research, development and tooling efforts that must be completed; in fact, the 1983 model year would be a difficult challenge for a change of this extent.

(*b*) Dr. Wildhorn's statement that ". . . our work indicates that 50 percent improvement in average new car fuel economy by 1980, over the 1974 figure of 14 miles per gallon, appears feasible, . . ." is consistent with the facts as we know them today when several modifying "if" phrases are added to that statement. First, "if" the industry model mix can be changed to emphasize the lower weight areas. Secondly, "if" more stringent emission requirements do not force fuel economy degrading systems and, thirdly, "if" other government or public pressures do not create large weight increases in vehicles. The first of these assumptions is speculative as the pressures of public demand will have a large influence on the type of cars produced in future years. American Motors strongly believes that the public will accept and desire smaller vehicles, not only for their benefits in terms of fuel economy and operating costs, but also for their lesser initial price. However, the true trend cannot be known and must remain speculative as of this writing. The second assumption is inconsistent with the requirements of the Clean Air Act as they exist today. Our current position must be that future models will have to meet very stringent standards for HC, CO and NO_x. These standards will create substantial reductions in fuel economy; especially if the .4 gm/mile NO_x requirement is not altered. The third assumption is likewise not in accord with current and proposed rulemaking in regard to safety and damageability. Proposals that will impose more severe test standards for bumper systems, barrier impacts, fuel systems, brakes and roll over situations will invariably add weight and add fuel penalties to vehicles. We fervently hope that relaxation of these proposals is forthcoming but, unless relief is granted, fuel losses must be expected.

A fifty-percent improvement in fuel economy would be the absolute upper limit of gain possible on American Motors' vehicles by the 1980 model year *if* all weight and efficiency factors relating to safety and emission standards could be ignored. As neither of these areas of control can be dismissed, our true potential improvement is far under that figure. This conclusion stems not only from considerations of technological feasibility but also from practical aspects of timing and economics.

Dr. Wildhorn's statement that ". . . after 1980, much higher average new car fuel economy appears feasible, if new technology is pursued vigorously, and R&D is successful. For example, fuel economy standards over 30 miles per gallon might be possible by 1985, . . ." must be viewed as extremely optimistic. In any field, if "technology is pursued vigorously" and if "R&D is successful," great benefits can accrue. However, the industry cannot plan on the basis of or predict technological breakthrough without some substantial basis for that hope. With the uncertainty created by the present legislative climate, it is virtually impossible to plan or predict the success of any power-train component for future model years. The reason is that the target that must be met are in constant flux with no defined end point promulgated. It is impractical to generate a dedicated research program for anything as complex as a new powerplant in this aura of confusion. Further, it is impossible to target such a project toward specific tooling dates, when such actions require commitment of extremely large financial resources, without knowledge of whether the components so planned will be capable of meeting legal requirements applicable to future products.

As mentioned previously, it is unrealistic to legislate fuel economy standards for future model years on the basis of undefined research claims founded on ambiguous and undocumented assumptions. It is necessary that both the base from which a percentage improvement number is to be obtained and the fully detailed test procedure for the base year and the future model year be objectively defined. The Rand inference that 25 mpg on a standard car and 40 mpg on a sub-compact car are attainable is virtually meaningless without sufficient modifying phraseology to define the specifications of these hypothetical vehicles and the procedures used to determine the fuel economy.

If we assume that no relief will be granted in the areas of emissions or safety standards, we must consider the Rand conclusions inaccurate. For our future products it will be extremely difficult to maintain the fuel economy levels of our 1975 vehicles while simultaneously reducing pollutants. With relaxation of the .4 NO_x requirement we can improve fuel economy in future years, but values as high as mentioned in the Rand study are not within our grasp.

(*c*) With regard to the statement that few incentives exist for the automobile industry to make technical improvements, we strongly disagree that this is a valid conclusion. It is clear to us that the trend is toward smaller, more fuel efficient vehicles, and at American Motors we have attempted to anticipate these demands in developing our new model program plans. Accordingly, as in the past, we will continue to direct our efforts toward meeting the market demand for more fuel efficient vehicles. Competition in the market place provides the strongest incentive a company could possibly have.

Since we do not know what the Rand Report means by "new technology," we have no estimate of what would be required to finance conversion to it. Therefore, it is difficult for us to comment on the statement that adequate capital resources are available to the industry. However, we can state very strongly that the total capital investment required by American Motors to convert to some of the new technology referenced in the report is not available to us. Capital investment for alternate powerplant or transmission systems would require investment beyond our current or foreseen average annual capabilities. The tremendous capital requirement is not available to us either through internal or external sources.

Sincerely,

R. A. Petersen,
Director, Powertrain Engineering

COMMENTS BY CHRYSLER CORPORATION

The following letter was written in response to quotations in Senator Warren G. Magnuson's letter of December 23, 1974, to Alan G. Loofbourrow, Vice President for Engineering, Chrysler Corporation.

Chrysler Corp.,
Detroit, Mich., January 10, 1975.

Hon. Warren G. Magnuson,
Chairman, Committee on Commerce,
U.S. Senate,
Washington, D.C.

Dear Senator Magnuson:

In reply to your letter of December 23, 1974, we are pleased to respond to your request for specific comments on the Rand Corporation Report entitled "How to Save Gasoline: Public Policy Alternatives for the Automobile" and answers to the enumerated questions attached to your letter. The quotations from your letter are indented and underlined below, followed by our comments.

(a) Chapter IV of the full report, entitled 'Per-Vehicle Comparisons of Auto Design Conservation Measures.' (We are especially interested in your comments on Rand's conclusions with regard to feasible technological improvements and the associated timescales for implementation, as well as their conclusions with regard to possible fuel savings.)

Our overall comment is that all of the values of fuel economy gains through technological changes presented in this report are gravely misleading. All errors are in the direction of predicting too much improvement. Specific examples are as follows:

1. No recognition is given to the approximate 30% loss in fuel economy that will result from the 1977–78 statutory emission standards compared to the 1975 standards.

2. The supercharged, stratified charge rotary engine is actually one of the least promising, with respect to fuel economy, of all internal combustion engines. Its thermal efficiency is inferior, blowby and seal wear is a problem even without supercharging, and the stratified charge is still too experimental to assume success.

3. The claimed potential fuel economy gain from the continuously variable transmission of 27–32% is greatly exaggerated. Assuming that such a transmission can ever be successfully developed, the maximum potential fuel economy gain is more in the order of 13–20%.

4. The Rand report claims a fuel economy gain for radial tires of 7–8%. Our experience averages about 3%.

5. An improvement of 13% is claimed for removing air conditioning from a full size car—9% to run the air conditioner and 4% for operation of the compressor and the weight effect is less than 1%.

6. A fuel economy improvement of 6% on the FDC Cycle and 9% on the OAP Cycle is claimed for a "minor" aerodynamic change reducing the drag coefficient from 0.5 to 0.38. Our experience indicates that the expected improvement would be more in the order of 1% on the FDC Cycle and 4% on the OAP Cycle. Moreover, on aerodynamic change of this magnitude would require major changes to the car and extensive retooling.

7. We fail to see how the extended use of aluminum in bodies and engines would result in a 12% reduced selling price. Except where it is already being used, every item that we have studied for converting to aluminum in engines and bodies is an indicated cost penalty that cannot be offset by secondary savings.

8. The effect of eliminating the trunk as a means of improving fuel economy is exaggerated. A direct saving of 150 lbs. might allow additional weight to be saved in tires, brakes, drivetrain, etc., to make a total saving of 2000 lbs. With a concurrent axle ratio change, an improvement in fuel economy of about 2–3% is anticipated. The 16–20% gain predicted is greatly overstated. Moreover, the elimination of the trunk would inevitably result in greater use of the roof for carrying baggage and other articles with concomitant aerodynamic losses and questions of vehicle stability.

9. The savings claimed for the combined effects of various vehicle design changes is exaggerated because it tends to count some effects more than once.

(b) The following two statements on page 22 of Dr. Wildhorn's written statement:

"Our work indicates that a 50 percent improvement in average new car fuel economy by 1980, over the 1974 figure of 14 miles per gallon, appears feasible."

"After 1980, much higher average new car fuel economy appears feasible, if new technology is pursued vigorously, and R&D is successful. For example, fuel economy standards over 30 miles per gallon might be possible by 1985."

These statements seem to be based on Figure 7–1, Page 80, of the full report. They assume complete elimination of full and intermediate size cars, with only compact and subcompact cars remaining by 1980. Also, they completely ignore the aforesaid estimated 32–40% negative effect of the 1978 emission standard. Every technological improvement cited in the entire report has been exaggerated for its beneficial effect.

For a realistic evaluation of what might be achieved by 1980, we would like to refer to our response of November 15, 1974, made to the Department of Transportation regarding a voluntary commitment to improve the average fuel economy of our U.S. manufactured cars from 13.8 mpg to 18.7 mpg by 1980. In that response we advised that if we are granted a carryover of 1975 emission standards through 1980 and if there are no overall weight increases due to regulations during this period, we believe we can meet the average fuel economy goal of 18.7 miles per gallon by 1980. It was pointed out that if we had to meet the statutory emission requirement of 0.4 grams per mile HC. 3.4 grams per mile CO, and 2.0 grams per mile NO_x, we would fall considerably short of their fuel economy objective, or an estimated average economy of 15.1 to 16.3 miles per gallon. Also, it was pointed out that the effect of any weight increases due to regulations would cause further decrease. In that response, no estimate was made of the still more serious deterioration that would result if the 1978 requirement of .41 grams per mile of NO_x had to be met, because the assumption suggested by DOT was that the NO_x requirement would be 2.0 grams per mile through 1980. Should the .41 grams per mile of NO_x have to be met, the further decrease in average fuel economy would be substantial—in the order of 20%, or 12–13 miles per gallon.

(c) The following statements from the executive summary:

"However, the most recent study of the market structure of the automobile industry argues that few incentives exist for making technological improvements. This conclusion is consistent with the results of our econometric analysis, which forecasts that large increases in real gasoline prices would lead to only small increases in average automobile efficiency." (Page 5)

We most emphatically disagree with the statement that few incentives exist in the automobile industry for making technological improvements, both in general and as it specifically applies to fuel economy. As I pointed out in my testimony before the Commerce Committee last December 10, at Chrysler the attainment of better fuel economy has been an important incentive for technological improvement in the past and continues to be even more so today. As I stated in that testimony, we estimate that Chrysler Corporation 1975 cars average 15% better fuel economy than 1974 models, and that we believe that we can meet the goal of a 40% sales weighted improvement in fuel economy by 1980 provided that there be no federally mandated weight increase from safety, noise, or damageability standards, and that emission standards remain at 1975 levels.

The accomplishment of this latter goal will represent a substantial technological achievement. We do not believe that any further increases in gasoline prices over present levels will provide any more incentive to accomplish this goal than we already have.

"The capital resources available to the auto manufacturing industry, either through internal reallocation (e.g., deferral of annual model changes) or from external sources (e.g., borrowing), appear adequate to finance conversion to new technology, such as an alternative type of power plant and transmission. Total capital investment required is roughly the same as a single year's capital expenditures by the motor vehicle industry." (Page 6)

Our response to this item is from the Corporate Comptroller's Office, and is included as an attachment to this letter.

Our analysis indicates that the supercharged rotary engine with charge stratification dominates all other engine types, including the diesel. Compared with the conventional SIE, it yields about twice the fuel economy, requires about 40 percent less lifetime energy, and reduces initial and lifetime per-vehicle costs by over 25 percent." (Page 7)

We cannot agree with these statements and it's incomprehensible to us that they could be made by anyone truly knowledgeable of this engine type. The stratified charge development, if successful, could help to offset the inherent *inefficiency* of the rotary engine in comparison to good piston engines at light loads, but these same advantages could also be realized by the piston engine. The weight and cost analyses of the rotary engine are unsupportable by the facts.

"The continuously variable transmission (CVT) can increase a conventional auto's fuel economy by about 27 to 32 percent, depending on driving cycle (urban or urban–rural driving) and auto size, all other things being equal. It does so by automatically selecting the most appropriate gear ratio between engine and wheels, thereby maximizing efficiency and fuel economy, without exceeding allowable nitrogen oxides (NO_x) emissions. Lifetime energy requirements of the auto can be reduced 10 percent: auto selling price can be reduced about 5 percent because the more efficient CTV can attain the same performance (i.e., acceleration) with a smaller engine and lighter vehicle, although the CVT itself is heavier and more expensive than a standard automatic transmission; and lifetime cost per vehicle can be reduced by 8 percent." (Page 7)

The continuously variable transmission is a good basic concept that has challenged the ingenuity of engineers and inventors for many years. Unfortunately, the problems of complexity, durability, noise, inefficiency, and cost have not been successfully solved despite the efforts of many people. If it could be successfully developed, our studies indicate a potential fuel economy improvement of 10–20%, in contrast to the 27–32% claimed in the Rand report. The efficiency of the transmission is a limiting factor, and during urban driving the periods of acceleration, deceleration and idling further reduce the benefit to be obtained. The added complexity of the CVT would add more cost than the savings resulting from a slightly smaller engine. Also, the increased weight of the CVT would tend to offset any weight savings realized in the engine.

"Our automotive design and analysis indicates that automobiles with new technology, but with the same acceleration and interior space characteristics as today's standard size cars, could achieve over 25 mpg, while subcompacts could achieve over 40 mpg. If a fuel economy standard is to be legislated, this finding suggests that the average range of 16 to 20 mpg standards, in recently proposed legislation, is perhaps unnecessarily low." (Page 8)

There is no "new" technology identified in the Rand report. Every proposed technological improvement is well known to automotive engineers and has been thoroughly analyzed and vigorously pursued. The projected levels of fuel economy are based on a combination of exaggerated benefit previously mentioned, and a drastic conversion to compact and subcompact cars. Further, they do not take into account the very large deterioration of the fuel economy that 1977–78 emission standards will impose. . . .

Very truly yours,

Alan Loofbourrow

*STATEMENT CONTAINED IN A JANUARY 10, 1975 LETTER TO SENATOR WARREN G. MAGNUSON FROM MR. ALAN G. LOOFBOURROW

STATEMENT

"The capital resources available to the auto manufacturing industry, either through internal reallocation (e.g., deferral of annual model changes) or from external sources (e.g., borrowing), appear adequate to finance conversion to new technology, such as an alternative type of power plant and transmission. Total capital investment required is roughly the same as a single year's current capital expenditures by the motor vehicle industry."

ANSWER

Available funds for capital expenditure within Chrysler are generated internally from write offs for depreciation and tooling amortization. Expenditures in excess of these amounts must be obtained from retained profits and/or borrowing. Chrysler's present level of long term debt and other borrowing negates any additional funds from external sources for capital expenditures. Profit levels have been significantly reduced due to rising economies and material shortages causing higher costs possibly influenced in part by materials added to vehicles for federally mandated standards. Based on our long term profit projections, it does not appear as though sufficient profits can be counted on to materially increase capital expenditures beyond those internally generated.

Even within these funds, the conclusion cannot be made that total capital expenditures would be deferrable to apply to a new engine and other drive train components.

Chrysler Corporation's total capital expenditures generated from depreciation and amortization would approximate $378 million. From this we would have to deduct replacement of worn out tools and facilities generally replaced for new model, facility maintenance including expenditures for EPA/OSHA. Nonautomotive operations, expenditures outside of the U.S. and Canada, and miscellaneous investments required for dealerships.

Consequently, approximately $150 million would be deferrable if we discontinued all expenditures for new model and expansion as well as planned expenditures for forthcoming additional federal mandated standards.

*Statement subtitle contains corrected date and correspondents identification.

The $150 million remaining is perhaps only 15–20% of the funds that would be needed for equipment, tools and rearrangement for new engines, transmissions and other drive train components.

COMMENTS BY FORD MOTOR COMPANY

The following letter was written in response to quotations in Senator Warren G. Magnuson's letter of December 23, 1974, to Fred Secrest, Executive Vice President/Operations Staff, Ford Motor Company.

Ford Motor Co.,
Dearborn, Mich., January 17, 1975.

Hon. Warren G. Magnuson,
U.S. Senate,
Committee on Commerce,
Washington, D.C.

Dear Mr. Magnuson:

In your letter of December 23, 1974, you asked us to answer some specific questions for the hearing record as supplements to the testimony I presented on December 10, 1974 at the Commerce Committee's hearing on an Energy Conservation Working Paper.

Most of your questions relate to the Rand Corporation report entitled "How to Save Gasoline: Public Policy Alternatives for the Automobile" and Dr. Sorrel Wildhorn's written testimony submitted to the Committee.

The Rand Report represents a major effort to analyze public policy alternatives relating to conservation of motor fuel. We agree in a *qualitative* way with its major conclusions:

A fuel price increase is the only effective near-term conservation strategy.

Improved new car fuel economy becomes the preferred strategy in the long-term, *provided* such improved fuel economy can be achieved at reasonable cost and without compromising the acceptability of the vehicle to the consumer.

This provision incorporated in the Rand recommendation is of great importance, and we endorse it without reservation. We are extremely concerned, however, that the *quantitative* results of the study have been given far more credibility than warranted by the methodology used. In our judgment, government policy predicated on those quantitative results would be ill-advised. Our general concerns are:

The inability of the simplistic model to generate reliable output.

The assumptions employed in connection with the input variables and with initial calibration of the model.

The dismissal in one sentence of the problems of raising the capital required to implement new technology, particularly in view of the fact that the Rand results depend on redesign and retooling of the entire automobile simultaneously with every engine and transmission change.

A confusing interpretation of feasibility and time-tables in which Rand considers a product to be capable of mass production at the same time that its feasibility is finally proven, with no consideration given to the risks involved in such a procedure.

An unwarranted and unsupported assumption that statutory emission standards will somehow be met without price, weight, fuel, and performance penalties for all forms of conventional and advanced technology.

Failure to recognize that the consumer has the option of keeping his existing car if a new car, however efficient, fails to offer the features he wants.

The lack of consideration of the need to recover capital investment, and the impact of this capital recovery on the cost of the car.

These points are developed further in our detailed response to your specific inquiries, which is attached. The attachment also includes our replies to your other questions on matters not involving the Rand Report. We appreciate the opportunity to provide comments on these important issues.

F. G. Secrest.

DETAILED ANSWERS TO QUESTIONS RAISED IN SENATOR MAGNUSON'S LETTER OF DECEMBER 23, 1974

RAND REPORT QUESTIONS

(a) "Chapter IV of the full report, entitled 'Per-Vehicle Comparisons of Auto Design Conservation Measures.' (We are especially interested in your comments on Rand's conclusions with regard to feasible technological improvements and the associated timescales for implementation, as well as their conclusions with regard to possible fuel savings.)"

Answer. If there is one lesson to be learned from this chapter of the Rand Report, it is that there is great uncertainty as to which of the alternatives offers the greatest promise for improved fuel economy in the shortest time at the lowest cost. In fact we have not depended solely on our judgment in this matter and have given the Jet Propulsion Laboratory, California Institute of Technology a grant to conduct an independent investigation and to report their findings directly to the public. For this reason, we believe it is imperative that no attempt be made to mandate technology. Such a course of action would stifle innovation and could result in a very expensive implementation of the wrong technology (as aptly demonstrated by the Morgantown People Mover installation). We have already stated in testimony before the Committee on Commerce that we believe market forces will provide sufficient incentive (particularly with increased gasoline prices) for improved fuel economy. To the extent that these market forces may not be sufficient, consideration should be given to tax incentives that would help shift market demand toward more efficient products. We believe that only under such a competitive environment will each of the promising technologies receive suitable development attention.

Finally, we are so seriously concerned about the quantitative accuracy of the Rand Report that we would caution against its use in support of any form of fuel economy standards. In particular, the effects on fuel economy of vehicle design changes as given in Chapter IV appear to be unjustifiably optimistic.

Before dealing with individual changes which fall into this category, it may be appropriate to discuss the reasons the Rand conclusions might err on the high side. To do this, it is necessary to evaluate the assumptions and input data upon which the Rand analysis is based. These are presented in another Rand document entitled "A Generalized Model for Comparing Automobile Design Approaches to Improved Fuel Economy," R–1562–NSF, by T. F. Kirkwood and Allen D. Lee, January 1975.

What are presented as conclusions in the executive summary and the full report are based on insufficient data and inadequate analysis. Furthermore, these conclusions must be placed in the context of the Rand assumptions regarding the automotive design process, and a proper interpretation also depends on an understanding of the inputs themselves.

It is clear that, for example, the use of radial tires *could* allow a slight decrease in the size of the engine required to attain a given performance level. Rand, however, goes beyond that observation and makes the implicit assumption that a decision to add radials can feed immediately into the design process, whereupon a slightly smaller engine, and shorter frame and body, will appear. In essence, then, Rand has, *in every case they analyzed,* assumed that all possible weight savings could be exploited. Without exception, they consider the vehicle to be redesigned from the ground up. Needless to say, the costs involved in such a procedure are prohibitive, and as a result the Rand estimates of potential savings are bound to be optimistic.

The reader of the Rand Report should bear in mind that many of the technological innovations analyzed by Rand, e.g., "supercharged rotary engine with charge stratification," have never been built, let alone tested. Consequently, Rand used estimates of possible performance specifications, rather than actual data. Estimation is, of course, unavoidable if one is attempting to project the impact of untried technology, but there is no escaping the fact that it is an estimation, and subject to wishful thinking. It is one thing to hypothesize that such an engine would have "37% of the weight, 90% of the volume and 53% of the cost per horsepower" of a conventional engine, it is quite another to build it and achieve those specifications.

In addition to the above observations, we note that the model is also deficient in these respects:

1. The approximation to the Federal Driving Cycle is incorrect.

2. The method of computing the fuel consumed based on this cycle is inadequate.

3. No consideration is given to the level of emission control as it influences fuel economy.

4. The overall model structure is unsound in that important constraints and objectives have been ignored.

5. The model has not been verified to the extent that its quantitative predictions can be believed with any acceptable level of confidence.

A comparison of the Rand approximations to the 1974 Federal Urban Driving Cycle can be made to the exact values. Figure 1 provides the comparisons. It may be seen that the Rand approximations are at wide variance to the true cycle parameters (see Clayton LaPointe, "Factors Affecting Vehicle Fuel Economy." SAE Paper No. 730791, September, 1973 and Arthur D. Little, Inc., "A Study of Technical Improvements in Automobile Fuel Consumption," February 1974). To expect the Rand approximations to reflect actual cycle characteristics is, therefore, unsupportable. Moreover, design changes which impact the separate cycle parameters in a non-uniform manner cannot be expected to be accurately evaluated.

In the Rand document, the calculation of fuel consumption over the cycle is in turn based on the consumption during the individual modes. This approach ignores the effect of transient operation and of cold operation during vehicle warm-up. Indeed, no computation scheme regardless of its complexity has been able to simulate these effects to date, and thus it has not been feasible to predict fuel economy performance over the Federal Driving Cycle. This is a failing common to all recent studies of fuel economy improvement potential.

The Rand computational method is the most primitive of those recently proposed. For example, the computation of fuel consumed during the idle mode is based on a simple assumption that idle flow rate is a function solely of peak engine power. The authors, in pursuing this assumed dependence, arrive at the illogical conclusion that idle fuel flow rate peaks for engines at 275 horsepower and declines as horsepower is increased beyond this value.

The actual idle fuel flow rate depends on the idle torque and the idle RPM. The product of these two quantities is the power required at idle to overcome friction and to power accessories such as the water pump, alternator, power steering pump, air conditioner, and air injection pump. This idle power requirement bears little relation to the peak power of the engine but does depend on emission control level. For example, idle RPM has been increased in recent years in order to reduce hydrocarbon emission both during idle and during deceleration modes. Rand's estimate of fuel consumption during idle is, therefore, incorrect.

The method used to compute fuel flow rate during acceleration modes is also incorrect. This partly due to the use of constant speed specific fuel consumption data to compute acceleration rates and times discussed earlier and the result is

Figure 1

RAND APPROXIMATION TO THE FEDERAL DRIVING CYCLE COMPARED TO THE
ACTUAL DRIVING CYCLE

Mode	Time (seconds)		Distance (miles)		Average rate	
	Rand	Actual	Rand	Actual	Rand	Actual
Acceleration	159	543	0.62	3.49	[1]3.0	[1]0.81
Deceleration	167	475	.67	3.08	[1]−3.0	[1]−.95
Cruise	770	109	6.11	.89	[2]28.6	[2]29.40
Idle	275	245	0	0	------------------	

[1] Miles per hour per second.
[2] Miles per hour.

totally misleading. It is not surprising that the authors found it necessary to adjust by 30% the fuel economy values computed by their model. This "calibration," moreover, was assumed to apply universally when, in fact, it is based on pre-1971 data and ignores many of the factors the authors seek to assess.

The authors have not attempted to account in any way for the impact of emission standards on fuel economy. (Perhaps the reason for this oversight is lack of data on future systems calibrated to more than one level of emissions control or perhaps because the prediction of emissions other than NO_x is analytically intractable). Whatever their reasons, the oversight is serious, and casts serious doubt on the validity of their results.

For details, the reader is referred to Ford's "Application (to the EPA) for Suspension of the 1977 Motor Vehicle Exhaust Emissions Standards." Briefly, this document shows that for a specific system, the level of emissions control dominates fuel economy behavior.

The effect is not secondary, but can actually determine whether technologically improved systems obtain better or worse fuel economy than present systems.

With regard to the overall model structure, we note that the single objective of the optimization routine in the Rand model is to minimize the length of those portions of the vehicle fore and aft of the passenger compartment, subject to approximate constraints on 0–60 acceleration time and range. In doing this, Rand has failed to appreciate the significance of packaging, handling, crashworthiness, ride quality, passing performance, and other such considerations having profound impact in vehicle design. In their singleminded devotion to minimum length, they adopt a view even more simplistic than that which gave us the claustrophobic, overweight vehicles under DOT's "Experimental Safety Vehicle" program in 1972. Rand would have us, for example, driving in "trunkless" cars with a sum of 18 inches fore and aft of the passenger compartment— totally inadequate to house wheel wells, engines, bumpers, etc., and absolutely impossible for occupant protection in a crash.

We take strong issue with the implication by Rand that "minor" changes can achieve a 25% reduction in drag coefficient without having significant impacts on the remaining components. For example, the underbody pan proposed by Rand, while attractive for racing applications, poses serious problems in maintaining ground clearance during entry/exit of parking garage ramps. It also can reduce airflow past brakes to the point that cooling is seriously impaired, requiring major redesign to avoid compromising safety.

As further evidence of the tradeoffs and constraints ignored by Rand, we offer the observation that the Honda Civic has a drag coefficient almost 20% higher than the value cited by Rand as typical of current domestic auto design, and 55% higher than the value assumed by Rand to be achievable with minor improvements" to subcompact design. As the Rand authors must surely know, it is virtually impossible to attain a low drag coefficient along with minimum vehicle length; the two objectives are to a substantial degree conflicting.

We would also point out that the 1972 Honda—which did not meet federal bumper standards—had a drag coefficient approximately 10% better than federalized (1973) model, another example of the undesirable side effects of mandated standards.

To calibrate the model (item 5), Rand arbitrarily adjusted parameters until they could reach satisfactory (general ±10%) agreement between the numbers output by the model and gross data from various sources on 1973 automobiles. Given the extremely simplistic view of the tradeoffs and constraints embodied in the model, and given that the fully calibrated model yields significant errors *even when applied to the data used to calibrate it*, extreme caution should be applied to interpretation of its predictions. This caution holds especially for predictions of the effects of radical departures from current technology and product attributes.

In conclusion, we view the Rand automotive design model as useful at best in a very limited sense, i.e., of providing the novice with a qualitative feeling for the kinds of gross interactions and tradeoffs possible in a world without government standards. As a tool upon which to base product or policy decisions (even to the extent of assignment of priorities) it is dangerously naive.

(b) "Comment on page 22 of Dr. Wildhorn's written statement 'Our work indicates that a 50 percent improvement in average new car fuel economy by 1980, over the 1974 figure of 14 miles per gallon, appears feasible'."

Answer. This statement is misleading. Not only is it based on faulty analysis discussed elsewhere, but the actions Rand postulates to accomplish this depend on invention.

Without the CVT or the supercharged rotary engine, it is not possible to find substantiation in the report for the claim that 50% improvement is feasible by 1980. Radial tires, major aerodynamic improvement and major incorporation of aluminum engine and structural components account for less than 30% fuel economy improvement by the authors' reckoning and less than 20% improvement by Ford's reckoning.

(b) Continued: "Further comment on page 22 of Dr. Wildhorn's written statement 'After 1980, much higher average new car fuel economy appears feasible, if new technology is pursued vigorously, and R&D is successful. For example, fuel economy standards over 30 miles per gallon might be possible by 1985'."

Answer. These statements should be considered in the context of Rand's 40 mpg subcompact design *according to their own published model results.* The total space available forward of the passenger compartment for packaging wheel wells, engine, radiator, front bumpers, and energy absorption necessary for crash protection, is 16 inches. The total space available behind the occupant for seat back, rear bumper, fuel tank, wheel wells, and crash protection is 2 inches.

(c) Comment on "The following statements from the executive summary:

1. 'However, the most recent study of the market structure of the automobile industry argues that few incentives exist for making technological improvements. This conclusion is consistent with the results of our econometric analysis, which forecasts that large increases in real gasoline prices would lead to only small increases in average automobile efficiency',"

Answer. The study referred to is the book "The Automobile Industry Since 1945" by Lawrence J. White. The statement above is simplistic and misleading.

White's actual argument is that, in order to minimize risk, the auto companies chose to compete in the area of styling change with moderate technological change, rather than in the area of fundamental technological change—an evolutionary, rather than a revolutionary, process. The facts suggest that policies of this general nature, independently adopted by various producers, were probably appropriate during the sixties when one considers the total system of car design, production, and repair. (Mechanics complain now about having to buy too many unique tools to repair cars with major technical changes.) Changes have occurred since White's book was published in 1971, however, Governmental regulations (especially the 1970 Clean Air Act Amendment), and the outlook for fuel prices and supplies, have changed the risk parameters significantly. Model changes have, therefore, been minimized and aimed at particular and fundamental needs; e.g., to have more desirable smaller cars such as the Pinto. Major technological changes, such as catalytic converter systems, have been installed. A quote from page 215 of White's own book gives some of the reasons why this is happening: "In cases of engineering developments that appeared to be the wave of the future and/or offered great potential for advertising and attracting interested customers into the showrooms, the companies (especially The Big Three) were usually quick to jump on the bandwagon and avoid being left out in the cold." Fuel economy and smaller cars would certainly fit these criteria. Safety and emission controls do not "sell" easily, while fuel economy will.

The change in the price of gasoline from 1973 to 1974 was approximately 25%. Simultaneously, considering U.S. cars only, the share of cars weighing less than 3,000 pounds increased from 12.7% of the 1973 model year output to

20.1% of the 1974 model year output, an increase of over 58%. At the same time, the cars weighing less than 3,500 pounds increased from 26.1% of '73's to 39.0% of '74's, an increase of over 49%,

2. "The capital resources available to the auto manufacturing industry, either through internal reallocation (e.g., deferral of annual model changes) or from external sources (e.g., borrowing), appear adequate to finance conversion to new technology, such as an alternative type of power plant and transmission. Total capital investment required is roughly the same as a single year's current capital expenditures by the motor vehicle industry."

Answer. Ford Motor Company's ability to finance the new technology that is required to achieve substantial improvements in automotive fuel economy depends, to a very large extent, on the investments that we must make to comply with government-mandated safety, damageability, and emission control standards. In addition to the $1.4 billion that Ford has previously invested for mandated standards, we would have to invest $2 billion more to meet the 1976–1980 car, truck, and plant standards. In our present financial condition, such an expenditure is, in itself, unacceptable—achieving fuel economy improvements of the magnitude outlined in the Rand Report would probably require additional investments by Ford Motor Company of more than $5 billion by 1985. This estimate, moreover, assumes a long-term (beyond 1980) NO_x standard that is no more stringent than the present 1977 statutory standard of 2.0 grams/mile. This assumption has been made because we do not even know how to comply with certification requirements for the 1978 statutory emission standards (0.41 HC/3.4 CO/0.4 NO_x grams/mile), irrespective of our ability to achieve fuel economy improvements at the 1978 standards or to finance the capital expenditures that might be required. Fuel economy and emissions requirements, together, are far beyond our financial resources, even after considering the potential for raising outside capital.

It is also important to understand more clearly the source and nature of the above statement on capital resources available to the auto manufacturing industry that was included in the Rand Report. The authors of the Rand Report "borrowed" this statement directly from a study that was conducted by the International Research and Technology Corporation (at the request of the U.S. Department of Transportation) for the purpose of evaluating the "Economic Impact of Mass Production of Alternative Low Emissions Automotive Power Systems." This study, undertaken in 1971–1972 and formally submitted to DOT on March 6, 1973, concerned the industry's ability to finance, produce, and sell engines with low emissions characteristics; the paper was not concerned with and did not attempt to evaluate the industry's ability to finance and achieve both low emissions and improved fuel economy. Instead, it concentrated its attention exclusively of alternative power sources that exhibited low emissions characteristics. Specifically, the study concluded that several power sources could be developed that would result in reduced automotive emissions—the authors noted, however, that the fuel economy of these engines (which were designed for use in standard-size cars) would range from 9.1 mpg for the least efficient engine to 12.4 mpg for the most efficient alternative that was studied. There was no evaluation of the potential investment that might be required to improve the fuel economy of these engines, primarily because at the cost of gasoline at that time fuel economy was not considered an issue of great importance relative to the automobile industry's ability to meet the statutory emission standards.

In summary, the financial requirements outlined by the International Research and Technology Corporation reflected their estimate of the capital investment levels required to achieve low automotive emissions with no consideration of the expenditures that might be required to also support even modest fuel economy improvements, let alone improvements of the magnitude outlined in the Rand Report. No effort was made to evaluate the automobile industry's financial or technical ability to support both the statutory emission standards and very large improvements in automobile fuel economy. We believe that it was inappropriate for the authors of the Rand Report to have dismissed the financing requirements of the automobile industry through reference to this much earlier study. We are surprised and disappointed, therefore, that the Rand Corporation did not itself attempt to determine and report both the requirements and the automobile industry's ability to support them in the present economic environment.

3. "Our analysis indicates that the supercharged rotary engine with charge stratification dominates all other engine types, including the diesel. Compared with the conventional SIE, it yields about twice the fuel economy, requires about 40 percent less lifetime energy, and reduces initial and lifetime per-vehicle costs by over 25 percent."

Answer. No one has built a supercharged rotary engine with charge stratification. Not only are the projected economies and costs conjectural, but the assumption of availability of a proven product in production quantities by 1980 is unrealistic. Curtiss-Wright has not been able to achieve even the fuel economy of a conventional SIE in their stratified-charge rotary development.

The rotary engine has poor fuel economy primarily because of seal leakage and inherent high heat transfer losses arising from its high surface to volume ratio. Nothing can change the latter and the former is *aggravated* by supercharging.

It is debatable whether such a hypothetical engine would exhibit improved fuel economy were it to be invested. The main effect would be a weight reduction rendered possible by its relatively smaller volume. The authors assume this weight reduction to amount to 1600 pounds. Even an adjustment of this extreme magnitude could not account for the 77% increase in fuel economy ascribed.

4. "The continuously variable transmission (CVT) can increase a conventional auto's fuel economy by about 27 to 32 percent, depending on driving cycle (urban or urban–rural driving) and auto size, all other things being equal. It does so by automatically selecting the most appropriate gear ratio between engine and wheels, thereby maximizing efficiency and fuel economy, without exceeding allowable nitrogen oxides (NO_x) emissions. Lifetime energy requirements of the auto can be reduced 10 percent; auto selling price can be reduced about 5 percent because the more efficient CVT can attain the same performance (i.e., acceleration) with a smaller engine and lighter vehicle, although the CVT itself is heavier and more expensive than a standard automatic transmission; and lifetime cost per vehicle can be reduced by 8 percent."

Answer. We agree in theory that a CVT could produce a fuel economy improvement of about 30 percent. This theoretical potential has triggered CVT research by Ford and by others over a period of many years. Realistically, however, problems of inefficiency, durability, noise, weight, size and customer acceptance make us extremely pessimistic about introduction of a CVT at any foreseeable future date for passenger cars or trucks. Arthur D. Little, in a study for the U.S. Department of Transportation, characterized the CVT as a high-risk technology probably not available in this decade.

It must be recognized that the CVT is a very old idea; in fact, some of the earliest U.S. automobiles were equipped with a primitive form. We now use a CVT on our low-horsepower garden tractors and have been working on the development of larger units since the 1940's (a CVT was installed in a 1946 Ford). Some examples of these development efforts are illustrated in Appendix A.

In order to achieve the weight saving and energy efficiency advantages claimed by Rand, the CVT must be controlled in a manner such that the engine will be heavily loaded at all speeds with resultant potential problems of noise, durability and NO_x emissions.

5. "Our automotive design analysis indicates that automobiles with new technology, but with the same acceleration and interior space characteristics as today's standard size cars, could achieve over 25 mpg, while subcompacts could achieve over 40 mpg. If a fuel economy standard is to be legislated, this finding suggests that the average range of 16 to 20 mpg standards, in recently proposed legislation, is perhaps unnecessarily low."

Answer. Same response as our answer to your question (b) above as follows: These statements should be considered in the context of Rand's 40 mpg subcompact design *according to their own published model results.* The total space available forward of the passenger compartment for packaging wheel wells, engine, radiator, front bumpers, and energy absorption necessary for crash protection, is 16 inches. The total space available behind the occupant for seat back, rear bumper, fuel tank, wheel wells, and crash protection is 2 inches. . . .

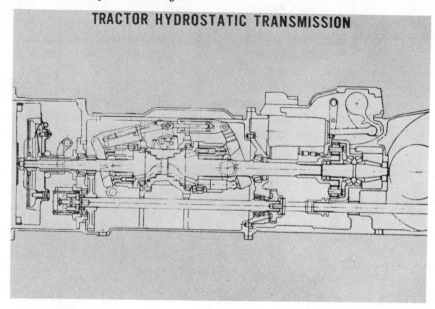

TRACTOR HYDROSTATIC TRANSMISSION

This photo shows a hydrostatic Infinitely Variable Transmission developed for use in Ford tractors in 1960. The system was never produced.

The transmission employed both a variable displacement hydraulic pump and motor. As can be seen by this photo, the unit was extremely complex and expensive and as with other hydrostatic transmissions, noise was a problem.

APPENDIX A

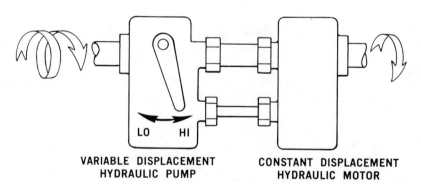

VARIABLE DISPLACEMENT   **CONSTANT DISPLACEMENT**
HYDRAULIC PUMP   **HYDRAULIC MOTOR**

There are several types of Infinitely Variable Transmissions which have been considered. One of the most popular types is termed Hydro-static and makes use of a variable displacement hydraulic pump and a constant displacement hydraulic motor to achieve infinitely variable operation.

This type of Infinitely Variable Transmission is currently used in Ford garden tractors.

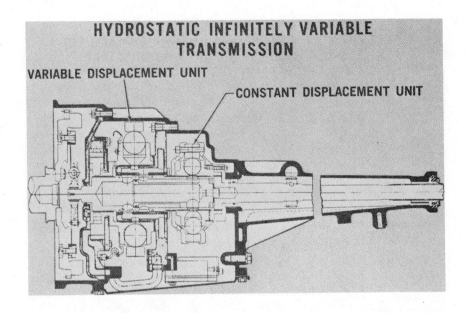

HYDROSTATIC INFINITELY VARIABLE TRANSMISSION

VARIABLE DISPLACEMENT UNIT

CONSTANT DISPLACEMENT UNIT

This photo shows a Split Path Ball Hydrostatic Infinitely Variable Transmission developed by T Division in 1962.

In this system, several steel balls are made to reciprocate within small cylinders. The unit rotates to form a variable displacement hydraulic pump and motor.

Tests conducted on vehicles with the transmission showed approximately 20% improved fuel economy during steady state operation. However, the system was very noisy and maintaining the proper clearance between the balls and the cylinders in order to prevent either excessive leakage or seizure of the unit was a major problem.

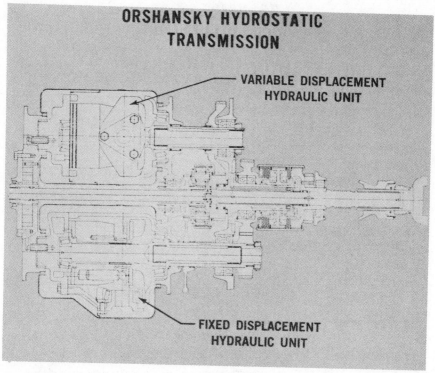

ORSHANSKY HYDROSTATIC
TRANSMISSION

VARIABLE DISPLACEMENT
HYDRAULIC UNIT

FIXED DISPLACEMENT
HYDRAULIC UNIT

One of the more recent hydrostatic transmissions is the development by Orshansky Transmissions Incorporated in California. This system uses a variable displacement hydraulic pump coupled to a constant displacement hydraulic motor in conjunction with a series of planetary gear sets to achieve infinitely variable operation.

The primary problems envisioned are excessive noise, complexity and cost.

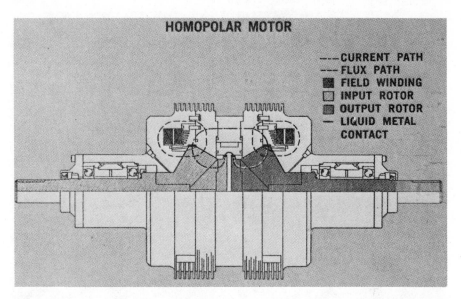

In addition to hydraulically operated Infinitely Variable Transmissions, Scientific Research Labs has proposed an Electrical Infinitely Variable Transmission using a "homopolar motor concept." Although the motor development was technically successful, the cost of the transmission was judged to be prohibitively high. Work was discontinued in 1964.

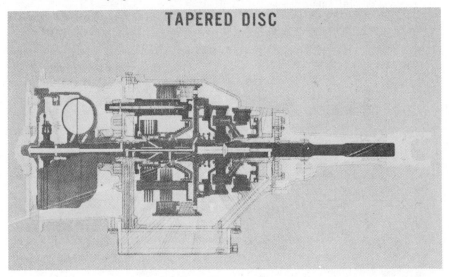

This photo shows a Tapered Disc Infinitely Variable Transmission. In this system, an assembly of tapered discs carries the transmission torque through an oil shear film. Moving of the "planetary disc unit" towards or away from the main shaft changes the ratio of the transmission.

The unit was built and tested by Ford during 1963. It was found to be quite inefficient and the program was discontinued.

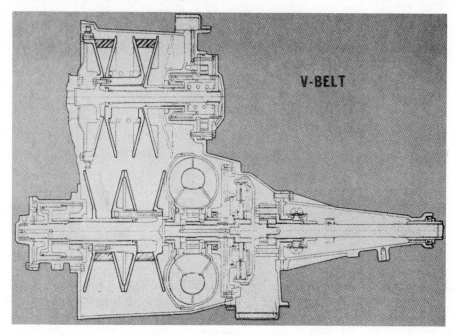

This photo shows a V–Belt Infinitely Variable Transmission using the same principal as that used in the DAF automobile made in Holland.

The belt portion of the transmission has been tested but belt life was completely unacceptable. Work was discontinued in 1958.

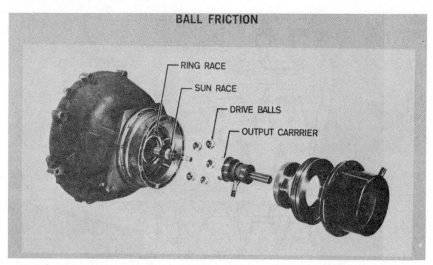

This transmission was developed at T Division from 1957 to 1958. The unit employes friction between a moveable "ring race" and "sun race" operating against several drive balls to continuously vary transmission ratio. The primary problem was deterioration of the friction surfaces when using loads sufficient to carry the required torque.

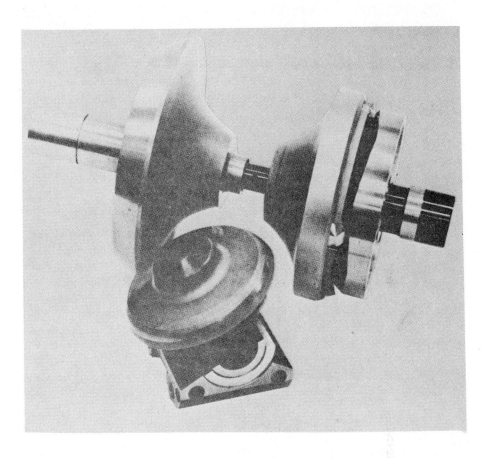

Another recent Friction Drive development is underway at Tracor in Austin, Texas. As can be seen, the Tracor system is quite similar to that used by General Motors except the configuration of the rotating members and the friction roller is different. This concept has also been under development for several years beginning at Curtis Wright in the early 1950s. A severe problem has been encountered in the Tracor system due to the very high thrust loading on the friction rollers. This requires a high pressure oil pump to supply the necessary lubrication and the resulting parasitic losses not only significantly depreciate the efficiency of the transmission but create an unacceptable noise condition.

COMMENTS BY GENERAL
MOTORS CORPORATION

The following letters were written in response to quotations in Senator Warren G. Magnuson's letter of December 23, 1974, to Henry L. Duncombe, Jr., Vice President and Chief Economist, General Motors Corporation.

General Motors Corp.,
Detroit, Mich., January 29, 1975.

Hon. Warren G. Magnuson,
U.S. Senate, Washington, D.C.

Dear Senator Magnuson:

In your letter of December 23, 1974, to Henry L. Duncombe, Jr., you requested General Motors' comments on a number of paragraphs from the Rand Report and from the testimony by Dr. Sorrel Wildhorn and answers to six questions. Since your request arrived at General Motors during the period when all corporate offices were closed for the holidays, we were unable to begin our preparation for response until after the first of January. Thus, it was necessary to advise your Committee Staff that our response would be delayed. We hope this delay has not caused any inconvenience to you or the Staff of the Senate Commerce Committee.

We are enclosing comments in response to the specific paragraphs from the Report, the Executive Summary and the Wildhorn testimony quoted in your letter.

To avoid repetition in these comments, they are grouped under three categories: (I) deals with technology, (II) concerns market structure, and (III) pertains to capital resources. Finally, each of the six numbered questions attached to your letter is answered separately and these answers are attached.

Sincerely,

Robert F. Magill.

COMMENTS BY GENERAL MOTORS CORPORATION IN RESPONSE TO QUOTATIONS AND QUESTIONS IN LETTER FROM SENATOR WARREN G. MAGNUSON TO HENRY L. DUNCOMBE, JR., DECEMBER 23, 1974

I. TECHNOLOGY

A. "Chapter IV of the full report, entitled Per-Vehicle Comparisons of Auto Design Conservation Measures. (We are especially interested in your comments on Rand's conclusions with regard to feasible technological improvements and the associated time-scales for implementation, as well as their conclusions with regard to possible fuel savings.)"

B. The following two statements on page 22 of Dr. Wildhorn's written statement:

"Our work indicates that a 50 percent improvement in average new car fuel economy by 1980, over the 1974 figure of 14 miles per gallon, appears feasible."

"After 1980, much higher average new car fuel economy appears feasible, if new technology is pursued vigorously, and R&D is successful. For example, fuel economy standards over 30 miles per gallon might be possible by 1985."

And the following statements from the Executive Summary:

"Our analysis indicates that the supercharged rotary engine with charge stratification dominates all other engine types, including the diesel. Compared with the conventional SIE, it yields about twice the fuel economy, requires about 40 percent less lifetime energy, and reduces initial and lifetime per-vehicle costs by over 25 percent." (Page 7)

"The continuously variable transmission (CVT) can increase a conventional auto's fuel economy by about 27 to 32 percent, depending on driving cycle (urban or urban–rural driving) and auto size, all other things being equal. It does so by automatically selecting the most appropriate gear ratio between engine and wheels, thereby maximizing efficiency and fuel economy, without exceeding allowable nitrogen oxides (NO_x) emissions. Lifetime energy requirements of the auto can be reduced 10 percent; auto selling price can be reduced about 5 percent because the more efficient CVT can attain the same performance (i.e., acceleration) with a smaller engine and lighter vehicle, although the CVT itself is heavier and more expensive than a standard automatic transmission; and lifetime cost per vehicle can be reduced by 8 percent." (Page 7)

"Our automotive design analysis indicates that automobiles with new technology, but with the same acceleration and interior space characteristics as today's standard size cars, could achieve over 25 mpg, while subcompacts could achieve over 40 mpg. If a fuel economy standard is to be legislated, this finding suggests that the average range of 16 to 20 mpg standards, in recently proposed legislation, is perhaps unnecessarily low." (Page 8)

GM COMMENT

Fuel economy predictions in this report are based upon a highly simplified analytical model of the engine-powertrain system of an automobile. Any conclusions drawn from such an analysis are, of course, entirely dependent upon the assumed empirical relationships between the many factors which control automobile fuel economy and acceleration performance. The type of relationships which were assumed by the authors, at best can be expected to yield qualitative, directional conclusions. Accurate numerical fuel economy predictions are impossible with such a crude analysis.

A more detailed critique of the assumptions used in this report is difficult, because there is insufficient information from which to judge the validity of the assumptions made. For instance, neither the basic report nor the supplementary report dealing with the Rand fuel economy calculation model contain adequate data to support the engine specific fuel consumption curves used. Data for existing engines would certainly show a wide scatter compared to the simplified curves used. Regarding the performance of future engine modifications, the assumptions made must be classed as pure speculation. Furthermore, the analysis ignores the interaction between exhaust emission control requirements and the design parameters of the engine, transmission and the vehicle. These interactions are very significant and can invalidate the results of even the most sophisticated analytical prediction techniques available today.

The specific conclusions regarding a "super-charged rotary engine with charged stratification" or a "continuously variable transmission" represents little more than an educated guess based upon numerous unsupported assumptions. Several examples can be cited of other recent studies, each of which have come to a different conclusion regarding the most promising "advanced" engine and powertrain components. Possibly the disagreement between these reports can be cited as evidence that the assumptions which have been made are not universally accepted by the technical community. In addition, of course, the automobile industry has had development experience with experimental components which are similar enough to the proposals being made, to conclude that the gains predicted are not available with existing technology.

Perhaps more important, fuel economy that can reasonably be obtained in real world situations is not determined by technological possibilities relating to that factor alone. Other technological goals exist which may well conflict with the fuel economy goal—e.g. emission control and safety regulations as explained in the testimony of H. L. Duncombe on December 10, 1974. In that same testimony it was also explained that consumer demands provide limits to what technological possibilities can actually be implemented in the marketplace.

MARKET STRUCTURE

(The following statement is from the Executive Summary)

"However, the most recent study of the market structure of the automobile industry argues that few incentives exist for making technological improvements. This conclusion is consistent with the results of our econometric analysis, which forecasts that large increases in real gasoline prices would lead to only small increases in average automobile efficiency."

GM COMMENT

This statement reflects the theoretical viewpoint of one structuralist economist who claims that the behavior of an industry can be predicted by looking at the number and size of firms in it. Not only is such a view strongly contested by other economists (see e.g., Harold Demsetz, *The Market Concentration Doctrine,* American Enterprise Institute: Columbia University Law School Conference on Industrial Concentration, Airlie House, Virginia), but it is not even endorsed by the Rand researchers.

The Rand study did not analyze the relationship between market structure and technological progress, but merely reported on the opinion of one author, L. J. White. Indeed they explicitly state:

"One may ask whether government mandated standards would be needed: would not competitive market processes achieve the same results? We did not have the resources to consider this question in detail, and sought only to look at impacts if mandated standards are imposed." (p. 5)

"This question would have required a detailed study of the market structure of the U.S. automobile industry and the effects of foreign competition on this industry. We did not have the resources to do such a study. Therefore, we cannot be sure that what could be achieved by mandating weight, technology, or fuel efficiency standards might not also be achieved through competitive market process." (pp. 76, 77)

"However, White's case is not completely air-tight. One could make several counter-arguments." (p. 78)

General Motors believes the structuralist view is wrong. Automobiles are designed to meet what consumers want and are willing to pay for. Any auto manufacturer who disregarded this fundamental reality would not survive. This is the way any competitive market works and the rivalry for patronage cannot be dismissed by a simple counting of existing firms. Attached is a GM document, *Competition in the Motor Vehicle Industry,* which fully supports this position.

As to the statement relating to the effect of gasoline prices on automobile efficiency, General Motors believes it also is in error. The econometric model referred to does not have the statistical base to reliably forecast the effect of large increases in gas prices on auto efficiency improvements. The criticism Rand makes of White would also seem applicable to their own work:

"White offers his analysis as a way of explaining the behavior of American automobile manufacturers during the postwar period. Some factors that could affect the behavior of the automobile industry did not change much from year to year; gasoline prices are an example. Consequently, it is risky to rely on White's analysis to predict auto manufacturers' future behavior when there are large year-to-year changes in these factors." (p. 78)

The reality has been that competitive rivalry has led to substantial mileage improvements on 1975 models. Current changing demand conditions due to our energy situation have caused further responses in GM's product plans which will allow for continued mileage improvement in future models.

III. CAPITAL RESOURCES

The following statement from the executive summary:

"The capital resources available to the auto manufacturing industry, either through internal reallocation (e.g., deferral of annual model changes) or from external sources (e.g., borrowing), appear adequate to finance conversion to new technology, such as an alternative type of power plant and transmission. Total capital investment required is roughly the same as a single year's current capital expenditures by the motor vehicle industry." (Page 6)

GM COMMENT

We agree that adequate capital funds are or can be made available to finance most new technological developments such as transmissions or alternative power plants. The main limitation to such new technology and component production is not capital but development, production lead time and feasibility, and user acceptance.

We would like to add that technological developments are, and will continue to be, limited because of present and proposed safety and emission regulations. Engineering and research skills are a limited resource: thus, to the extent that these scarce resources must be allocated to meeting safety and emission regulations, this will detract from the allocation of these skills to technological developments that would have potential market-determined returns.

An additional factor of the currently mandated emission standards is that these—rather than capital availability—delay the development of alternate engines that have potential for fuel economy improvements.

This judgment is not limited to the automobile industry. For example, the National Academy of Sciences has said: "The 0.4 g/mi NO_x level mandated by the Federal 1978 Emissions Standards is expected to inhibit the development of these technologies." (Report by the Committee on Motor Vehicle Emissions. National Academy of Sciences. November 1974. P. 3.)

General Motors Corp.,
New York, N.Y., February 4, 1975.

Hon. Warren G. Magnuson,
U.S. Senate
Committee on Commerce,
Washington, D.C.

Dear Senator Magnuson:

As indicated by the questions you raised in your letter of December 23, 1974, you have a particular interest in the Rand Report titled *HOW TO SAVE GASOLINE*. While Mr. Magill's letter of January 29th responded to your specific questions, I wanted to provide some overall comments about the report.

If the report were to be viewed as an attempt by researchers to develop analytical tools in an area where they lacked experience and any particular expertise, it could simply be dismissed as a first, but incomplete, effort. Our comments then could have been limited to suggestions for improving the research. Such comments would point out that the scope of the problem is not carefully defined, important previous research has been overlooked, and there are problems of methodology, of data, and statistical analysis.

Unfortunately, the Rand Report purports to go beyond a research effort and to develop "policy implications." Even though they are duly denoted as tentative and are qualified throughout the report, we believe that such speculative policy implications are not only erroneous, but are highly misleading as a basis for public policy alternatives that are being considered by your Committee.

In the first of the findings of the report, it was concluded that the only effective short-term gasoline conservation measure would be price increases in gasoline. As would be expected, the higher the price, the lower the gasoline consumption. While we are not as confident as the Rand researchers as to the exact gasoline price elasticities which exist, we do agree that gasoline price increases offer an effective means of reducing consumption in the next few years. This is one of the reasons why GM has often recommended decontrol of domestic petroleum prices. It does not follow, however, that the only way to achieve higher prices is through a gasoline tax.

To confuse the effects of a price increase with the effects of a gasoline tax is both incorrect and misleading. To say that gasoline taxes offer the "only hope" in the short term ignores issues now being debated, such as decontrolling the price of domestic petroleum and natural gas, a tax on oil imports, and a tax on all petroleum uses. The effects of these different policies would be quite different on petroleum demand and supply relationships. In short, to say that higher gasoline prices will reduce gasoline consumption is redundant—to say that gasoline taxes are the "only hope" is naive.

A second finding of the report is that a tax on only new cars—whether a fixed tax or graduated to discourage the purchase of less fuel-efficient autos—offers little promise of gasoline conservation in the near-term. The report recognizes that such a policy would encourage retention of older, less fuel efficient, larger cars and thus have dubious effectiveness as an energy conservation measure. This is a finding arrived at in the GM deliberations of this issue as discussed in my testimony of December 10, 1974, and in our responses to your questions.

A third finding reported is that in the longer term, the most significant fuel economy improvements will be obtained through new automobiles that utilize technological improvements, that do not sacrifice comfort or performance, and that can be sold for the lowest price. It surely does not take any analytical models to arrive at such a conclusion. It is because we have hopes of achieving such results that GM has committed and will continue to commit extensive resources to technological improvements.

Rand goes on, however, to state that there are "several types of policies" that may achieve improvements in new car fuel economy. We strongly disagree that the "several" policies enumerated by Rand which involve artificial regulatory product prohibitions would provide gasoline conservation results equivalent to market responses without excessive costs and substantial disruptions to the economy. For example, the report states, on page 94, that:

"Although all of the policy instruments examined offer some potential for energy conservation, because of their varied social, economic, and environmental impacts, there is no clear dominance of one policy over others in the medium and long term."

If the policies had been fully and properly analyzed, we do not believe that there would be a lack of dominance of one policy versus another. To imply, as the report does, that relying on market processes would not be preferred to a policy that prohibits the manufacture of products now demanded by the market, is to place little value on the rights of consumers to purchase the products of their choice.

The highly publicized new car fuel efficiencies discussed in the Rand Report are based on either product restrictions (e.g., no new cars above a compact size) and/or the success of yet-to-be-proven research and development efforts.

For the first of these, if there were to be severe prohibitions on the sale of new cars above a certain weight class, then it is likely that widespread consumer resentment would result. Obviously it is *possible* to enact such drastic measures in 1975—simply prohibit the sale of all cars larger than the subcompact Vega size. While sales-weighted new car fuel economies would obviously be sharply increased, it is unlikely that the gasoline consumption would be reduced in quite the simplistic way predicted by the Rand models. The models ignore the fact that many persons would refuse to purchase the new smaller models and would retain their older cars.

The second way in which the Rand Report states exaggerated claims of fuel economy improvements is on the assumption that their theoretical guesses on new technology will be developed as they have predicted. It is difficult to see how or why Rand can assume that the success of research and development projects can be guaranteed by government regulations.

More importantly, even if such projects were to be successful, there must be market acceptance of such technological developments. As I stressed in my testimony, ". . . the most fuel efficient car it is possible to produce would make no contribution to our national energy goals unless our customers were willing to buy it." I do not see how this basic fact can be ignored when considering governmental regulations.

The Rand Report asks the question whether or not market processes would achieve the same results as governmental regulations. They say they couldn't really answer such a question but that "... *we cannot be sure that what could be achieved by mandating weight, technology, or fuel efficiency standards might not also be achieved through competitive market process.*" It is unfortunate that more thought was not given to such an important topic. Perhaps the Rand researchers would have at least thought more carefully about the problems of trying to regulate technological developments or to restrict consumer choice.

In conclusion, we are sorry that such a preliminary research effort by Rand was published without the researchers giving more careful consideration to the implications of their technological and economic speculations. It would indeed be unfortunate if such a report were to be used as a basis for any legislation by your Committee.

Sincerely,

Henry L. Duncombe, Jr.

Chapter Ten

Response to the Auto Makers' Comments

Sorrel Wildhorn,
Thomas Kirkwood, and
Burke Burright

INTRODUCTION AND SUMMARY

During the December 10th, 1974, hearing on the Senate Commerce Committee's Energy Conservation Working Paper, automobile industry witnesses were requested to comment in writing on, among other things, several sections of a recent Rand Corporation report (R-1560-NSF), "How to Save Gasoline: Public Policy Alternatives for the Automobile" and on two statements in Sorrel Wildhorn's (a principal author of the Rand report) written testimony to the Committee. The Commerce Committee asked us, in turn to respond to the auto makers' comments on our work.

As the following discussion indicates, there are some points of apparent disagreement that we attempt to resolve by clarification and others by provision of further information. On still other points we disagree.

The auto makers' comments covered a variety of points. Here, we respond to all of their major comments and to most of their more restricted points as well.

In sum, we believe that the auto makers' comments have not affected our major qualitative, directional conclusions, and we stand by them. In our published report, How to Save Gasoline, and in Sorrel Wildhorn's written testimony to the Committee, we did not make definitive recommendations as to the advisability of adopting particular, specific policies, such as mandated fuel economy standards or various new car taxing schemed because our project, limited

This chapter contains the authors' written response to the auto manufacturers' comments on the study, as requested by the U.S. Senate Committee on Commerce. See the Committee's *Energy Conservation Working Paper*, pp. 341–52.

211

in both time and resources, was unable to evaluate adequately all of the impacts of alternative policies. Among the limitations of our analysis (as well as other analyses we are acquainted with) are many of the points made in the auto makers'* [sic] comments. For example, they indicated, and we recognized in our work, that if such policies resulted in a dramatic shift toward the production of small cars, consumers might react by retaining their older gas guzzlers.

There remains the question of how the auto makers' comments have affected our major conclusions regarding our quantitative estimates. In our published report and written testimony we stated that we chose to estimate the potential gasoline savings, if certain measures or policies were undertaken, given certain assumptions. Having such potential savings in mind might stimulate needed action. For example, as we made clear in our report and statement, our conclusions regarding the feasibility of a 50 percent improvement in average new car fuel economy by 1980, over the 1974 figure of 14 miles per gallon, and higher fuel economy after 1980, were based on the assumptions that future safety and emission control standards would not impose additional penalties over and above those we considered in our analysis, that research and development was successful and that new technology could be introduced on the schedule we explicitly assumed. If actual performance falls short of our assumptions, actual savings may be less than we predict and/or may be delayed in time.

The automobile manufacturers have in varying degree questioned the realism of our assumptions. Our analysis was unable to go very far in determining this. We are unable to predict the course of emission control standards, or the problems that may arise in connection with control systems. R&D is inherently uncertain and we are not prepared to predict the outcomes of specific projects. We are reasonably confident, however, that a diversified R&D program will produce a menu of successful developments that offer approximately the degree of improvement that we estimate. Finally, the schedule we have assumed for the introduction of new technology is distinctly different from what might be described as "business as usual" in the industry. We have not yet analyzed the impact on the industry of incentives to achieve such a schedule, the industry's response to such incentives, or the appropriate form of government action to provide them.

One must recognize, however, that the issues involved are extremely complex and any policy analysis of distant future courses of action involves important uncertainties—uncertainties stemming from

*A typographical error contained in the Commerce Committee's Working Paper has been corrected here.

incomplete data, from alternative interpretations of existing data and from the limitations of any analytical technique. We have tried to set forth the qualifications regarding such uncertainties to prevent policymakers from accepting all of the quantitative results without question. These qualifications are emphasized in Mr. Wildhorn's written statement to the Committee, summarized on page xviii of our published report, How to Save Gasoline, (R-1560-NSF) and repeated wherever relevant throughout our reports. However, in spite of the many uncertainties in our analysis, we believe that our analysis made substantial qualitative, quantitative and methodological contributions that will help resolve the problems before us regarding the costs and benefits of alternative public policies for conserving gasoline used by the auto.

We are pleased that the Ford Motor Company and General Motors Corporation agree with the qualitative conclusions of our report, that:

> An increase in the pump price of gasoline is the only effective near-term conservation strategy, short of rationing.
>
> Improved new car fuel economy is an attractive long-term strategy provided such improved fuel economy can be achieved at reasonable cost and without compromising the acceptability of the vehicle to the consumer.

General Motors also agreed with our conclusion that a fixed excise tax on new cars offers little promise of gasoline conservation in the near term because it would encourage the retention of older gas guzzlers and that such an effect would reduce the effectiveness of a graduated (by fuel efficiency, weight or horsepower) tax. One could design policy instruments to deal with this problem, e.g. graduated taxes with subsidies for highly efficient cars, graduated taxes on used cars or combined new and used car graduated taxes with or without mandated fuel economy standards. (Regarding the graduated excise tax on new and/or used cars, we should emphasize at the outset that, to date, the impacts of alternative graduated taxing schemes on supply and demand for new cars by market class, on total auto travel, on retention of older cars by market class and on total gasoline consumption of the auto fleet are largely unknown in quantitative terms. Such policies need to be analyzed too, and we and other researchers have begun to do so. When such work is completed, the basis for selecting energy conservation policies for the auto should be much clearer.)

General Motors and Ford both argue that a law inhibiting the sale of large cars would also encourage retention of older gas guzzlers. We agree this might occur. This problem is complex and requires a similar analytical approach to the estimation of new and used car demand by market class as does the graduated excise tax policy.

Since we were unable to include it in our empirical work because of study resource limitations, our research did not provide any empirical estimate of the likely magnitude of the retention effect. We believe such estimates should be made before any action is taken to inhibit the sale of larger cars.

The comments and criticisms of the auto makers fall into three categories:

First, there were comments focused on the major questions posed by the Committee. The auto makers generally agreed that: our estimates of potential improvements in new car fuel economy were optimistic; more efficient transmissions and engines could not be introduced as early as we had assumed; government regulation is not needed, since market forces will be adequate to improve mileage, because fuel economy "sells"; and capital funding for new technology will be limited because of competing claims for these funds arising from present and proposed safety and emission regulations.[a]

Second, some of the auto makers—particularly Ford and GM—contended that the analytical tools we employed were unable to generate reliable estimates or that, at best, they could be expected to yield qualitative, directional conclusions.

Third, the remaining comments by the auto makers can best be characterized as detailed criticisms of specific technological, economic or methodological aspects of our work.

We shall address these three categories in turn, although we do not comment on every point raised by the auto industry.

COMMENTS ON MAJOR QUESTIONS POSED BY THE SENATE COMMERCE COMMITTEE

Fuel Economy Improvement

One major criticism voiced by the auto makers was that we assumed that emission and safety standards would be met without major price, weight, fuel economy and performance penalties for all forms of conventional and advanced technology. Consequently, our estimates of potential fuel economy improvements are held to be optimistic. Our estimates of improvements feasible by 1980 and 1985 are based on the assumption (noted on pp. 121–122 of R–1560–NSF) that no further fuel economy penalties are implied beyond those associated with compliance with 1973 safety standards

[a]Of the four auto makers, only General Motors indicated that adequate capital funds are or could be made available to finance new technological developments, but that the really scarce resources were engineering and research skills. To the extent that these skills are allocated to meeting safety emissions regulations, General Motors said, this would detract from technology development.

and the use of a catalytic converter and exhaust gas recirculation for emission control. We chose this assumption because of lack of data on more advanced emission controls, and the uncertainty as to the magnitude and timing of specific future emission and safety standards. We suspect that these requirements will have similar impacts on fuel economy of autos with different technology, so that our broad conclusions regarding the relative effectiveness of different technical advances in improving fuel economy will hold.[b] Whether emission and safety requirements will result in a loss in future fuel economy or not, depends on the specific standards and design approaches used to meet them. We feel that the tradeoff between emissions, safety, and fuel economy should be studied much more extensively than they have been to date.

The auto makers' responses differed sharply as to our conclusion that a 50 percent improvement in average new car fuel economy by 1980, over the 1974 figure of 14 miles per gallon, appears feasible. American Motors indicated that this statement was consistent with the facts if: the market class mix shifted toward smaller cars; more stringent emission standards do not penalize fuel economy; and government or public pressures do not create large vehicle weight increases. Chrysler indicated that a 35 percent increase was possible with similar qualifications. Both Ford and GM simply rejected our conclusions on the basis of our allegedly inadequate analytical methodology, offering no counterestimates of their own.

To clarify the basis for our conclusion, we note that a 50 percent improvement by 1980 implies both a large shift toward smaller cars and the introduction of near-term improved design features, such as radial tires, minor aerodynamic improvements, horsepower reductions, and improvements to the conventional spark ignition engine.[c] If there is only a modest shift toward small cars, then additional technological improvements, such as better transmissions and major improvements to the spark ignition engine (charge stratification, supercharging) may be necessary.

Another criticism shared by most of the auto makers has to do

[b]Ford doubts this, and certainly it is true that relaxing the requirements on emissions of different species will affect various engines differently. For example, relaxing the hydrocarbon requirements would favor rotaries more than reciprocating designs. The question is a quantitative one, however—will a reasonable set of emission standards, which are acceptable from the point of view of both air quality and fuel economy result in favoring one engine type over another so as to *dominate* the choice of engine types? We think not.

[c]We did not consider improvements to the spark ignition engine in our study. Because of our study time frame (1975–1995), we were interested in more advanced, longer-term possibilities. However, examination of the possible near-term improvements has convinced us that the above estimate is reasonable.

with the basis for comparing alternative technological options. They point out accurately that the basis of comparison we used requires that each car be completely redesigned to maximize the fuel economy improvement when a new change is introduced. Thus, for example, if air conditioning is added, our procedure results in redesigning the entire car to provide the increased strength required by the weight of the air conditioning equipment, and the increased power required to obtain the specified acceleration when carrying the additional weight. We agree that this will not be the case in all situations; for example, the same auto will be sold either with or without air conditioning. However, so far as the major design changes are concerned, we believe that our approach mirrors the actual situation better than the simple substitution of the new component in an existing auto. As an example, a new engine or transmission may be first introduced as an optional feature of an existing model. If it proves successful, however, and if we maintain a strong continuing motivation toward improved fuel economy, in subsequent model years the design will be modified to capitalize on the potential weight and volume savings due to the new component. Moreover, our method of comparison more accurately measures the potential relative improvement of different technological options.

Timing

As stated in our report (for example, see p. 7 of R–1560–NSF), our estimates apply to the gains which might be obtained at the result of a maximum effort to improve fuel economy as rapidly as possible, without regard to the financial risk or the availability of capital. Our estimates of the performance of various technical advances assume that future research on them is successful and that they perform up to their potential. We recognize (and agree with the auto makers) that there is risk involved—that the research may not be successful or may take longer than we have allowed. We chose this type of analysis, however, because it serves two purposes: first, it indicates those areas in which research effort may result in large improvements in fuel economy, and second, it provides some indication as to whether there is a large gain to be achieved, or whether even successful research would lead to only minor gains. As we interpret the results of our study, they say that potential gains in fuel economy due to improved transmissions, internal combustion engines and structural materials are quite large. The adoption of policies to achieve these potentials should be based on a balancing of the urgency of achieving gasoline savings against the risks inherent in their development.

The industry is concerned that we have not allowed sufficient time for the conversion to mass production once the feasibility of a new device has been demonstrated. As we have stated, we attempted to estimate the shortest possible time required considering only technical feasibility. While such estimates are highly uncertain, the recent rapid conversion of several plants to small cars by the industry in the aftermath of the embargo indicates to us that the industry may be much more flexible than is often believed. We recognize, of course, that none of the new models involved the introduction of radically different or new technology: nevertheless, the ability to shift production to new models at the recent rate represents a very impressive accomplishment.

If the potential improvements in fuel economy are to be achieved it will call for active pursuit of advanced technology development soon. In their comments on our estimates the industry offers no alternative estimates of what the future potential might be and how long it will take, nor do they reveal in what ways they are now pursuing advanced technology development. Thus, their comments offer no basis for evaluating whether current auto industry behavior is adequate.

Their comments show very little optimism regarding the potential for improved fuel economy that might result from technology advanced beyond the improvements of the current spark ignition engine. They also indicate great concern over the loss in fuel economy which they expect will accompany more stringent emission requirements. While we recognize that the conventional spark ignition engine may be severely limited, we feel that there is now sufficient technical data to establish the fact that substantial gains in fuel economy can be made, even if stringent emission standards are to be met. We refer primarily to Ford's and Texaco's tests on advanced stratified-charge engines that demonstrated improved fuel economy in combination with emission levels comparable to the ultimate federal standards, Curtiss–Wright's work on stratified rotary engines that has demonstrated better specific fuel consumptions than a conventional spark ignition engine, and, work by Orshansky and Tracor on advanced transmissions. (Other work in the areas of new engine concepts, advanced materials, aerodynamic refinement, and radial tire design is covered in our published report). We recognize, however, that none of these developments are currently advanced to the point that they could be introduced into production.

In our study of alternative policies we made no judgment as to the advisability of mandating fuel economy standards, for two reasons. First, in our work, we did not study (and others have not yet studied) how the auto industry would respond to such standards. Second, other potentially effective policies, such as excise taxes on new and/or used car price, graduated by fuel economy or weight or horsepower, have not yet been studied in enough depth to provide meaningful estimates of how demand and supply of new and used cars and overall gasoline consumption would change relative to changes induced by the policies we did study. However, if policies to stimulate greater fuel economy are to be adopted they should be designed so that industry can recognize now that they will eventually have to introduce technology more advanced than improvements to the conventional spark ignition engine. Thus, they can initiate the necessary research early enough to allow them to meet the mandate.

It also seems reasonable to us that the federal government should expand its research activities in the area of improved fuel economy to the point of demonstrating at various times in the future a number of automobile types with improved fuel economy, emissions, and safety features. The major purpose of this effort would be to provide government with a knowledge of what levels of fuel economy could be obtained so that, in the future, policy decisions can be based on the information from sources independent of, as well as within, the industry. This thinking is consistent with that developed in a study at the Massachusetts Institute of Technology and is partially consistent with at least certain views within the current administration.[d]

Market Structure

In their comments the auto makers asserted that government regulation is not needed, since market forces will be adequate to improve mileage, because better fuel economy "sells." It is important to be clear about the question at issue. It is not whether American auto makers compete in some ways. American automakers could compete in certain ways and not in others.[e] For example, American auto makers might compete on the basis of price, styling, and some kinds of technological innovations but might not compete on the basis of

[d]See John B. Heywood, Henry D. Jacoby, Lawrence H. Linden, "The Role of Federal R&D on Alternative Automotive Power Systems," Energy Laboratory Report MIT–EL–74–103, Massachusetts Institute of Technology, November, 1974: and "The Role of the Federal Government in Automotive R&D," Energy Research and Development Office, Federal Energy Administration, November 6, 1974.

[e]In its comment, General Motors argues that the auto market is competitive because "automobiles are designed to meet what consumers want and are willing to pay for." This is not a standard for determining whether a market is competitive; even a pure monopolist (one seller) would have to provide products that consumers want and are willing to pay for.

other kinds of technical innovations. Nor is it a question of whether American auto makers will make some improvements in new car fuel efficiency without government action. In their comments, the auto makers say that they are trying to improve the fuel efficiency of their new cars, and we believe them.

The question is how far American auto makers will improve new car fuel efficiency, consistent with maintaining the performance and comfort of today's cars, without government action. The case for government action hinges on this question. If national energy conservation policy implies more than industry would normally do, then government action would be needed.

We did not have the resources to study how auto makers would respond to higher real gasoline prices. Therefore, we did not want to guess how far American auto makers would improve new car fuel efficiency without government action. In our study we found that improving new car fuel efficiency substantially (without sacrificing the performance and comfort of today's cars) would require significant changes in engines and transmission. We noted that there are some reasons to believe that American auto makers are reluctant to adopt new engine and transmission technology in their cars. Consequently, they might be reluctant to improve new car fuel efficiency substantially if doing so meant significant changes in engine and transmission technology.

We drew the reasons why American auto makers might be reluctant to adopt new engine and transmission technology from Lawrence J. White's book[f] and noted that his analysis is consistent with the results of our econometric modeling.[g] Note that in its comment, Ford appears to agree with White's analysis as a description of the American auto industry during the 1960s.

As General Motors emphasized in their comments, we do not fully endorse White's analysis. Because we only estimated the potential improvement in new car fuel economy over today's level and because we did not address the issue of how far auto makers would go toward that potential without government action, we cannot say (and did not say in our published report) whether government action is needed.

---

[f]Lawrence J. White, *The Automobile Industry Since 1945* (Cambridge, Mass.: Harvard University Press, 1971).

[g]"Consistent" in the sense that White's analysis and the outcome of our economic modeling do not contradict each other.

The Availability of Adequate
Capital Resources

In contrast to our statement, Ford, Chrysler and American Motors all asserted that sufficient capital funding would not be available to finance alternate powerplant or transmission systems in addition to the capital resources required to meet presently mandated federal safety, damageability and emission control standards. Although General Motors indicated that adequate funds are or can be made available to finance most new technological developments, they indicated that the really scarce resources were engineering and research skills. To the extent that these skills are allocated to meeting mandated safety and emission control standards, this would detract from allocation to developing technology for improved fuel economy.

Ford correctly observes that Rand did not study the issue and that our statement regarding the availability of adequate capital resources for improving fuel economy derives from the International Research and Technology Corporation study cited. This was the only independent (i.e., non-automotive industry) estimate available in 1973–74, when we were conducting our study. It is true that the IRT study was aimed primarily at new automotive powerplants that exhibited low emissions, and not necessarily good fuel economy. But the technological options studied by IRT were at least as advanced as any we addressed in our study. Moreover, the only other independent estimates we are aware of is the Congressionally-mandated DOT–EPA 120-day study, and it was available only after our report went to press. The DOT–EPA study estimated that additional capital funds required by the auto industry to improve new car fuel economy would vary between $50 million and $200 million per year, depending on the set of fuel economy options pursued. These figures compare to recent auto industry expenditures for longer lasting capital goods of between $2.0 and $2.5 billion annually.

In his letter to Senator Magnuson, Mr. Fred Secrest of Ford makes a related point. Mr. Secrest writes that he is concerned about lack of consideration of the need to recover capital investment. He does not develop this point. Since we feel it could have important distributional implications, we want to go into it further.

We interpret Mr. Secrest's comment as follows: auto makers have purchased some types of capital equipment that can be used only in the production of large, inefficient cars. Equipment used to produce large engines is an example. A law which reduces the number of large cars that can be built and sold would reduce the value of such equipment; in other words, such a law would inflict a lump-sum capital loss on auto makers. The size of the losses will be a function particularly of how quickly the law is to go into effect. The further into the future the losses, the less the losses, providing the companies begin to adjust now.

It is not clear how large these lump-sum capital losses would be. To be able to judge their likely importance one would need a detailed study of the impact on capital equipment requirements of changes in the composition of automobile output. This is yet another consideration that needs to be weighed in making a legislative decision.

Methodology

A general comment by some of the automakers was that our analytical methodology was too simplistic or inaccurate to generate reliable output and that, at best, the analytical tools could be expected to yield qualitative, directional conclusions.

With regard to our generalized auto design model, we purposely designed it to be a relatively simple tool capable of systematically comparing a wide variety of alternatives, by illustrating the major interactions of performance, design and cost parameters. Our model was intended to produce a reasonable "first cut" at alternative auto designs, to relate such factors as auto weight, fuel economy, dimensions, selling price, operating cost, etc. We believe it does this successfully. Its primary purpose was to enable relative comparisons to be made and broad conclusions to be drawn among design alternatives that promise varying improvements in fuel economy. Since the model was calibrated with current (1973) design and technology, we feel that its accuracy in predicting relative differences among near-term alternatives is quite acceptable for the purposes intended, and in our detailed comments in a subsequent section of this testimony we show why we believe this. As to its accuracy in forecasting substantially different technologies, all analytical models share the same limitations, because of the lack of accurate input data. The best that can be done is to attempt to discern whether large differences exist among new alternatives, since small differences are swamped by the uncertainties in the input data. And in our conclusions regarding very advanced engines, such as the Stirling, Rankine or gas turbine, we noted our reservations that flowed from such uncertainties (e.g., see p. 38 of R–1560–NSF), even though we predicted large differences in fuel economy among these engines.

While all of the auto makers commented on our generalized auto design model, only General Motors commented on our econometric model. General Motors feels that our econometric model lacks the statistical base to reliably forecast effects of large increases in gas prices. What they mean by statistical base is not clear; from the context, we take their comment to mean the following:

During the period (1954 to 1972) over which the model was estimated, the price of gasoline in terms of constant-buying-power dollars fluctuated relatively little.

When estimates with such data are used to forecast the impacts of large changes in gasoline prices, one has limited confidence in its forecast.

We agree (and we noted this qualification on p. xviii of our published report) that econometric estimates using future ranges of a variable (such as gasoline prices) that are large compared to the historic range of variation may be open to question. This is not a problem of our model alone; it is shared to varying degrees by all econometric work in the area. But while this is a source of uncertainty in our estimates, there is no implication that our results are biased in either direction.

SPECIFIC INDUSTRY COMMENTS

We now turn to the more detailed auto industry comments.

Advanced Engine Technology

The industry believes that our projected improvements in fuel economy from the supercharged stratified rotary engine are conjectural, since no one has built such an engine. We recognize that such an engine has not yet been built and thus its performance cannot be predicted with great certainty—and we said so in our report. However, there is some empirical basis on which to base such estimates. The Curtiss–Wright Corporation has been working on the development of stratified charge rotary engines since 1962 at a modest pace (they have a total of only about 1000 test hours to date). In spite of this relatively early state of development, the results have been encouraging.

Ford's statement that Curtiss–Wright has not been able to achieve the fuel economy of a conventional spark ignition is not correct. Curtiss–Wright demonstrated a carburated rotary engine which matched the fuel consumption of a conventional automobile spark ignition engine ten years ago.[h] More recent designs have resulted in a stratified charge engine having specific fuel consumptions (using

[h]"A Progress Report on Curtiss–Wright's Rotary Stratified Charge Engine Development," Charles Jones, Curtiss Wright Corporation, SAE Paper No. 741206, November 1974.

gasoline) that are more than ten percent lower than a conventional engine. When JP fuel is used, this advantage increases to close to 20 percent. We recognize that these comparisons are between engines operating without emission controls and that Curtiss–Wright has not made any extensive investigation of emissions. Their recent tests, however, on engines using dual fuel injection have achieved a degree of firing regularity which, when taken with the extreme lean mixtures typical of stratified charge engines, may indicate low emission levels. This is in line with Ford's work on the PROCO reciprocating stratified charge engine which demonstrated improved fuel economy in combination with emission levels comparable to the ultimate Federal standards.[i]

We stated in our report that, to our knowledge, no stratified rotary engine has been tested with supercharging. However, the Texaco stratified charge reciprocating engine was tested with and without turbocharging. The results of adding turbocharging to the stratified charge engine were quite analogous to those obtained by adding it to a conventional carbureted engine, and we know of no reason to expect a drastic difference if it is added to a rotary engine. Consequently, we feel satisfied that our estimates for this type of engine are generally reasonable.

We recognize, as Ford points out, that sealing and high surface to volume ratio in the combustion chamber are problems with current rotaries. How well the sealing problem will be solved can only be determined by future research. We suspect that the surface to volume effect may be less serious on stratified charge engines, and this may account for Curtiss–Wright's success, but further research is needed before any more definite statement can be made.

Advanced Transmission Technology

The industry recognizes the potential of the Continuously Variable Transmission for improved fuel economy, but fears that inefficiency, durability, noise, weight, size, and customer acceptance make their use unlikely. The two most promising CVTs at present appear to be under development by Orshansky and Tracor. Objections to the Orshansky design are excessive noise, complexity, and cost. We believe that none of these objections are serious enough to justify the pessimism apparently felt by industry regarding the introduction of

[i]E. Mitchell, A. Alperstein, J. M. Cobb and C. H. Faist, "A Stratified Charge Multifuel Military Engine—A Progress Report," SAE Paper No. 720051, January 1972. See also A. Simko, M. A. Chima, and L. L. Repko, "Exhaust Emission Control by the Ford Programmed Combustion Process," PROCO, SAE Paper No. 720052, January 1972.

these transmissions. Our work indicates that the increase in cost is more than offset by the savings in fuel cost over the life of the car and by the reduction in selling price due to the smaller size engine required for a specified acceleration. If fuel price increases in the future, the cost advantage of the CVT will also increase. Admittedly, the hydromechanical transmission is more complex than current automatic transmissions. However, Orshansky points out that the majority of the parts are similar to those used in conventional transmissions, so that it should be possible to convert existing transmission plants to the manufacture of CVTs.

We agree that noise remains a problem, and this problem is currently being addressed in research. Without trying to judge the success of this research, we observe that engine noise will be reduced due to the lower operating rpm's with this transmission, that engine sizes may become smaller in the future (thus reducing both engine and transmission noise), and that even the present noise levels may be acceptable in the future as the desire for better fuel economy increases.

Ford's judgment about the Tracor transmission also seems unnecessarily pessimistic to us. They state that high thrust loadings on the traction surfaces require high pressure lubrication which results in a parasitic power loss and a noise problem. We have discussed this situation with Tracor and they state that the recent tests on a Pinto equipped with a CVT were made with a single cavity design equipped with an oversize aircraft hydraulic pump—which was noisy, but conveniently available. Tracor is now proposing a dual cavity design primarily to improve their efficiency at the low power settings which are so important for automobile use. They estimate that the oil pump will be about the size of a conventional power steering pump and that the oil pressure will be lower than that used in the Pinto application (about 1200 psi compared to 1400–1500 psi). Tracor recently has proposed a research program to EPA based on this new design. While it is much too early to evaluate the success of the new design, the prospects appear to us to be favorable enough to justify a vigorous research effort in this area.

We understand that Ford has also proposed a research program on a continuously variable transmission to EPA, indicating that they too see possibilities in advanced transmission technology.

The Effects of Auto Weight Reduction

The industry doubts that the use of advanced technology, such as the rotary stratified charge engine, or advanced transmissions, can result in the large increase in fuel economy which we estimate.

The effect of a weight change on fuel economy is strongly dependent on the conditions under which the charge is made. We have investigated this under three different sets of constraints.

If we assume that weight is changed with no other change in the auto (as would be the case if only a ligher weight component were substituted for a heavier one), our results indicate that a one percent reduction in curb weight results in about 0.3 percent improvement in fuel economy. This compares with a value of 0.25 percent given by AMC.

If in changing weight, only the dimensions of the passenger compartment and the acceleration time from 0 to 60 mph are held constant, our results indicate that a one percent change in weight results in .55 to .60 percent improvement in fuel economy.

Finally, if passenger compartment size and acceleration are varied with weight, as is current practice between different market classes, our results indicate that a one percent reduction in weight results in a one percent improvement in fuel economy. This is in agreement with the results of EPA tests on current autos.

In order to clarify the steps that result in the large fuel economy improvements we show, we have summarized in Figure 1 [Fig-

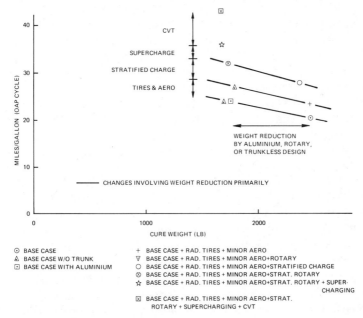

Figure 10–1. Effect of Design Changes on Fuel Economy of Subcompact Cars with No Air Conditioning.

Source: Adapted from Figure 1, *Energy Conservation Working Paper,* p. 349.

ure 10–1 of this volume] the effects of changes in weight and other design alternatives (as we predict them) for subcompact cars without air conditioning. The figure shows how the curb weight and miles per gallon (on the OAP cycle) vary as design changes are made. We drew lines connecting designs in which only changes in weight are involved; i.e., there is no change in engine efficiency or road or air resistence. These lines apply to a situation in which the passenger compartment size (and thus the frontal area) of the car is held constant as weight is reduced, as described above. The slopes of these lines indicate that, for this situation, a 1.0 percent reduction in weight results in about 0.55 to 0.60 percent improvement in miles per gallon. The points in the figure show how various changes made to the base can combine to result in a doubling of miles per gallon in the most advanced case. It should be noted we would predict even further gains if aluminium were used in the most advanced design, or if the trunk were eliminated.

Overall Dimensions

Ford concludes that the objective of our design model is to minimize the length of the auto. We do not minimize length in the sense that we believe a short auto is superior to a longer one; our purpose in estimating length is to provide a basis for determining the weight of the body, and eventually, of the entire auto. It is true that we provide no more length than is required to house the fuel, passenger and trunk compartments, and the engine with an efficiency of volume utilization representative of current (1973) autos.

Ford objects to two of our designs. One is a trunkless car, and Ford comments that there is only 18 inches of length fore and aft of the passenger compartment. The second is a subcompact (with trunk) using the supercharged stratified rotary engine. The first of these cars is much smaller than any auto in large production at present. It weighs only 1,053 pounds, has an overall length of 7.7 feet, has a 39 horsepower engine and a six gallon gasoline tank, and it retains a standard subcompact passenger compartment but has no trunk. While our model does not estimate the size of the wheels, they are small—possibly one foot in diameter. Remembering that the rear wheel wells may be at least partially recessed under the sides of the rear seat, as is the conventional practice on subcompacts, and that the engine is a highly compact type (supercharged rotary with charge stratification), we feel that the dimensions predicted by our model are a reasonable first estimate of what can actually be achieved. Our purpose in considering the trunkless small car was simply to estimate the gains in fuel economy when the trunk is eliminated. Autos like the Honda and other current small hatchback designs closely approach the type of auto we had in mind.

Ford also feels that another model we analyze, the 40 mph subcompact, is impractical. Our results indicate that such a car is about twelve feet long, weighs 1600 pounds, and has a 50 horsepower engine, while having a standard subcompact passenger compartment and trunk. The length of the trunk and fuel tank section is 4.3 feet and the length of the engine compartment is 1.5 feet, which we believe is adequate to house the compact 50 horsepower supercharged rotary engine.

Although our weight estimates are based on auto designs using the conventional arrangement with the engine in the front and the trunk in the rear, a car of this type lends itself to a rear engine arrangement, and we suspect that the difference in weights between front and rear engine arrangements is small and within the accuracy of our model.

Autos very similar to this design (except for the engine and transmission) are already on the market. The following table [see Table 10–1 of this volume] compares our subcompact design using the supercharged stratified rotary engine with the 1975 Volkswagen Rabbit. The comparison shows that there is nothing unreasonable about the weight and dimensions of our car—they are very similar to the VW. We show a much better fuel economy than the VW due to a lower acceleration capability and a much more advanced engine and transmission.

Air Conditioning

AMC and Chrysler believe that our estimate of the effect of air conditioning on fuel economy is too high (AMC estimates 1 to 2 percent average loss during the year, while Chrysler estimates 4 to 5 percent). We show 13 percent, of which 4 percent is due to the

Table 10–1. Comparison of Model Subcompact with 1975 VW Rabbit

	Rand Advanced Subcompact	VW Rabbit
Length (feet)	12.0	12.9
Width (feet)	5.3	5.3
Height (feet)	4.1	4.6
Horsepower	50.6	75
Weight (pound)	1,601	1,680
Time from 0 to 60 miles per hour (second)	20	11.3
Miles per gallon (urban)	36.5	24

Source: Adapted from *Energy Conservation Working Paper*, p. 350.

weight of the air conditioning equipment and 9 percent due to its operation. Our estimate is based on EPA laboratory tests of full size cars with and without operation of the air conditioning.[j] These show a 9 percent loss in fuel economy over the Federal Driving Cycle in 70°F ambient temperature. They estimate the penalty may go as high as 20 percent or may, of course, be zero if the air conditioner is not used. We used the 9 percent figure as representative of the nation-wide year round average for cars of all sizes which are equipped with air conditioning. However, we recognize that this may overstate the fuel economy penalty attributable to air conditioning, if the average temperature nationwide is lower than 70°F. In estimating the effect of air conditioning on the fuel consumption of the entire fleet, we assumed that the fraction of each market class equipped with air conditioning remains the same as at present.

Radial Tires

Both Chrysler and AMC make lower estimates than ours for the effect of radial tires. Chrysler estimates 3 percent improvement in fuel economy, AMC estimates 4 percent, and we show 4 to 8 percent. We suspect the difference is primarily due to our assumption of redesigning the car completely as opposed to the substitution of radial for bias-ply tires on the same car. The power saving due to radial tires during the acceleration of zero to 60 mph results in a lower power-to-weight ratio when radials are used. This in turn results in better specific fuel consumptions around the driving cycle and a gain in fuel economy which is greater than that due to the direct reduction in road resistance obtained from radial tires.

Aerodynamic Improvements

Industry generally doubts that aerodynamic improvements can result in as large an improvement in fuel economy as we show. AMC believes that the fuel economy improvement due to the minor aerodynamic changes that we consider could not be more than 2–3 percent and Chrysler estimates 1–4 percent. Again, we believe that our estimates are greater than those industry predicts because of the effect of comparing on the basis of equal acceleration time. The drag coefficient affects the power required during the high speed portion of the 0 to 60 mph acceleration, and thus a reduction in drag coefficient results in a design with a smaller power to weight ratio. This results in higher power settings in city driving, as well as some saving in weight—both of which contribute to better fuel economy in city

[j]*Fuel Economy and Emission Control*, United States Environmental Protection Agency, November 1972.

driving. Thus, even though the change in drag in low speed driving is small, drag reduction can result in improved fuel economy when the comparison is based on equal acceleration.

Ford expressed doubt that a 25 percent reduction in drag can be obtained by aerodynamic improvements which they would consider "minor." The modifications that we assumed would accomplish this were the rounding (primarily in plan view) of the front end of the car and the use of an underbody "dam" across the front end to lower flow velocities over the underbody. The sources on which we base these estimates are described on page 8 of R–1560–NSF. We do not consider the complete underbody fairing a "minor" aerodynamic improvement (as Ford misunderstood)—we considered it as part of the "major" aerodynamic improvements which lead to a 50 percent reduction in drag coefficient, but which we rejected as too extreme a modification.

Ford also points out, and we agree, that our model does not adjust the drag coefficient to allow for the shape of each auto body as it is designed. We recognize that the model could be improved in this respect (assuming sufficient data were available) but we do not feel this a serious shortcoming. Its effects would be to make small (short) cars somewhat less attractive in comparison to larger cars than we show them to be. In comparisons between cars of approximately the same size in which other features are varied, it would have little effect, since both autos in the comparison would be similarly affected.

The Approximation to the Federal Driving Cycle

Ford suggests that our approximation to the Federal Driving Cycle is not accurate and they suggest a different set of accelerations and times in cruise and idle. Our study employs the DHEW Urban Dynamometer Driving Schedule, which is used for measuring emissions.[k] There is no "exact" value of acceleration used in the schedule. In Figure 3 we show the only acceleration from 0 to 50 mph, which occurs in the schedule. It can be seen that the Ford value of .84 mph/sec is a reasonable estimate of the overall average acceleration from 0 to 50 mph, but that the actual schedule involves several much higher accelerations combined with several nearly constant

[k]This schedule is defined in one second intervals in the *Federal Register*. Vol. 35, No. 219, Part II, Nov. 10, 1970. Since our study began, the EPA has defined driving cycles for measuring fuel economy in city, suburban, and highway driving. These cycles all involve accelerations similar to those we have used, and we feel that the use of these cycles in place of the DHEW emission cycle would not affect the major conclusions of our study.

speed cruises and even some deceleration. Our approximation to the schedule, which is made up of accelerations at 3 mph/sec and constant speed runs at 25 to 50 mph, is also shown in Figure 2 [Figure 10-2 of this volume]. Clearly, it is more accurate than the overall average acceleration proposed by Ford.

Actually, so far as fuel economy is concerned, it makes very little difference which acceleration schedule is used. We calculated the fuel consumed by a full size car (the "base case" in R-1560-NSF) using both Rand and Ford approximations to the acceleration for 0 to 50 mph (enough distance in cruise at 50 mph was added to make the total distance covered in both cases equal) and found only a 7 percent difference in fuel consumed. Considering the wide difference in accelerations, this indicates an extreme insensitivity to acceleration. This does not imply, of course, that stop and go driving does not consume more fuel than constant speed driving. It does, however, imply that the most important characteristic of a driving cycle so far as fuel economy is concerned, is the total speed change (i.e., the number of accelerations and the speed increment in each acceleration) rather than the level of acceleration used in changing speed.

We examined decelerations on the schedule again and found values ranging from -.94 mph/sec to -3.26 mph/sec with most of the values being between -2.0 mph/sec and -3.0 mph/sec as we have used in our approximation to the driving cycle.

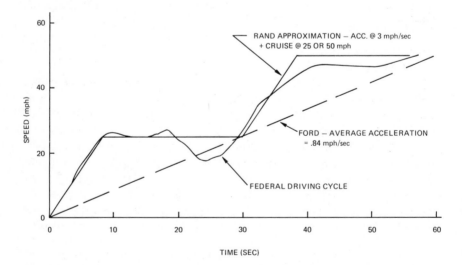

Figure 10-2. Approximations to the Federal Driving Cycle.

Source: Adapted from Figure 2, *Energy Conservation Working Paper,* p. 351.

The differences in cruise time between our estimates and Ford's are a direct result of the differences in acceleration and deceleration—since in our approximation we accelerate and decelerate faster (covering less distance in these modes) and we cover the remaining distance in cruise. In summary, we are quite satisfied that our approximation represents the driving cycle with sufficient accuracy for the purpose of our study.

The Use of Constant Speed Engine Data

Ford points out, and we agree, that our use of constant speed engine test stand data does not allow for cold starts, engine inertia, and the effect of the acceleration pump. They also point out, however, that "no computational scheme regardless of its complexity has been able to simulate these effects to date." Recognizing this, we chose to calibrate our model with data on 1973 (not pre–1971 as Ford states) auto fuel economy, as described in our report. We believe this results in a satisfactory basis for comparing autos using conventional engines. The use of this method on more advanced engines is less certain, but we think it is adequate for the first order comparisons we make. The losses due to the choke and acceleration pump are presumably eliminated, or at least reduced, in an engine using fuel injection and charge stratification—but we have no method for estimating them.

Idle Fuel Flow

As Ford points out, we have correlated the fuel flow in idle with the engine size, as measured by its maximum power. As described in our report, the data we used were based on tests of idle fuel consumption made by the Highway Research Board. The data indicate that fuel flow in idle increases more or less linearly with engine size at low horsepower, but becomes almost independent of size at the higher powers. For convenience, we fitted this with the curve shown in the report, which has a slight peak in it. This does not imply that we believe that idle fuel flow decreases for larger engines. The largest spark ignition engine used in our study was 214 horsepower, and thus lay well below the peak.

We recognize that emission requirements affect idle fuel flow, but we have not been able to quantify this. Since our results show that idling consumes between 5 and 12 percent of fuel, we feel that modification of the idle fuel flows would not affect first order conclusions drawn from the study.

Chapter Eleven

Testimony: Alternative Public Policies for Conserving Gasoline

Sorrel Wildhorn

Thank you for your invitation to appear before this Committee to discuss the potential problems and benefits of alternative public policies for conserving gasoline.

During the past fiscal year I led a team of economists and engineers in a national-level study comparing several alternative public policies for conserving gasoline used by the personal automobile. The work, conducted at The Rand Corporation, was sponsored by the National Science Foundation, Office of Research Applied to National Needs. The study that I will discuss is part of a larger research program at Rand that analyzes a wide range of energy policy issues. The findings, views, and conclusions expressed in this testimony are those of the author and should not be interpreted as representing those of the Rand Corporation or any of the agencies sponsoring its research.

The purpose of this testimony is to expose the different layers of the problem and to outline the impacts of several alternative public policies for conserving gasoline. Additionally, I will describe how our work was used and the interaction we had with the auto industry.

The necessity or desirability of adopting specific new energy conservation policies rests on the answers to four questions:

1. Should we conserve gasoline?
2. If so, how much should we conserve and by when?
3. Can we rely on existing private incentives to accomplish specific conservation goals?

This chapter contains the testimony submitted to the California Assembly Committee on Energy and Diminishing Materials, April 2, 1975, Hearing on bills related to auto fuel economy regulation.

4. If government conservation policies are needed, how do *all* of the alternatives compare?

In our work we did not address the first three questions. With respect to the fourth, we compared *some*, not all, of the alternative public policies on the *assumptions* that conservation was needed and that the private sector would respond to future gasoline prices consistent with their past responses.

The purposes of our study were twofold: to develop analytical tools, then to apply the tools in a systematic comparison of the impacts of several alternative conservation measures and policy instruments. Previous studies of auto conservation policies, conducted over the past couple of years, have generally focused on either technology or on economic policy, but usually not on both. In this study, therefore, we designed an approach in which both aspects of policy could be evaluated on a comparable basis.

SCOPE

A fairly comprehensive list of public policies for conserving gasoline, either by inducing a reduction in total auto travel or by improving the fuel economy of the auto fleet, would surely include:

1. Regulatory: (a) mandated maximum weight standards; (b) mandated technology standards; and (c) mandated average fuel economy standards for new car production.
2. Additional Taxes: (a) on gasoline; (b) fixed or flat excise taxes on new and/or used cars; and (c) graduated (by weight, horsepower, or fuel economy) excise taxes on new and/or used cars.
3. Limit supply of gasoline (e.g., rationing, import limitations).
4. Alternative tax treatment of oil companies (e.g., different depletion allowance).
5. Transportation management or control policies (e.g., carpooling, congestion relief).
6. Public transit improvement or fare reduction.
7. Land use policies.

We decided to limit our analysis to two kinds of policies: regulatory policies aimed at improving the fuel economy of the auto fleet, and price-change policies on gasoline and new cars. Of course, these are not independent or mutually exclusive policies, since price increases in gasoline or new cars may induce technological change, and technological changes in autos may affect new car prices.

The three types of regulatory policies we analyzed were (1) maximum weight standards that are introduced in the latter half of the 1970s; (2) mandated technology changes, which assume that among other things a new engine and a new transmission are introduced into the fleet in the early 1980s; and (3) average fuel economy standards for new car production.

One way to change prices is through additional taxes. We analyzed different levels of additional gasoline taxes and *average* or flat new car excise taxes, both applied over the twenty-year period between 1975 and 1995. We did *not* analyze new car excise taxes that are graduated with respect to either weight, horsepower, or fuel economy.

Our basic approach was to compare various economic, social, and environmental impacts of alternative policies over the next twenty years with the impacts projected for a Base Case. In the Base Case projection, we made specific assumptions about future gasoline and new car price levels in the absence of additional governmental intervention.

The policy impacts we considered in our analysis included: gasoline consumption; total energy consumption (in the production, distribution, and use of gasoline and in the production, distribution, sales, repair, and scrappage of automobiles); user costs (assuming auto lifetimes of ten years and 100,000 miles of driving); vehicle miles traveled; weighted emissions (which is a proxy for air quality); new car sales; and total auto ownership. Finally, we made only partial and initial estimates of employment and income distributional effects. We made estimates of initial employment changes in only five auto-related sectors of the economy, which in 1971 employed close to 3 million workers, or about 4.5 percent of the total non-agricultural work force. Fewer jobs in a particular sector may be a negative impact in the short run, but not necessarily in the long run, because most displaced workers will move into other sectors.

As to income distributional effects, we estimated the initial impact on different earnings groups of additional expenditures for gasoline used only for work trips. We emphasize strongly here that although we did not study alternative uses to which the additional tax revenues could be put for alleviating distributional inequities or auto sector unemployment resulting from increased prices, there are many ways to do this.

Other potential policy impacts, such as auto safety, auto damageability, or balance-of-trade implications were not considered at all. A summary of the quantitative findings is given in our study's executive summary (R–1560/1–NSF) and in previous written testimony to the

U.S. Senate Commerce Committee—both of these documents are being submitted to this Committee as part of this testimony.

A QUALITATIVE SUMMARY OF THE STUDY'S FINDINGS

Let me summarize here our major findings in largely qualitative terms.

In the short term, apart from rationing, only higher gasoline prices will achieve significant conservation of gasoline. Early gasoline conservation would be mainly due to reduced travel; there would be persistent reductions in auto ownership, travel, emissions, and in employment (mainly in the auto parts and service sectors).

In the longer term, apart from extremely high gasoline taxes, we find that policies that improve fuel economy without raising new car prices—preferably lowering them—offer the best promise for conservation. Under such policies new car sales will rise, and people will scrap their older gas hogs more quickly. With better fuel economy will come more driving because the cost per mile driven falls. More driving will mean more emissions and more employment in the auto-related sectors.

A number of alternative policies might have such an effect. Regulatory standards are one example, provided that they do not diminish the consumer appeal of the resulting product line. Subject to the same qualification, a graduated excise tax, perhaps with subsidies for the most efficient models, might be another. A combination of a graduated excise tax on new cars and a gasoline tax might be yet another. In our study, we made quantitative comparisons only among regulatory standards, a flat excise tax on new cars, a gasoline tax, and combinations of regulatory standards and a gasoline tax.

Because each of the policies considered in this study has different social, economic, and environmental impacts, combinations of policies, such as gasoline taxes and regulatory standards may be more effective, *if* a national objective is to achieve significant levels of gasoline conservation over the *entire* twenty-year period we examined.

Under a flat excise tax on new cars, new car prices will rise, sales will fall, people will retain their older gas hogs longer, and as a result, total auto ownership and the amount of driving will be virtually unchanged—with little or no reduction in gasoline consumption. A graduated excise tax, without subsidies for most efficient cars, will also increase average new car prices.

New technology offers great promise. In addition to relatively minor improvements like radial tires and better aerodynamic design for new cars, we find that if a new internal combustion engine and a new transmission, such as the continuously variable type, are introduced, individual full-size cars may achieve over 25 miles per gallon and subcompacts may achieve over 40 miles per gallon on a combined urban–rural driving cycle. Then, too, depending on the technological option pursued, this can mean lower new car prices and lower lifetime costs. These results suggest that if federal R&D support is necessary, a new internal combustion engine and transmission should not be neglected. (Under EPA sponsorship, the federal government already is sponsoring R&D on more unconventional engine types such as the gas turbine, steam engine, and the Stirling engine— but no R&D on advanced internal combustion engines is currently being undertaken. Private R&D activities include work on some variants of the internal combustion engine.)

If new car fuel economy standards are to be mandated, our analysis indicates that with a combination of new technology and a shift to small cars, an average of up to 38 miles per gallon for new car production is possible in the longer term (after 1985). By 1980, under our assumptions, we find that it is feasible to improve average new car fuel economy by roughly 50 percent over the 1974 national average of 14 miles per gallon. Our assumptions were that future safety and emission standards would not impose additional penalties over and above those we considered, that R&D would be successful, and that new technology could be introduced on the tight schedule we assumed. If actual performance falls short of our assumptions, actual savings may be less than we predict and/or may be delayed in time.

Mandated fuel economy standards are probably preferable to specific mandated weight or technology standards, for several reasons. An important consideration is the uncertainty about the performance of specific new technologies, resulting in the risk that highly specific technological standards would not be achieved, or would lead to high costs. Under mandated miles per gallon standards, a greater variety of technological and weight limiting approaches could be pursued by manufacturers, which would improve conservation possibilities and offer the consumer a greater variety of choices in automobile characteristics.

An alternative policy to mandated fuel economy standards is the graduated (by weight, horsepower, or fuel economy) excise tax on new car price, perhaps with subsidies for the most efficient, lightest or smaller-engined autos. When subjected to close analysis, it may prove to be more attractive than mandated fuel economy standards.

But the methodology for analyzing the impacts of such a policy is only now being developed.

In our published report, *How to Save Gasoline* (R–1560–NSF), we did not make definitive recommendations as to the advisability of adopting particular, specific policies, such as mandated fuel economy standards or various new and/or used car taxing schemes because our project, limited in both time and resources, was unable to evaluate adequately all of the impacts of the alternative policies.

HOW THE STUDY WAS USED

I believe that it is useful to provide the Committee with a short account of how our work has been used and how the auto industry reacted to it.

Our published report was one among several sources used by federal agencies such as FEA, DOT, and the Treasury Department in forming and solidifying their views on energy policy.

The U.S. Senate Commerce Committee invited me to submit written testimony on our work to their Hearings (in late November and early December 1974) on their Energy Conservation Working Paper. (I have included it with my testimony today.) Automobile industry witnesses also testified at the same Commerce Committee Hearings. During their testimony the auto industry witnesses were asked to comment in writing on, among other things, several sections of our published report and on two statements in my written testimony. The Commerce Committee asked me, in turn, to respond to the auto makers' comments on our work. (Our written response to the auto makers' views is also included along with my testimony today.)

Before describing the auto makers' views and our response to their views, I should make it clear that all of these documents—my original testimony, the auto makers' comments, and our response to their comments—will be published shortly, as part of the public record of these Commerce Committee hearings.

Now, what was the nature of the auto makers' comments? First, General Motors and Ford both agreed with two of the qualitative conclusions of our study—that (1) an increase in the pump price of gasoline is the only effective *near-term* strategy, short of rationing, and (2) improved new car fuel economy is an alternative *long-term* strategy, provided it can be achieved at reasonable cost and without compromising the acceptability of the vehicle to the consumer. General Motors also agreed with our conclusion that a fixed or flat excise tax on new car price offers little promise of gasoline conservation in the near term, because it would encourage the retention of older gas guzzlers.

On the critical side, the auto makers made five major points; we summarize each of their points and our response below:

First, our estimates of potential improvements in new car fuel economy were optimistic for the short run because we assumed that emission and safety standards would be met without major price, weight, fuel economy, and performance penalties. We chose this assumption because of lack of data on more advanced emission controls and the uncertainty as to the magnitude and timing of specific future safety and emission standards. Whether emission and safety standards will result in a loss in future fuel economy depends on the specific standards and design approaches used to meet them—a subject that needs much more extensive study than has been the case to date.

Second, new technology, such as more efficient transmissions and engines could not be introduced as early as we assumed. Our timing estimates were based on a maximum effort to improve fuel economy, with little regard to financial risk—a schedule distinctly different from what might be termed "business as usual" in the industry. We chose this approach to indicate those areas in which R&D may result in large improvements and those areas where even successful research would lead to only minor gains. The adoption of policies to achieve these potentials should be based on a balancing of the urgency of achieving gasoline savings against the risks inherent in their development.

The auto makers' comments offered no alternative estimates of what the longer-term potential of new technology might be, no estimate of how long it will take, nor did they reveal in what ways they are now pursuing advanced technology development beyond short-term improvements to conventional design or the conventional engine. Thus, their comments offer no basis for evaluating whether current auto industry behavior is adequate.

Third, the auto makers asserted that government regulation is not needed, since market forces will be adequate to improve mileage, because better fuel economy "sells." The case for government action hinges on whether national energy conservation policy implies *more* than industry would normally do to improve fuel economy. We did not have the resources to study how auto makers would respond to higher gasoline prices in the absence of other government action. But we noted that a recent study of the industry by Lawrence White (an economist) indicated that American auto makers are reluctant to adopt major new (engine and transmission) technology. We don't fully endorse White's analysis. Because we only estimated potential improvements in new car fuel economy over today's level and because we didn't address the issue of how far auto makers would go toward that potential without government action, we cannot say (and did not say in our published report) whether government action is needed.

Fourth, Ford, Chrysler, and American Motors all asserted that sufficient capital funding would *not* be available to finance alternate power plant or transmission systems in addition to the capital resources required to meet presently mandated federal safety, damageability, and emission control standards. Although General Motors indicated that adequate funds are or can be made available to finance most new technological developments, they indicated that the really scarce resources were engineering and research skills.

It is true that we did not study the issue independently, but our statement that adequate capital resources could be available derives from the only independent (i.e., non-automotive industry) study available when we were doing our work. Subsequently, the Congressionally mandated DOT–EPA 120-day study indicated that *additional* capital requirements between $50 million and $200 million annually were needed to improve fuel economy depending on the set of fuel economy options pursued. These figures compare to recent industry expenditures for capital goods of between $2.0 and $2.5 billion annually.

Fifth, some of the auto makers felt that our analytical methodology was too simplistic or inaccurate to generate reliable quantitative output and that at best the tools could be expected to yield qualitative, directional conclusions. Our auto design methodology was intended to produce reasonable "first cut" estimates, and we believe it does this successfully. Our econometric model shares the same problems felt in varying degrees by all econometric work in this area, but there is no implication that our results are biased in either direction.

In sum, we believe that the auto makers' comments have not affected our major qualitative, directional conclusions and we stand by them. As to how our quantitative estimates stand up, we made clear that we chose to estimate *potential* gasoline savings, if certain measures or policies were undertaken, given certain assumptions. Having such potential savings in mind might stimulate needed action. If actual performance falls short of our assumptions, actual savings may be less than we predict and/or might be delayed in time. We were unable to go very far in determining the realism of our assumptions, since we are unable to predict the course of emission control standards, the problems that may arise in connection with control systems or the outcome of specific R&D projects for improving fuel economy. We are reasonably confident, however, that a diversified R&D program will produce a menu of successful developments that offer approximately the degree of improvement we estimate.

Appendixes

Appendix A

Summary Description and Validation of the Generalized Automobile Design Model

This appendix provides a general description of the automobile design model we used to evaluate the effects of technological changes.[a]

THE GENERALIZED AUTOMOBILE DESIGN MODEL

The Generalized Automobile Design Model relates automobile resource and energy requirements and the cost of auto ownership to auto size, performance, and design characteristics (i.e., type of engine, transmission, fuel, and so forth). The purpose of the model is to allow the effects of changes in auto size, performance, or design to be assessed when one of these variables is changed while the others are held constant. The literature on automobile design abounds with descriptions of point designs in which a new engine type (or other design feature) has been tested, and differences in fuel consumption measured, by installing it in an existing automobile body and chassis. The difficulty in interpreting the results of such tests lies in the fact that the modified auto usually shows differences not only in fuel consumption but also in performance and sometimes in the amount of useful space inside the car. Examples of this are (1) diesel powered autos that have lower acceleration but better fuel consumption than gasoline cars of the same size, because of the greater weight of the diesel engine, and (2) automobiles that have been equipped with continuously variable transmissions that improve both acceleration

[a]A more detailed description containing a complete exposition of the equations as well as a discussion of the inputs and data base is given in Thomas F. Kirkwood and Allen D. Lee, *A Generalized Model for Comparing Automobile Design Approaches to Improved Fuel Economy*, R–1562–NSF, The Rand Corporation, January, 1975.

and fuel economy. Our model will allow the results of tests of this type to be used to determine the comparative fuel consumption of automobiles designed to have the *same* performance and useful space characteristics.

The input quantities used in the model to define an automobile are of three types: (1) those that define the size of the passenger and trunk compartments and whether or not the auto is air conditioned, (2) those that define the car's ability to accelerate and its unrefueled range, and (3) those that define the design features used. The first group may be considered to define the comfort of the car. (While comfort also depends on the suspension system, no changes in suspension design are considered in this study; thus all autos are assumed to be equipped with suspensions typical of existing autos of the same weight.) The second group defines the performance of the car as observed by the owner, and the third defines the options open to the designer of the automobile.

The outputs of the model consist, first, of a description of the car. This includes its weight, overall dimensions, installed horsepower, its fuel economy over two different driving cycles, and its purchase price. Second, the outputs include a list of the materials necessary to produce the car. Third, they include an itemized list of all the energy consumed in producing, distributing, selling, and operating the auto throughout its lifetime. Finally, the model gives a breakdown of the total cost of buying and operating the auto throughout its lifetime.

Design options the model can evaluate include:

New engine types;
Tire design and pressure;
Aerodynamic design;
New transmission types;
New fuels;
New materials;
Changes in the size of the passenger compartment and trunk.

The design model ensures that each auto will meet three basic requirements:

1. Sufficient power to provide the desired acceleration (The desired time to accelerate from zero to sixty miles per hour is input.);
2. A body large enough to enclose the desired passenger compartment, trunk volume, engine, and fuel;
3. A curb weight equal to the sum of the weights of its compartment parts.

To ensure that these three conditions are met, it was necessary to develop (1) a method for calculating the time required to accelerate from zero to sixty mph, (2) a method for calculating the fuel consumed on the specified driving cycles, and (3) techniques for estimating the component weights and dimensions required to house the components. These three basic tools are described in the following paragraphs, and outlined in Figures A–1, A–2, and A–3. The following description applies to the model as it is used to define automobiles using conventional spark ignition engines with three speed automatic transmissions. The other technologies are described in Appendix B.

Calculation of Acceleration Time

Figure A–1 defines the calculation of acceleration time. This requires a knowledge of the variation of full throttle power (P_{WOT}), required power (P_R), transmission efficiency (η), and engine rpm, with road speed. These relations, which are obtained from data on actual engines and transmissions, are, after being normalized, represented by the points plotted in Figure A–1. Also required is the

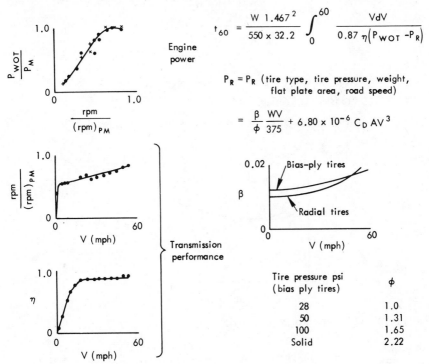

$$t_{60} = \frac{W \; 1.467^2}{550 \times 32.2} \int_0^{60} \frac{V dV}{0.87 \, \eta \left(P_{WOT} - P_R\right)}$$

$P_R = P_R$ (tire type, tire pressure, weight, flat plate area, road speed)

$$= \frac{\beta}{\phi} \frac{WV}{375} + 6.80 \times 10^{-6} \, C_D \, A V^3$$

Tire pressure psi (bias ply tires)	ϕ
28	1.0
50	1.31
100	1.65
Solid	2.22

Figure A–1. Calculation of Acceleration Time.

weight of the auto, W, and the engine maximum power, P_M. The maximum engine power is reduced by 13 percent to allow for differential and rear axle bearing losses, imperfect engine tune, and the fact that the gasoline available to the average driver is less than test quality.

Calculation of Miles per Gallon

The calculation of miles per gallon is outlined in Figure A–2. The required power (P_R) is determined from the equation in Figure A–1, except that an allowance for acceleration[b] is added. The two major inputs to the miles per gallon calculation are the variation of specific fuel consumption (SFC) with power and the definition of the driving cycle.

The variation of specific fuel consumption with power is determined by available data on the performance of the engine-transmission combination and is represented by two relations indicated in Figure A–2. The first relation gives the specific fuel consumption at

$$mpg \sim \frac{\text{CYCLE LENGTH}}{\int_{\substack{\text{DRIVING}\\\text{CYCLE}}} \frac{\text{SFC} \times P_R}{\eta_T} \, dt}$$

P_R = P_R (tires, weight, flat plate area, road speed, acceleration)

η_T = η_T (transmission design, road speed)

SFC = SFC (engine type, size, throttle setting, transmission design)

t = time

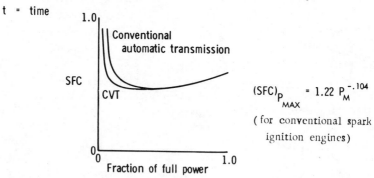

$$(SFC)_{P_{MAX}} = 1.22 \, P_M^{-.104}$$

(for conventional spark ignition engines)

Figure A–2. Calculation of Miles per Gallon.

[b]$\dfrac{W}{g} \dfrac{Va}{550}$, where g = acceleration due to gravity, V = road speed, a = acceleration; all units in the foot, pound, second system.

rated power as a function of the engine rated power; this accounts for the effect of engine size on specific fuel consumption. The second relation describes the variation of specific fuel consumption of a fixed size engine with throttle setting. This is done for a road load condition using the characteristics of the particular transmission being considered. Curves are shown in Figure A–2 for a conventional spark ignition engine equipped with a three speed automatic transmission and with a continuously variable transmission.[c]

Two driving cycles are considered: the Federal Driving Cycle, representing urban type driving, and a second cycle defined by the EPA's Office of Air Programs, which represents a mixture of urban and rural driving. We refer to this as the OAP cycle.

We have approximated the Federal Driving Cycle by the following series of operations:

17 accelerations from 0 to 25 mph;
17 decelerations from 25 mph to 0;
1 acceleration from 0 to 50 mph;
1 deceleration from 50 mph to 0;
275 seconds of idling;
110 seconds at 50 mph;
660 seconds at 25 mph;
Accelerations are at 3 mph/sec;
Decelerations from 25 mph are at 3 mph/sec;
Deceleration from 50 mph are at 2 mph/sec.

The OAP cycle consists of the Federal Driving Cycle, plus a number of constant speed runs defined as follows: one third of the time is split equally between 20, 30, and 40 mph; two thirds of the time is split equally between 50, 60, and 70 mph.

While we have computed miles per gallon over both driving cycles, we consider the OAP cycle to be more representative of "national" driving habits. We have also found that when the Auto Design Model is used to generate current autos of current size and performance characteristics, mixed in the proportions found in the present fleet, the resulting estimate of average fleet miles per gallon is in reasonable agreement with the actual national average. Thus, we have used the OAP cycle in estimating national annual fuel consumption.

---

[c]The determination of these curves from test data on engine/transmission is described in detail in Kirkwood and Lee, *A Generalized Model for Comparing Automobile Design Approaches to Fuel Economy.*

Component	Equation
Running gear	0.2 x curb weight
Tires	0.04 x curb weight
Engine (spark ignition)	$22.03 \, P_M^{.611}$
Engine section	0.2 x engine weight
Transmission (3 speed automatic)	$11\sqrt{\text{installed power}}$
Fuel	Range / mpg
Fuel system (gasoline)	0.2 x fuel weight
Glass	Function of surface area of passenger compartment
Body (5% plastics)	$0.102 \, (\text{body surface area})^{1.64}$
Emission control	$7.0\sqrt{\text{installed power}}$
Air conditioning	112
Battery	Function of engine power
Curb weight	Sum of above
Pass. weight	Input
Inertial weight	Sum of above

Figure A–3. Weight Estimation.

Estimation of Component Weights

Estimates of the weights of various automobile components are based primarily on data obtained by contract from Rath and Strong, Inc. These basic data were correlated with pertinent parameters to

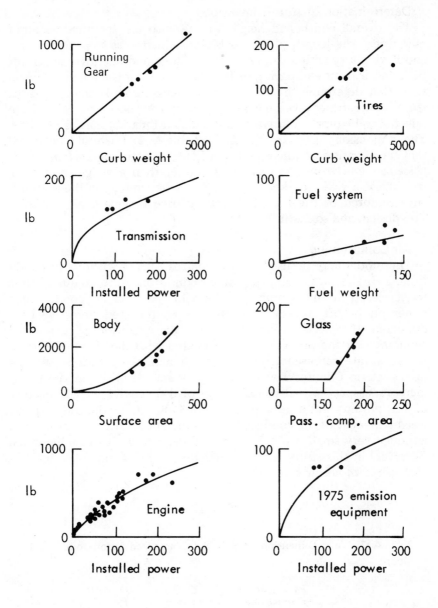

yield a set of weight equations used in the model. The components considered, and the weight equations used, are summarized in Figure A–3, which also shows the actual data points and the fitted equations.

Determination of Auto Dimensions

The overall width and height of the auto are specified as input quantities. The length of the car is determined so as to provide a rear end having a specified (input) trunk volume and adequate space for fuel, and a front end having sufficient volume for the engine. Dimensions that determine the size of the passenger compartment and the trunk compartment volume are input, and in most cases have been selected to be representative of four standard market classes of autos. The dimensions used are shown in Table A–1. It should be noted that specification of a market class of auto denotes *dimensions of the passenger and trunk compartments* rather than a weight class. The weights of a given market class may vary depending on the performance required or the technical options used (engine type, transmission design, and so forth.

Air Conditioning

The model may be used to design autos with or without air conditioning. If they are equipped with air conditioning, the required time to accelerate to sixty mph may be achieved with air conditioning either on or off; however, in the results reported here, we have evaluated the acceleration with the air conditioning off. Fuel economy, on the other hand, is evaluated with the air conditioning on at a rate representative of average annual operation (see the discussion in Chapter Two). This is represented in the model by an increase in specific fuel consumption of 9 percent, a weight increase of 112 pounds and a price increase of $400.00. We did not vary the weight or cost of air conditioning equipment with the size of auto, although very small cars might require smaller air conditioning units. However, in this study we have designed all autos smaller than subcompact *without* air conditioning.

Table A–1.   **Auto Dimensions Used in the Generalized Automobile Design Model**

Market Class	Passenger Compartment Length (ft)	Overall Width (ft)	Overall Height (ft)	Trunk Volume (ft³)
Subcompact	6.2	5.3	4.1	15
Compact	6.5	6.0	4.3	20
Intermediate	6.6	6.5	4.4	25
Full-Size	6.7	6.6	4.4	29

Emission Control Equipment

The weight associated with exhaust emission control equipment includes an oxidizing catalytic converter and exhaust gas recirculation equipment. We also assume that because of the presence of the converter, the engine may be returned from the lean mixtures in use in 1973 to improve drivability and fuel economy and that this results in a 15 percent *improvement* in fuel economy on engines of 200 horsepower or greater, no effect on engines under 130 horsepower, and a linear variation in between [1].

Estimates of the effect of emission controls on the fuel economy of future engines are quite uncertain [2]. All estimates agree, however, that small engines will be unaffected and that large engines will benefit (relative to 1973) from the use of catalytic converters. The improvement of 15 percent for large engines implies that they will obtain essentially the same fuel economy as when no emission controls are applied. While this estimate may seem somewhat optimistic, we have used it here because no more authoritative estimate is available at present.

In estimating the amount of exhaust emissions we assume that this equipment, or other equipment, will achieve the 1976 statutory emission levels.

Auto Design Synthesis

Once the procedures for calculating acceleration time, fuel economy, component weights, and dimensions have been established, an automobile can be designed to meet any specification of size, performance, fuel type, and technical options. The procedure followed is outlined in Figure A-4. As the figure shows, a double iteration, once on engine power, and once on curb weight, is made until all three of the basic requirements (power sufficient for the required acceleration; dimensions adequate to house passengers, engine, trunk, and fuel; total curb weight equal to the sum of the component weights) are met. When the design iteration is completed, the weight, power, and dimensions of the auto are defined, and we can proceed to determine the lifetime energy requirement and cost of ownership. Before we describe this step, however, we discuss the validation of the design portion of the model.

Design Model Validation

The design model has been validated by comparing its results with a group of twelve actual 1973 autos. In doing this, it was necessary to modify the weight and cost of current emissions equipment from that used in obtaining the study results, when units were designed to

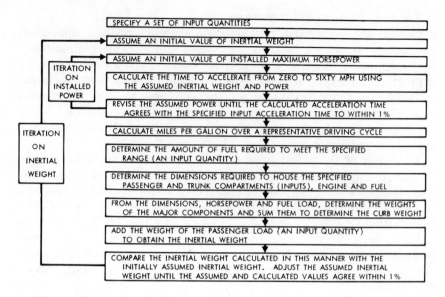

SPECIFY A SET OF INPUT QUANTITIES

ASSUME AN INITIAL VALUE OF INERTIAL WEIGHT

ASSUME AN INITIAL VALUE OF INSTALLED MAXIMUM HORSEPOWER

ITERATION ON INSTALLED POWER

CALCULATE THE TIME TO ACCELERATE FROM ZERO TO SIXTY MPH USING THE ASSUMED INERTIAL WEIGHT AND POWER

REVISE THE ASSUMED POWER UNTIL THE CALCULATED ACCELERATION TIME AGREES WITH THE SPECIFIED INPUT ACCELERATION TIME TO WITHIN 1%

ITERATION ON INERTIAL WEIGHT

CALCULATE MILES PER GALLON OVER A REPRESENTATIVE DRIVING CYCLE

DETERMINE THE AMOUNT OF FUEL REQUIRED TO MEET THE SPECIFIED RANGE (AN INPUT QUANTITY)

DETERMINE THE DIMENSIONS REQUIRED TO HOUSE THE SPECIFIED PASSENGER AND TRUNK COMPARTMENTS (INPUTS), ENGINE AND FUEL

FROM THE DIMENSIONS, HORSEPOWER AND FUEL LOAD, DETERMINE THE WEIGHTS OF THE MAJOR COMPONENTS AND SUM THEM TO DETERMINE THE CURB WEIGHT

ADD THE WEIGHT OF THE PASSENGER LOAD (AN INPUT QUANTITY) TO OBTAIN THE INERTIAL WEIGHT

COMPARE THE INERTIAL WEIGHT CALCULATED IN THIS MANNER WITH THE INITIALLY ASSUMED INERTIAL WEIGHT. ADJUST THE ASSUMED INERTIAL WEIGHT UNTIL THE ASSUMED AND CALCULATED VALUES AGREE WITHIN 1%

Figure A–4. Sequence of Operations in the Design Model.

meet ultimate statutory emission standards. This was done by eliminating the weight and cost of a catalytic converter and thus reducing the weight of emission equipment from $7\sqrt{\text{max power}}$ (Figure A–3) to $2\sqrt{\text{max power}}$, and reducing the cost of emission equipment from $1.22 \times$ Power (Figure A–6) to .35 × Power. In addition to this, the specific fuel consumption of the engine was increased by 15 percent for engines above 200 horsepower [3]. This increase was scaled down linearly with horsepower, so that engines below 130 horsepower are unaffected. The cost of ownership was also modified by removing the cost of replacing one catalytic converter in 100,000 miles. The inputs used to define the twelve autos used (three in each major weight class) are shown in Table A–2 [4].

Comparisons of the curb weight, overall length, installed horsepower, miles per gallon, and sticker price of the autos predicted by the model and the actual auto are shown in Figure A–5. The weight, length, power, and price of the actual autos is obtained from *Consumer Reports*. The miles per gallon are obtained from tests by the EPA [5] using the Federal Driving Cycle.

It will be noted that, as shown in Figure A–5, the calculated miles per gallon have been corrected to the actual weight of the tested vehicles. Although the design model estimates the initial weight by adding an allowance for passengers and baggage (usually 350 lbs) to the curb weight, the actual cars were tested by *Consumer Reports*

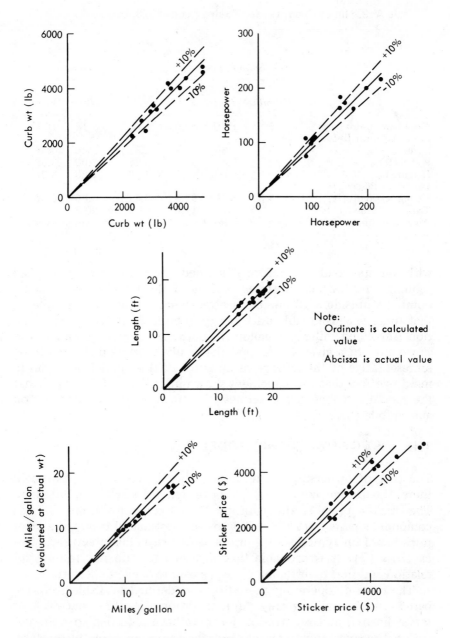

Figure A–5. Design Model Validation (Calculated versus Actual Auto Properties).

Table A-2.   Input Quantities for Twelve Actual 1973 Autos

	Auto Model					
	Subcompact			*Compact*		
	Gremlin	*Pinto*	*Vega*	*Valiant*	*Nova*	*Maverick*
Time from 0–60 (sec)	15	19.5	18.5	16.5	18	16.5
Range without Refuel (mi)	378	230	208	288	346	288
Width (ft)	5.92	5.42	5.73	5.92	6.00	5.92
Height (ft)	4.08	4.00	4.00	4.33	4.25	4.25
Length of Passenger Compartment (ft)	6.13	6.25	6.38	6.54	6.46	6.50
Trunk Volume (ft^3)	15.4	15.3	12.4	21.8	20.2	18.8
Air conditioning	no	no	no	yes	yes	yes

with varying loads; therefore it seemed reasonable to correct fuel economy to the actual tested weight of the vehicles. While some points lie outside a 10 percent scatter band, it must be remembered that there is considerable uncertainty in both the measured acceleration times and miles per gallon. In both cases, tests are based on a single auto of a given model and the results must be presumed to be representative of the average of all autos of that model. With this in mind, we feel that the agreement shown in Figure A–5 indicates that the model satisfactorily describes the effects of input quantities on automobile characteristics.

THE COST OF OWNERSHIP MODEL

The cost of ownership model is described in Table A–3. As shown there, the lifetime cost is evaluated over ten years and 100,000 miles. The sticker price is the sum of the price contributions of the component parts [6]. The selling price is estimated from the sticker price based on typical selling prices of American-manufactured autos in 1973 [7]. It is probable that foreign autos do not follow this relation and that their selling price is closer to their sticker price.

The costs of operating the auto, also defined in Table A–3, are based on Federal Highway Administration data [8], except that taxes, license, and registration fee have been modified to represent national average values rather than the values appropriate to Maryland (used by the FHWA).

The cost of fuel is an input to the model. For the per-vehicle comparisons described in Chapter Four, a fuel cost of 38 cents per

Table A–2. continued

Auto Model					
Intermediate			*Full-Size*		
Buick Century	Metador	Dodge Comet	Mercury Marquis	Ford LTD	Buick Electra
13	11.5	12.5	11.5	13	11
285	273	292	264	286	312
6.50	6.41	6.50	6.67	6.67	6.58
4.38	4.38	4.25	4.50	4.54	4.42
6.58	6.58	6.46	6.92	6.79	6.87
25.2	24.2	24.0	27.8	28.1	29.1
yes	yes	yes	yes	yes	yes

gallon (27 cents base cost plus 11 cents federal and state tax) was used as representative of fuel costs in recent years before the fuel shortage of late 1973. In the cases described in Chapter Seven, where the effect of an increase in fuel tax is explored, fuel cost is varied by the approximate procedure described in Appendix D.

The annual cost of ownership includes lost interest (figured at 7.5 percent), selling price, and operating cost (which includes insurance). No allowance for garaging or parking fees has been included—partly because of the uncertainties in estimating them on a national basis and partly because these costs are relatively insensitive to changes in auto design or miles driven.

THE LIFETIME ENERGY MODEL

The lifetime energy model estimates the total energy consumed in building the auto, operating it for ten years and 100,000 miles, and the energy recovered when the auto is scrapped. The items included are summarized in Table A–4 and the procedure for estimating production energy is outlined in Table A–5. In Table A–5, the energy required for extraction, refining, and fabrication of the various materials used in auto construction is given. To determine the amount of energy used for each auto *component*, it is necessary to define the amounts of each type of material used in each component. The distribution of materials by component, which we have used for autos powered with conventional spark ignition engines, is shown in Table A–6. The values shown are combined with the material energy requirements of Table A–5 to yield the auto component energy

Table A–3. Lifetime Cost Model (100,000 Miles in 10 Years)

Purchase

Running Gear	.87 $/lb
Tires	.90 $/lb
Engine	1.13 $/lb
Transmission	.77 $/horsepower
Emission Control Equip	1.22 $/horsepower
Fuel System	.95 $/lb
Glass	1.80 $/lb
Body	1.13 $/lb
Air Conditioning	400 Dollars
Sticker Price	Total

Selling Price = .91 x Sticker Price
-25×10^{-6} (Sticker Price)^2

10 Year Operation

Repairs and Maintenance	
Engine	820 + 2.6 power
Other	500 + .09 x curb wt
Tires	1.25 Dollars/lb
Accessories	200 Dollars
Gasoline (input)	.27 Dollars/gallon
Oil (input)	.75 Dollars/quart
Insurance	1150 + .05 x curb wt
Taxes	
State	
Gasoline	.07 Dollars/gallon
Sales	.028 Dollars/dollar
Registration and License	281 Dollars
Federal	
Tires	10 Dollars/lb
Oil	.06 Dollars/gallon
Gasoline	.04 Dollars/gallon

ANNUALIZED COST OF OWNERSHIP

$$= Selling\ Price \left[\frac{i(1+i)^{10}}{(1+i)^{10}-1} - \frac{.07\,i}{(1+i)^{10}-1} \right] + \frac{10\ Year\ Operating\ Cost}{10}$$

Available interest rate = .075

Table A–4. Lifetime Operating Energy (100,000 Miles in 10 Years)

Production	Table A–5	
Gasoline		
Consumption	127650	Btu/Gallon
Refining and Extraction	.089	Btu/Btu of Gasoline Heat Content
Transport	39100	Btu/Dollar of Gasoline
Oil	67350	Btu/Dollar of Oil
Transport and Sales	30100	Btu/Dollar of New Car Selling Price
Tires	62800	Btu/Dollar of Tires
Repairs and Maintenance	27900	Btu/Dollar of Maintenance and Repair
Scrap		Table A–5

Sources: "Direct and Indirect Energy Requirements for Automobiles" Eric Hirst,
      unpublished draft;
      "Census of Manufacturers," Census Bureau 1967;
      "Environmental Impacts of Polystyrene Foam and Molded Pulp Meat
      Trays" W. E. Franklin, R. G. Hunt, Midwest Research Institute,
      April 1972.

requirements shown on the right side of Table A–5. These are then combined with the weights of components, as determined by the design model, to yield the total production energy required.

As seen in Table A–4, all the operating energy items (except those associated with gasoline) are referred to the dollar amount of business involved in each area. We have allocated this energy among individual vehicles on a dollar cost basis. Thus the energy involved in repairs and maintenance for a particular auto is obtained from the appropriate factor in Table A–4 multiplied by the cost of repair and maintenance obtained from the cost model.

In estimating the energy of gasoline consumption, the amount of gasoline consumed was determined by dividing 100,000 miles of driving by the miles per gallon over the OAP cycle as determined in the design model.

NOTES TO APPENDIX A

1. "A Report on Automotive Fuel Economy," Environmental Protection Agency, Office of Air and Water Programs, Office of Mobile Source Air Pollution Control, October 1973.

2. A number of estimates are given in "Motor Vehicle Emission Standards and Fuel Economy," Congressional Hearings before the Subcommittee on Public Health and Environment of the Committee on Interstate and Foreign Commerce, December 3, 4, and 5, 1973.

3. "A Report on Automotive Fuel Economy," EPA, October 1973.

4. *Consumer Reports*, January 1973, February 1973, March 1973, April 1973, June 1973.

5. *Federal Register*, "Control of Air Pollution from New Motor Vehicles and Engines, Federal Certification Test Results for 1973 Model Year," May 2, 1973.

Table A–5. Production Energy Model

Material	Energy for Extraction Refining, Fabrication
Carbon Steel	26366 Btu/lb
Sheet Steel	27400 Btu/lb
Forging	38000 Btu/lb
Alloy Steel	27676 Btu/lb
Cast Steel	23400 Btu/lb
Cast Iron	12500 Btu/lb
Pig Iron	8332 Btu/lb
Aluminum	107,086 Btu/lb
Copper	63975 Btu/lb
Zinc Die Casting	43853 Btu/lb
Stainless	39466 Btu/lb
Glass	9125 Btu/lb
Lead	5600 Btu/lb
Steel Wire	30563 Btu/lb
Copper Wire	53108 Btu/lb
Rubber	62800 Btu/Dollar

Component	
Running Gear	27890 Btu/lb
Engine and Section	25492 Btu/lb
Transmission	22613 Btu/lb
Emission Control	27400 Btu/lb
Air Conditioning	63400 Btu/lb
Fuel System	27400 Btu/lb
Glass	9125 Btu/lb
Body	27803 Btu/lb
Battery	5600 Btu/lb
Tires	62800 Btu/Dollar
Fabrication	8580 Btu/lb
Transport of Parts and Assembly	of curb weight
TOTAL PRODUCTION ENERGY	Sum

Energy recovered from Scrap = 1850 x wt of Steel + 12,000 x wt of cast iron −144 x Curb wt

Source: R. Stephen Berry and Margaret Fulton Fels, "The Production and Consumption of Automobiles," University of Chicago, July 1972.

6. Provided under subcontract by Rath and Strong, Inc., Management Consultants.

7. *Consumer Reports*, April 1973.

8. "Cost of Operating an Automobile," Federal Highway Administration, Department of Transportation, April 1973.

Table A–6. Material Used by Component

Component	Fraction of Component Weight
Running Gear	
Carbon Steel	.52
Sheet Steel	.23
Forgings	.10
Alloy Steel	.15
Tires	
Rubber	1.00
Engine and Engine Section	
Cast Steel	.04
Cast Iron	.65
Sheet Steel	.06
Forgings	.07
Pig Iron	.02
Aluminum (cast)	.05
Copper	.07
Zinc (die castings)	.04
Transmission	
Forgings	.43
Pig Iron	.18
Cast Iron	.39
Emission Control System	
Sheet Steel	1.00
Air Conditioning	
Sheet Steel	.53
Aluminum	.35
Stainless Steel	.12
Fuel System	
Sheet Steel	1.00
Glass	
Glass	1.00
Body	
Sheet Steel	.95
Steel Wire	.03
Copper Wire	.003
Zinc (die castings)	.02
Battery	
Lead	1.00

Note: These proportions were estimated at The Rand Corporation from informatopm on weight breakdowns and materials required in the manufacture of a typical automobile.

Summary Description of Inputs for Automobile Design Measures

This appendix describes the modifications of the design model made to define the alternative design measures considered. They were applied to the basic version of the model described in Appendix A, which considered automobiles having the following design features:

No speed limit;
Bias-ply tires;
Aerodynamic cleanliness representative of 1973 model year body design;
Three speed automatic transmission;
Conventional spark ignition engines;
Conventional materials;
Gasoline fuel.

This appendix presents only the *mathematical* changes made in the model. For a short discussion of the *engineering* aspects of each design feature, and of the sources of our estimates, see Chapter Four.

SPEED LIMIT (55 MPH)

Allowance for the effects of a 55 mph speed limit is made by changing the driving cycle definition to exclude all speeds over 55 mph. While this has no effect on the Federal Driving Cycle (because in our representation of this cycle there are no speeds above 50 mph), it does affect the OAP cycle, which has speeds as high as 70 mph. In modifying this cycle, the total distance driven is held constant, but all distances originally covered at speeds above 55 mph are now covered at 55 mph.

Table B–1.   Ratio of Rolling Resistance to Gross Weight

Speed (mph)	Resistance/Weight	
	Bias-Ply Tires	Radial Tires
0	0.0154	0.0125
20	0.0162	0.0126
40	0.0173	0.0148
60	0.0188	0.0190
80	0.0206	0.0251

RADIAL TIRES

The changes used to account for radial tires are as follows:

1. The power required to overcome rolling friction is modified so that resistance at zero speed is reduced by 19 percent, with the variation of rolling resistance to gross weight ratio shown in Table B–1.
2. The weight of radial tires for a given automobile is increased 35 percent over bias-ply tires.
3. The price of radial tires on a new car is increased from 90 cents a pound to $1.29 a pound.
4. In determining the cost and energy consumed in the manufacture of the replacement tires required during a 100,000 mile lifetime, the life (in miles) of radial tires is assumed to be 2.1 times that of conventional tires.

MINOR AERODYNAMIC CHANGES

The value used for drag coefficient is reduced from 0.5, typical of present autos, to 0.38.

MAJOR AERODYNAMIC CHANGES

The value used for drag coefficient is changed to 0.25 and the body weight is increased 2.5 percent.

CONTINUOUSLY VARIABLE TRANSMISSION

1. The relation between engine rpm (as a fraction of rpm for maximum power) and road speed was changed as shown in Table B–2. This results in greater power transmitted to the wheels at a given speed and consequently greater acceleration with the CVT.

2. The expression for specific fuel consumption is changed to allow for the more favorable engine operating conditions. The comparison is shown in Table B–3.
3. The transmission weight was increased from $11\sqrt{\text{max power}}$ to $13.3\sqrt{\text{max power}}$.
4. The cost of the transmission (in dollars) was increased from $0.77 \times (\text{max power})$ to $0.96 \times (\text{max power})$.

INTERNAL COMBUSTION ENGINES

Rotary engines are handled by corrections to the weight and volume of an equivalent reciprocating engine. Rotary engine weight is 53 percent, and its volume is 84 percent, of a reciprocating engine of the same power. Carbureted versions of the rotary engine are assumed to be limited to a compression ratio of 9 (as are carbureted reciprocating engines). It is assumed here (although current mass-produced rotary engines do not achieve this) that rotary and reciprocating

Table B–2. Relationship between Engine RPM and Road Speed

| | *Rpm* | |
| | $\dfrac{Rpm}{(Rpm)_{Max\ Power}}$ | |
Road Speed (mph)	*Conventional Three Speed Automatic*	*Continuously Variable Transmission*
0	0.13	0.13
10	0.56	0.71
15	0.585	1.0
50	0.76	1.0
70	0.81	1.0

Table B–3. Relationship between Specific Fuel Consumption and Power

| | *Specific Fuel Consumption* | |
| $\dfrac{Operating\ Power}{Max\ Power}$ | $\dfrac{Specific\ Fuel\ Consumption}{Specific\ Fuel\ Consumption\ at\ Max\ Power}$ | |
	Conventional Three Speed Automatic	*Continuously Variable Transmission*
0.05	1.56	1.14
0.1	1.13	0.92
0.2	0.93	0.825
0.4	0.84	0.81
0.6	0.86	0.86
0.8	0.91	0.91
1.0	1.0	1.0

engines of the same compression ratio have the same specific fuel consumption. Rotary engines using a stratified charge and fuel injection are assumed to operate at a compression ratio of 11.

Stratified Charge Engines

1. The specific fuel consumption is 0.85 times that of a conventional spark ignition engine without emission controls, because the stratified charge engines can operate with a compression ratio of 11 compared with 9 for the conventional spark ignition engine. This results in corrections to specific fuel consumption as a function of engine size as shown in Table B–4.
2. The weight of an engine of specified power is reduced to 95 percent of a conventional spark ignition engine. This allows for the extra weight of fuel injection equipment and for the power increment obtained from the higher compression ratio.
3. The engine cost per pound is increased by 30 percent relative to a conventional spark ignition engine.

Supercharged Carbureted Engines

When supercharging (sufficient to increase the power obtained from a given displacement by 40 percent) is applied to conventional carbureted spark ignition engines, it is assumed that the compression

Table B–4. Specific Fuel Consumption as a Function of Engine Size

Max Power	*Stratified SFC* / *Reciprocating SFC* *(with 1976 emission controls)*
Less than 115 hp	0.85
140	0.94
180	0.89
Over 200	0.83

Table B–5. Supercharging Power Increases

Power / *Max Power*	*Factor by which Power Required is Increased*
0	1.0
0.2	1.3
0.4	1.23
0.6	1.15
0.8	1.07
1.0	1.0

ratio must be reduced from 9 to approximately 6 to prevent pre-ignition. To account for the effect of supercharging, we use the same relation between SFC and fraction of max power that applies to a conventional spark ignition engine, but enter this curve at a value of power that is increased over the actual power required by the factor shown in Table B–5.

1. The weight of an engine of specified power is 74 percent of the weight of a conventional spark ignition engine of the same power. This allows for the additional weight of the supercharger, which is offset by the higher power obtained from a given displacement.
2. The volume required by an engine of a specified power is 10 percent less than that of a conventional spark ignition engine of the same power.
3. The engine cost per pound is increased 10 percent over that of a conventional spark ignition engine due to the higher cost of the supercharging equipment.

Supercharged Rotary Stratified Charge Engines

When supercharging is applied to a stratified charge engine, it is assumed that pre-ignition is avoided by using fuel injection. In this case, the SFC curve for a conventional spark ignition is used but it is entered with a value of power 40 percent greater than the actual power required.

1. Engine weight is 37 percent of a conventional spark ignition engine of the same power.
2. Engine volume is 10 percent less than that of conventional spark ignition engine of the same power.
3. Engine cost per pound is 43 percent higher than for a conventional spark ignition engine, due to the cost of supercharging and fuel injection equipment. However, engine cost per horsepower is only 53 percent that of a conventional engine due to the greater horsepower per pound.

Advanced Engines

The most important variables needed to define a new engine type in the design model are engine weight, volume, specified fuel consumption at maximum power, the variation of SFC with power setting, and the variation of full throttle power with engine rpm. The values used for these quantities for the diesel, Rankine, gas turbine, and Stirling engines are summarized in Table B–6, which also

Table B–6. Engine Inputs

Engine Type	Engine Weight	Engine Volume	SFC at Max Power
		Equations for:	
Conventional spark ignition	$22.0\,P_M^{0.611}$	$0.785\,P_M^{0.624}$	$1.22\,P_M^{0.104}$
Gas turbine	$100 + 0.24\,P_M$	$4.0 + 0.06\,P_M$	$1.26\,P_M^{-0.15}$
Rankine	$23.8\,P_M^{0.672}$	$0.862\,P_M^{0.624}$	$3.70\,P_M^{-0.325}$
Stirling	$13.9\,P_M^{0.73}$	$0.865\,P_M^{0.624}$	$0.92\,P_M^{-0.104}$
Diesel	$26.1\,P_M^{0.645}$	$1.32\,P_M^{0.55}$	$0.717\,P_M^{-0.0318}$ (100 hp) $0.600\,P_M^{-0.0318}$ (200 hp)

Variation of SFC with Power Setting

$\dfrac{Power}{Max\ Power}$	$\dfrac{SFC}{SFC\ at\ Max\ Power}$				
	Conventional Spark Ignition	Gas Turbine	Rankine	Stirling	Diesel
0.05	1.56	2.15	1.00	1.35	1.35
0.10	1.13	1.60	0.78	0.96	0.99
0.20	0.93	1.20	0.76	0.76	0.83
0.40	0.84	1.02	0.82	0.70	0.82
0.60	0.86	1.00	0.88	0.70	0.86
0.80	0.91	1.00	0.94	0.74	0.91
1.00	1.00	1.00	1.00	1.00	1.00

Variation of Full Throttle Power with Rpm

$\dfrac{Rpm}{(Rpm)_{max\ power}}$	$\dfrac{Full\ Throttle\ Power}{Max\ Power}$				
	Conventional Spark Ignition	Gas Turbine	Rankine	Stirling	Diesel
0.2	0.19	0	0.32	0.19	0.19
0.4	0.41	0	0.61	0.41	0.41
0.5	0.55	0.058	0.73	0.55	0.55
0.6	0.69	0.123	0.84	0.69	0.69
0.8	0.91	0.400	0.98	0.91	0.91
1.0	1.00	1.000	1.00	1.00	1.00

includes the conventional spark ignition engine for comparison. All of the advanced engines are assumed to be equipped with continuously variable transmissions.

In addition, a number of other changes were included to allow for characteristics of particular engine types. These are as follows:

1. For the *Rankine* engine the fuel flow at idle is 0.02 × max power. The weight of the engine section is changed from 1.2 to 1.1 times the engine weight, because the condenser weight is included in the estimated engine weight and the standard auto radiator is not required. For lack of better information, the engine cost per pound is taken to be the same as for conventional spark ignition engines.
2. The cost per pound of *diesel* engines is taken as 50 percent higher than that of conventional internal combustion engines to allow for the heavier construction required by the higher operating pressures. Diesel engine maintenance, on the other hand, is reduced to 60 percent of a conventional spark ignition engine of the same power.
3. For *gas turbine* engines the fuel flow at idle is 0.055 times the engine power. The engine cost per pound is taken as $3.00 (~2.6 times the cost per pound of conventional spark ignition engine), and engine maintenance cost is reduced to 0.6 of that of a spark ignition engine of the same power.
4. For *Stirling* engines, the fuel flow during deceleration is taken as the average between that at cruise prior to deceleration and at idle. (For the other engines, fuel flow during deceleration is taken as being equal to that at idle.) This change was made to allow for the power required to pump the hydrogen working fluid from the engine into a high pressure storage container when engine power is reduced. The cost per pound of the Stirling engine is taken as twice that of a conventional spark ignition engine.

ADVANCED FUELS

Two advanced fuels—methanol and liquid hydrogen—are considered. The input quantities needed to define these fuels for the purposes of the design model are given in Table B-7, where they are compared with gasoline. It is assumed that engine efficiency is unchanged by the use of these fuels (i.e., the specific fuel consumption on a Btu basis is unchanged).

Table B-7. Inputs Describing Advanced Fuel

	Gasoline	Methanol	Liquid Hydrogen
Relative Btu/gallon	1.000	0.45	0.24
Weight of fuel system per pound of fuel (lb/lb)	0.200	0.36	6.00
Cost per pound of fuel system ($/lb)	0.850	0.85	2.00
Cost of fuel per gallon, without tax ($)	0.280	0.21	0.20
Energy of fuel extraction and refining per Btu of heat content	0.098	0.67	1.96

Appendix C

Effectiveness of Emission Controls

To assess the effects of changes in auto size and design on future air pollution, we must estimate the effectiveness of future emission control systems. At the time of the study, no combination of internal combustion engine and emission control system had been developed that would be capable of meeting the ultimate 1976 federal statutory emission standards (0.41 gm/mi of hydrocarbon, 3.4 gm/mi of carbon monixide, and 0.4 gm/mi of NO_x) for 50,000 miles of operation. Consequently, it is not possible to describe the design, weight, or cost of emission control equipment adequate to accomplish this goal.

As of January 1974, the major manufacturers had demonstrated the ability to meet the 1976 hydrocarbon and carbon monoxide requirements only for mileages of 15,000 to 25,000 miles, with one automobile meeting these requirements for 43,900 miles. The NO_x emissions, however, were over the statutory limit, but usually under 2.0 gm/mi [1]. These results were accomplished, for the most part, with systems using exhaust gas recirculation and catalytic oxidizing reactors.

Tests on a full-size auto using a stratified charge engine show similar results over a distance of 8,900 miles. Tests on stratified charge engines in the development stage indicate that they will require a catalytic converter to meet the 1976 statutory standards, although they can meet the interim standards (2.0 gm/mi of NO_x) without exhaust recirculation or catalytic converters [2].

While the hydrocarbon and carbon monoxide standards can be met with current equipment, meeting the statutory NO_x standards will require the development of additional equipment, possibly a reducing catalytic converter. However, Congress may modify the law

to allow NO_x emissions of 2.0 gm/mi, in which case further development of currently demonstrated equipment may be adequate to meet
the standards.

Consequently, we have assumed that all autos produced from
1975 on will meet, or exceed, the 1976 statutory requirements. The
weights and cost of emission control equipment required to do this
are described in Appendix B. This assumption may be somewhat
optimistic in the early years, but is expected to be a reasonable
estimate over the twenty-year period covered in our fleet mix analysis.

The approach described above is applied to all engine types that
will incur significant cost penalties to meet the emission standards.
This includes all internal combustion engines, whether they use a
stratified charge approach, are rotary or piston type design, or are
supercharged or naturally aspirated.

For the more advanced engine concepts, however, the emission
levels will be lower than the standards. The Rankine cycle engine and
the Stirling engine both promise to give substantially lower emissions
than the statutory standards, and the gas turbine may give less than
the required emission levels of hydrocarbons and carbon monoxide.
In this situation, the emissions produced should vary with the size of
the engine, approximately in proportion to the airflow required and,
to be useful for our purposes, should be integrated over an appropriate driving cycle. The data available on these engines, however, is not
sufficient to allow a trend with engine size to be determined. For
example, data from different sources on engines of the same basic
type, but of different specific designs, show a scatter large enough to
mask any size effect. Consequently, a single value of grams per mile
was determined for each engine type regardless of size.

The data used in estimating the emissions of various engine types
are summarized in Table C-1. The grams per mile values selected for
each engine type are given in Table C-2. It will be noted that somewhat higher emissions have been selected for the Stirling than for the
Rankine engine, although, since both are external combustion
engines, they might be expected to have the same emissions. It is not
intended to imply that the Rankine has lower emissions than the
Stirling. Table C-1 shows that different references on the Rankine
engine give values that bracket those selected for the Stirling engine
and that Reference 8 would have justified a lower set of estimates for
the Stirling. The values from Reference 7 were selected to represent
the Stirling, because they represent the goals of the Ford-Philips
development program.

Because our study is not primarily a study of emissions, it was felt
to be highly desirable to combine the emissions of various species

Table C-1. Emission Characteristics of Advanced Engines

	Grams per Mile			
Engine Type	*Hydrocarbons*	*Carbon Monoxide*	*Oxides of Nitrogen*	*References*
Diesel	0.100	0.500	1.000	(1)
Rankine	0.410	3.500	0.400	(2)
	0.056	0.333	0.137	(3)
	0.170	0.210	0.275	(4)
	0.130	0.200	0.260	(5)
Gas Turbine	0.120	0.700	0.400	(5)
	0.2–0.61	0.7–2.11	0.2–2.86	(6)
Stirling	0.040	0.100	0.260	(1)
	0.200	1.100	0.150	(7)
	0.100	0.310	0.170	(8)

(1) *Final Report Hybrid Heat Engine/Electric Systems Study, Vol. I*, The Aerospace Corporation, prepared for Division of Advanced Automotive Power Systems Development, U.S. Environmental Protection Agency, June 1971.
(2) System Presentation, Scientific Energy Systems Corporation, June 1973.
(3) *Organic Rankine Cycle Automotive Propulsion System Turbine Expander*, Aerojet Liquid Rocket Company, June 1973.
(4) *Rankine Cycle Power System with Organic-Based Working Fluid and Reciprocating Expander for Passenger Vehicles*, Presentation Material for Eighth Rankine Cycle Contractors Meeting, Ann Arbor, Michigan, Thermo Electric Corporation, June 5–6, 1973.
(5) *A Technology Assessment of the Transition to Advanced Automotive Propulsion Systems*, HIT–541 (Draft), Hittman Associates, Inc., November 1972.
(6) *Energy/Environmental Factors in Transportation 1975–1990*, The MITRE Corporation, April 1973.
(7) Norman D. Postma (Ford Motor Company), Rob Van Giessel, and Fritz Reinink (N. V. Philips, Holland), *The Stirling Engine for Passenger Car Applications*, SAE 730648, June 1973.
(8) C.B.S. Alm, S.G. Carlqvist, P.F. Kulmann, K.H. Silverqvist, and F.A. Zacharias, *Environmental Characteristics of Stirling Engines and their Present State of Development in Germany and Sweden*, presented at the International Congress on Conbustion Engines (CIMAC), Washington, D.C., April 1973.

Table C-2. Selected Emission Rates for Advanced Engines

	Grams per Mile		
Engine Type	*Hydrocarbons*	*Carbon Monoxide*	*Oxides of Nitrogen*
Internal Combustion (ultimate statutory 1976 standards)	0.41	3.4	0.40
(Interim 1976 standards)	0.41	3.4	2.00
Diesel	0.10	0.5	1.00
Rankine	0.13	0.2	0.26
Gas Turbine	0.12	0.7	0.40
Stirling	0.20	1.1	0.15

into one number that could serve as a relative index of total emissions. Past attempts to do this have not met with general acceptance, because different emissions species have different effects on the health and comfort of human beings, and their absolute and relative effects on health are still poorly understood [3]. However, three weighting schemes that have been proposed in the past were examined to see whether they would lead to a usable index number. The weighting schemes used were those proposed by Caretto and Sawyer, Babcock and Nagda, and Walthers. The weights employed by these authors are given in Table C-3.

We first applied these weighting factors to the federal statutory standards for 1976 and to the interim 1976 federal standards (these are the same as the 1976 statutory standards except that the NO_x requirement is relaxed to 2.0 grams per mile). The factors were then applied to the emission estimates for new engine types given in Table C-2. Two sets of emission index ratios were formed relating each engine type to the internal combustion engine—one based on the assumption that the internal combustion engine meets the 1976 statutory standards, and one based on the assumption that it meets the interim 1976 standards. The ratios thus obtained are shown in Table C-4.

In all cases the spread between weighting systems in a particular engine type is less than a factor of three, and in most cases, the spread is less than 50 percent. In view of the subjective nature of the weighting process, the uncertainty of much of the emission data on new engines, and the uncertainty of the actual fleet performance of emission control equipment for internal combustion engines, this level of agreement seems adequate for the purposes of this study.

Because the Caretto–Sawyer system gives results that are intermediate between those obtained from the two other systems in every case, it was chosen for use in the analysis of fleet emissions made here. However, in our screening analysis of new engine types we consider the sensitivity of our results to the weighting scheme used.

In addition to estimating the emissions resulting from the introduction of new engine types, it is necessary to estimate emissions

Table C-3. Specie Weighting Factors

	Specie		
Weighting System	Hydrocarbons	Carbon Monoxide	Oxides of Nitrogen
Caretto and Sawyer	62	1.0	44
Babcock and Nagda	10	1.0	24
Walthers	124	1.0	22

Table C–4. Ratio of Weighted Emissions

Engine Type	Ratio to Federal 1976 Statutory Requirements			Ratio to Federal 1976 Interim Requirements		
	Caretto–Sawyer	*Babcock–Nagda*	*Walthers*	*Caretto–Sawyer*	*Babcock–Nagda*	*Walthers*
Internal Conbustion	1.00	1.00	1.00	1.00	1.00	1.00
Diesel	1.09	1.49	0.55	0.43	0.46	0.55
Gas Turbine	0.56	0.67	0.39	0.22	0.21	0.25
Stirling	0.43	0.39	0.46	0.18	0.12	0.30
Rankine	0.42	0.45	0.35	0.17	0.14	0.22

that will be produced by the fleet already in existence at the beginning of the time period of the study (1975). This was done using the MOVEC emission model developed at The Rand Corporation [4]. The model produced overall fleet average grams per mile of each specie from 1960 to 1973 and a set of predicted values for 1974.

In the Fleet Mix Model used in this study, the initially existing fleet is treated on an overall average basis, with a single average value of emissions per mile being used to represent the entire existing fleet. It was recognized, however, that older cars, with the highest emission levels, will be the first to be retired from the fleet. Thus, it was clearly not appropriate to use the 1974 average emission values as representing the fleet in the future.

After all cars manufactured before the start of 1975 have been retired, the remaining cars will meet the 1974 emission standards. About 90 percent of the 1975 fleet will be retired in ten years. Thus, by 1985, the cars remaining from the initial fleet will meet the 1974 emission standards.

Based on this reasoning, the emission characteristics of the fleet at the end of 1974 were averaged with the 1974 standards to obtain an average estimate of the emissions of the initial fleet from 1975 to 1985. No modification of this average was made for the years after 1985, because such a small fraction of the initial fleet will remain. As with the advanced engine emissions, the various species were combined into a single emissions index using the Caretto–Sawyer weighting factors. The values used are summarized in Table C–5.

Table C–5.   Initial Auto Fleet Emissions

	Specie			
	Hydro-carbons	Carbon Monoxide	Oxides of Nitrogen	Caretto–Sawyer Weighting
1974 Fleet as Predicted by the Rand MOVEC Model	6.5	45.4	2.9	575
1974 Federal Standards	2.6	23.0	3.1	320
Average Value Used to Represent the Initial Fleet in 1975[a]				448

[a]Reduced to 438 in 1976 and 429 in 1977 to allow for the introduction of radial tires.

NOTES TO APPENDIX C

1. *Third Quarterly Report on the Effort and Progress of the Vehicle Manufacturers on Meeting the 1976 and 1976 Model Year Exhaust Emission Standards*, State of California Air Resources Board, January 9, 1974.

2. "Symposium on Low Pollution Power Systems Development," NATO Document No. 32, October 1973.

3. Lyndon R. Babcock, Jr. and Niren L. Nagda, "Cost Effectiveness of Emission Control," *Journal of the Air Pollution Control Association*, March 1973.

4. W. T. Mikolowsky, *Vehicle Emission and Cost Model (MOVEC): Model Description and Illustrative Applications*, R–1364–SD, The Rand Corporation (Appendix 2), December 1973.

Appendix D

Summary Description of the Automobile Fleet Mix Model

DETERMINATION OF AUTO FLEET MIX

The Automobile Fleet Mix Model determines the mix of the auto fleet each year from 1975 to 1995 by use of the equation:

$$n_{wiy} = n_{wi(y-1)} + \theta_{wy}\beta_{wiy}P_y - \sum_{j=0}^{18} KS_j(\theta_w\beta_{wi}P_y)_y + N_{F(y-1)}[1 - KS_y],$$

where n_{wiy} = Number of autos in the fleet at the end of the year y in weight class w with technological features i;

θ_{wy} = Fraction of the annual production (in year y) in weight class w;

β_{wiy} = Fraction of the production (in year y) in weight class w with technological features i;

P_y = Total annual production in year y;

K = Scrappage rate correction factor to allow for the difference between anticipated scrappage rates and those based on past experience;

S_j = Fraction of autos of age j scrapped in their j^{th} year;

n_{Fy} = Number of autos in the original fleet (i.e., the fleet existing at the start of 1975), remaining at the end of year y;

S_y = Fraction of the original fleet retired in year y if retirement occurred at a rate typical of past experience.

The total number of cars at the end of year y is obtained by summing over w and i.

The annual production and scrappage rates in future years are both estimated by the NAV model described in Chapter Three and Appendix E. The values of θ and β, which define the nature of each year's production in terms of weight class and technological features, are inputs to the Fleet Mix model used to define each case. The values of S, the scrappage rate based on past experience [1], are tabulated in Table D–1.

The number of autos remaining from the original fleet (n_{Fy}) was determined by applying the scrappage rates, based on past experience, to the fleet estimated to exist in 1975. The fleet at the start of 1975 was estimated by the NAV Model to consist of a total of 90,794,000 autos, and the breakdown of the fleet by age was estimated [2] and tabulated in Table D–1.

The resulting decay of the 1975 fleet, plotted in Figure D–1, shows an almost linear decay for the first eight years, at which time only about 20 percent of the original fleet remains. Decay rates then decline; the number of autos from the original fleet in use after ten years is relatively small, and only a few autos remain after eighteen years.

The scrappage rate values used are modified by the factor K to conform the *overall* fleet scrappage rate with that estimated and the NAV Model. (Note that the aggregate NAV Model specifies the *total* scrappage rate but does not deal with the scrappage rates disaggre-

Table D–1. Scrappage Rates Based on Past Experience and Age Distribution in 1975 Fleet

Age of Auto	Fraction of Fleet at the Start of the Year that Is Scrapped during the Year (S_j)	Estimated Fraction of Autos by Age at the Start of 1975
1	0.005	0.126
2	0.010	0.120
3	0.020	0.115
4	0.040	0.110
5	0.080	0.101
6	0.080	0.090
7	0.100	0.078
8	0.120	0.065
9	0.110	0.053
10	0.090	0.041
11	0.120	0.031
12	0.060	0.023
13	0.060	0.016
14	0.050	0.012
15	0.030	0.009
16	0.015	0.005
17	0.008	0.004
18	0.002	0.001

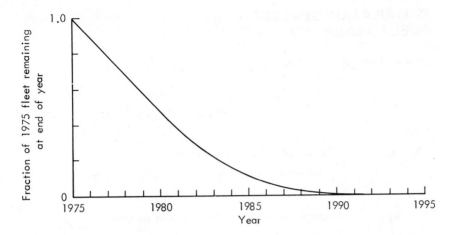

Figure D–1. Decay of 1975 Fleet.

gated by age of auto.) The value of K is determined by first calculating the overall scrappage rate for the fleet in a particular year assuming that scrappage rates based on past experience apply. This overall fleet scrappage rate is determined as

$$S_y = \frac{n_{y-1} + P_y - n_y}{n_{y-1}},$$

when n_y is calculated using K = 1.0. The value of K is then determined as α_y/S_y, where α_y is the inferred scrappage rate from the NAV Model.

DETERMINATION OF AUTO FLEET PROPERTIES

Once the mix of autos in the fleet is determined as a function of time, the calculation of annual emissions, cost of ownership, annual and cumulative fuel consumption, and annual energy consumed is determined from per-vehicle results obtained from the design model. It was necessary to modify these results to allow for the variations in annual vehicle miles traveled (obtained from NAV Model) and in the cost of fuel,[a] which was varied to assess the effects of various gasoline tax levels. This modification was accomplished by making approximate corrections to the design model outputs.

[a]The results obtained from the design model are based on an average of 10,000 miles a year per vehicle and a fuel cost of 27 cents per callon, plus tax.

CALCULATION OF FLEET
FUEL CONSUMPTION

The annual gallons of fuel used is calculated as:

$$g_y = \sum_{w,i} \frac{(VMT_y/n_y)}{mpg_{wi}} n_{wiy} + \frac{(VMT_y/n_y)}{mpg_{F_y}} n_{F_y},$$

where g_y = Gallons of fuel consumed by the fleet in year y;

VMT_y = Total vehicle miles driven by the fleet in year y;

n_y = Total number of vehicles in the fleet in year y;

n_{F_y} = Number of vehicles in 1975 fleet remaining in year y;

n_{wiy} = Number of vehicles in weight group w with technological features i;

mpg_{wi} = Miles per gallon of autos in weight group w with technological features i;

mpg_{F_y} = Miles per gallon of autos in the 1975 fleet.

The quantity VMT_y was input from the NAV Model result, and the mpg quantity was obtained from the appropriate design model result.

The existing (1975) fleet was represented by a single average value of 13.9 miles per gallon; however, this value was modified in 1976 and 1977 as owners of autos five years old or less (about 57 percent of the 1975 fleet) converted to radial tires over a two-year period as their present tires wore out. It was assumed that owners of older cars would not convert to radials. This resulted in an increase in miles per gallon to 14.1 in 1976 and 14.5 in 1977. Thereafter, the miles per gallon of the original fleet did not vary.

CALCULATION OF FLEET EMISSIONS

Annual emissions are calculated from the equation:

$$E_y = \frac{1.1}{10^6} \sum_{w,i} \left(e_{wi}(VMT_y/n_y) n_{wiy} \right) + \frac{1.1}{10^6} e_f n_f(VMT_y/n_y),$$

where E_y = Emissions in year y, expressed in equivalent tons of carbon monoxide by the Caretto–Sawyer weighting system;

e_{wi} = Emissions in gm/mi of vehicles in weight class w, with technological features i;

VMT_y = Total vehicle miles driven in year y;

n_y = Total number of autos in the fleet in year y;

n_{wiy} = Number of autos in weight class w with technological features i in year y;

e_F = Average emissions in gm/mi of the autos in the existing fleet;

n_F = Number of autos in the original fleet that remain in the year y.

The values of e_{wi} represent per-vehicle emission values for autos equipped with emission control equipment to allow them to meet the 1976 statutory standards. Using the Caretto–Sawyer weighting system,[b] the value is found to be $e_{wi} = 46.4$.

The 1975 fleet is made up of old cars having high emissions and relatively few late model cars that meet the 1973 and 1974 standards. As explained in Appendix C, Table C–5, a value for e_F of 448 is used in 1975, and this is reduced to 438 in 1976 and to 429 in 1977 to allow for the replacement of conventional tires. Beyond that time, it is held constant.

CALCULATION OF FLEET ANNUAL COST

The annual cost of operating the fleet is obtained from the equation:

$$C_y = \sum_{w,i} (c_{wi} n_{wiy}) + C_F n_F,$$

where C_y = Total cost of operating the fleet in year y;

C_{wi} = Annual cost of a single auto of weight class w with technological features i;

n_{wiy} = Number of autos of weight class w and technological features i in year y;

C_F = Average per vehicle cost of operation for autos in the 1975 fleet;

n_F = Number of autos in 1975 fleet that remain in the fleet in the year y.

The quantity C_{wi}, individual vehicle annual cost, was based on the results of the design model which applied to an annual driving distance of 10,000 miles per vehicle and a fuel cost of 38 cents per

[b]See Appendix C for a discussion of values used for per-vehicle emissions and of emission weighting systems.

gallon. Examination of the outputs of the design model indicated that about 57 percent of the annual cost of ownership is independent of the number of miles driven or the cost of fuel, about 23 percent (primarily repair and maintenance) varies with the amount of driving, but not with the fuel consumed, and about 20 percent varies with the price and amount of fuel consumed. Thus the per-vehicle annual cost of ownership was obtained from the design model results by:

$$C_{wi} = \left[0.57 + 0.23 \left(\frac{VMT_y}{n_y \times 10,000} \right) + 0.20 \left(\frac{VMT_y}{n_y \times 10,000} \right) \left(\frac{f}{0.38} \right) \right] C'_{wi},$$

where C'_{wi} = Annual cost of ownership obtained from the design model for 10,000 miles of driving and a fuel cost of 38 cents per gallon;

f = Fuel price per gallon (dollars);

VMT_y = Total fleet vehicle miles driven in year y;

n_y = Total number of autos in the fleet in year y.

Autos in the original 1975 fleet were handled differently, because their procurement costs had been sunk before the time period we consider (1975–1995). Examination of the design model results indicated that the recurring costs (operation plus lost interest) were about 75 percent of the total. Thus, for the 1975 fleet, the annual cost became:

$$C_F = \left[0.32 + 0.23 \left(\frac{VMT_y}{n_y \times 10,000} \right) + 0.20 \left(\frac{VMT_y}{n_y \times 10,000} \right) \left(\frac{f}{0.38} \right) \right] C'_F,$$

where C'_F = Average annual cost of autos in the 1975 fleet as predicted by the design model (this value was $1130);

f = Fuel price per gallon (dollars).

The cost of fuel used was based on the NAV Model estimate of 67 cents per gallon at the start of 1975, of which 4 cents was federal tax and 7 cents was state tax. The value was modified to allow for inflation effects on the base fuel price and for (input) variations in federal tax rate. The fuel cost was thus expressed as:

$$f_y = 0.56I_y + 0.11 + T_y,$$

where f_y = Fuel price per gallon (dollars) in year y;

I_y = Inflation factor; the number of dollars in year y required to obtain the same purchasing power as a dollar in 1975;

T_y = *Incremental* tax per gallon (dollars).

The values used for the inflation factor I_y are determined from the following schedule of inflation rates: 1976, 5.5 percent; 1977, 4.8 percent; 1978, 4.1 percent; 1979, 3.4 percent; 1980 (and beyond), 2.6 percent.

CALCULATION OF FLEET ENERGY CONSUMPTION

The total annual energy consumed by the automobile fleet is determined as:

$$\Phi y = \sum_{w,i} \frac{\Phi_{wi}}{10} n_{wiy} + n_{F_y} \frac{\Phi_f}{10}$$

where Φ_y = Annual energy consumed by the fleet (millions of Btu);

Φ_{wi} = Lifetime (ten years) energy consumed by a single vehicle in weight class w with technological features i;

n_{wiy} = Number of vehicles in weight class w with technological features i in year y;

n_{F_y} = Number of vehicles in the 1975 fleet that are still in operation in the year y;

Φ_f = Average annual energy consumed by vehicles in the 1975 fleet.

The values of Φ_{wi} are the per-vehicle lifetime (ten years) energy requirements as given by the appropriate design model case. The value Φ_F was obtained by averaging results from the design model for the types of autos in the current fleet. This led to a value of 1,310 million Btu per vehicle in 1975. The introduction of radial tires reduced this to 1,295 million Btu in 1976 and to 1,278 million Btu in 1977. Thereafter it remains constant.

Table D–2. Inputs Defining the Original Fleet *(Total number of autos in fleet on January 1, 1975: 90, 794, 000)*

	1975	1976	1977 and on
Average Miles per Gallon	13.9	14.1	14.5
Emission Index (Caretto–Sawyer Weighting System)	448	438	429
Average Per-Vehicle Annual Cost of Ownership (dollars)	1130	1121	1112
Total Annual Energy Consumed per Vehicle (million Btu)	1310	1294	1278

INPUTS FOR SPECIFIC CASES

The inputs used to define the cases described in Chapters Five and Seven are given here. The real world situations these inputs represent are discussed in those sections.

All of the inputs for the *1975 fleet* are the same in all cases, with the exception of the scrappage rate, which is adjusted to make the overall fleet scrappage rate equal to that obtained from the NAV Model. The remaining inputs that define the original fleet are shown in Table D–2.

INPUTS OF PRODUCTION, SCRAPPAGE RATE, VEHICLE MILES, AND TAX INCREMENT

The input values for annual production, scrappage rate, vehicle miles, and tax increment for all the cases considered are shown in Table D–3. It can be seen that these quantities are the same for all the cases considered in Chapter Five; (the Base Case plus Cases A through I). Further, these same production inputs apply to Cases 1, 2, and 3 in Chapter Seven.

The values of θ define the fraction of the year's production in each weight class. The values of β define the breakdown of each weight class in autos having differing technical features.

The weight classes considered are summarized as follows:

Φ_{SCO}, Subcompact; $\quad$ Φ_{FUL}, Full-size;

Φ_{COM}, Compact; $\quad$ Φ_{RSC}, Trunkless subcompact;

Φ_{INT}, Intermediate; $\quad$ Φ_{2PX}, Two passenger vehicle.

Table D–3. Input Values of Production, Scrappage Rates, Vehicle Miles, and Tax Increment

| Year | Chapter Five, Base Case + Case A through I | | | Case 1, 2, 4[a] | Case 1 | | Case 2 | | Case 4 | |
	Annual Production (million vehicles)	Scrappage Rate	Annual Vehicle Miles (billion miles)	Annual Production (million vehicles)	Scrappage Rate	Annual Vehicle Miles (billion miles)	Scrappage Rate	Annual Vehicle Miles (billion miles)	Scrappage Rate	Annual Vehicle Miles (billion miles)
1975	10.62	0.139	787	10.62	0.140	781		781		781
1976	11.78	0.109	805	11.78	0.110	814		811		814
1977	12.68	0.098	836	12.68	0.099	865		860		865
1978	13.38	0.095	871	13.38	0.095	914		904		914
1979	14.02	0.092	911	14.02	0.093	971		953		971
1980	14.74	0.090	953	14.74	0.090	1033	Same as Case 1	1009	Same as Case 1	1038
1981	15.05	0.092	993	15.05	0.092	1092		1071		1109
1982	15.38	0.092	1032	15.38	0.093	1151		1135		1184
1983	15.78	0.092	1070	15.78	0.092	1209		1206		1269
1984	16.24	0.091	1109	16.24	0.092	1267		1284		1363
1985	16.72	0.091	1149	16.72	0.091	1321		1373		1460
1986	17.29	0.091	1188	17.29	0.091	1376		1461		1561
1987	17.70	0.091	1227	17.70	0.092	1427		1549		1659
1988	18.15	0.091	1266	18.15	0.092	1479		1632		1754
1989	18.64	0.091	1306	18.64	0.091	1529		1718		1854
1990	19.11	0.090	1346	19.11	0.091	1576		1803		1945
1991	19.73	0.087	1387	19.73	0.091	1627		1882		2034
1992	20.17	0.090	1428	20.17	0.090	1675		1957		2115
1993	20.66	0.090	1469	20.66	0.090	1723		2032		2195
1994	21.18	0.089	1510	21.18	0.090	1772		2102		2271
1995	21.72	0.089	1553	21.72	0.090	1826		2167		2344

Table D–3. continued

	Case 5a				Case 5b			
Year	Annual Production (million vehicles)	Scrappage Rate	Annual Vehicle Miles (billion miles)	Tax Increment (dollars per gallon)	Annual Production (million vehicles)	Scrappage Rate	Annual Vehicle Miles (billion miles)	Tax Increment (dollars per gallon)
1975	9.06	0.216	669	0.15	7.51	0.292	571	0.30
1976	11.39	0.137	676	0.15	11.00	0.173	566	0.30
1977	12.56	0.112	706	0.15	12.45	0.129	594	0.30
1978	13.32	0.104	742	0.15	13.26	0.116	631	0.30
1979	13.97	0.101	782	0.15	13.92	0.111	671	0.30
1980	14.67	0.098	824	0.15	14.61	0.109	721	0.30
1981	14.98	0.100	864	0.15	14.92	0.109	751	0.30
1982	15.32	0.100	902	0.15	15.26	0.109	790	0.30
1983	15.72	0.099	940	0.15	15.65	0.107	827	0.30
1984	16.18	0.098	979	0.15	16.12	0.105	867	0.30
1985	16.66	0.097	1019	0.15	16.60	0.104	906	0.30
1986	17.24	0.097	1059	0.15	17.18	0.103	946	0.30
1987	17.64	0.096	1098	0.15	17.59	0.103	985	0.30
1988	18.09	0.096	1138	0.15	18.04	0.102	1025	0.30
1989	18.58	0.096	1178	0.15	18.53	0.101	1065	0.30
1990	19.06	0.095	1219	0.15	19.01	0.100	1106	0.30
1991	19.68	0.094	1260	0.15	19.63	0.099	1148	0.30
1992	20.13	0.094	1302	0.15	20.09	0.099	1190	0.30
1993	20.61	0.094	1343	0.15	20.57	0.098	1232	0.30
1994	21.13	0.093	1386	0.15	21.09	0.097	1275	0.30
1995	21.67	0.093	1429	0.15	21.63	0.096	1319	0.30

Table D-3. continued

Year	Case 5c				Case 6			
	Annual Production (million vehicles)	Scrappage Rate	Annual Vehicle Miles (billion miles)	Tax Increment (dollars per gallon)	Annual Production (million vehicles)	Scrappage Rate	Annual Vehicle Miles (billion miles)	Tax Increment (dollars per gallon)
1975	7.00	0.374	484	0.45	9.81	0.210	662.8	0.140
1976	10.65	0.216	469	0.45	11.52	0.130	691.0	0.126
1977	12.34	0.152	495	0.45	12.76	0.100	752.0	0.112
1978	13.20	0.132	532	0.45	13.50	0.093	813.0	0.098
1979	13.86	0.125	572	0.45	14.16	0.090	882.0	0.084
1980	14.54	0.122	613	0.45	14.87	0.087	956.0	0.078
1981	14.86	0.122	652	0.45	15.10	0.092	1019.0	0.066
1982	15.20	0.119	690	0.45	15.50	0.089	1091.0	0.052
1983	15.59	0.118	727	0.45	15.90	0.088	1162.0	0.038
1984	16.09	0.115	766	0.45	16.40	0.087	1236.0	0.024
1985	16.53	0.113	805	0.45	16.90	0.082	1307.0	0.010
1986	17.13	0.111	845	0.45	17.40	0.084	1374.0	0
1987	17.54	0.110	884	0.45	17.70	0.090	1427.0	0
1988	17.99	0.109	924	0.45	18.20	0.091	1479.0	0
1989	18.47	0.108	964	0.45	18.60	0.091	1529.0	0
1990	18.96	0.106	1005	0.45	19.10	0.090	1576.0	0
1991	19.58	0.104	1047	0.45	19.70	0.090	1627.0	0
1992	20.05	0.103	1090	0.45	20.20	0.090	1675.0	0
1993	20.52	0.103	1132	0.45	20.70	0.090	1723.0	0
1994	21.04	0.101	1175	0.45	21.20	0.089	1772.0	0
1995	21.58	0.101	1219	0.45	21.70	0.089	1826.0	0

Table D–3. continued

	Case 7				Case 8			
Year	Annual Production (million vehicles)	Scrappage Rate	Annual Vehicle Miles (billion miles)	Tax Increment (dollars per gallon)	Annual Production (million vehicles)	Scrappage Rate	Annual Vehicle Miles (billion miles)	Tax Increment (dollars per gallon)
1975	7.43	0.296	546.3	0.31	6.49	0.342	492.7	0.410
1976	11.07	0.170	556.0	0.30	10.75	0.200	490.8	0.400
1977	12.55	0.122	602.3	0.29	12.42	0.141	532.4	0.395
1978	13.37	0.109	652.1	0.28	13.26	0.124	579.6	0.385
1979	14.03	0.104	705.3	0.27	13.95	0.116	634.6	0.380
1980	14.74	0.101	764.4	0.26	14.81	0.102	707.5	0.360
1981	15.04	0.102	828.0	0.25	15.05	0.106	777.6	0.345
1982	15.38	0.101	894.0	0.24	15.44	0.103	857.1	0.325
1983	15.79	0.099	966.6	0.23	16.00	0.094	957.4	0.290
1984	16.24	0.098	1050.5	0.22	16.26	0.100	1049.2	0.280
1985	16.92	0.089	1153.3	0.19	16.83	0.095	1155.0	0.260
1986	17.55	0.087	1264.7	0.16	17.59	0.086	1284.0	0.232
1987	17.98	0.086	1380.5	0.13	17.79	0.094	1388.4	0.210
1988	18.44	0.084	1496.6	0.10	18.27	0.092	1497.7	0.190
1989	18.94	0.084	1617.0	0.07	18.85	0.088	1623.4	0.160
1990	19.43	0.082	1740.7	0.04	19.36	0.086	1747.2	0.130
1991	20.06	0.081	1861.2	0.01	20.16	0.080	1894.3	0.090
1992	20.34	0.087	1954.4	0	20.45	0.084	2010.8	0.06
1993	20.70	0.089	2030.9	0	20.99	0.082	2138.6	0.035
1994	21.19	0.089	2101.5	0	21.51	0.081	2264.3	0
1995	21.72	0.090	2167.3	0	21.79	0.087	2342.2	0

Note: If no tax increment is specified, it is zero.

aCase 3 is the same as Case 2, but is interpreted differently (see Chapter Seven). Case 3a and 3b use the same production, scrappage rates, and vehicle miles as Case 2.

Two things are required to define the β's: a number, which is the fraction of a particular weight class equipped with a specified technical feature, and a description of the technical feature.

The θ's and β's used in each case are defined below.

Base Case.   Both β's and θ's are constant for all years.

Φ_{SCO}	0.28	Φ_{INT}	0.18
$\beta_{(1)}$	0.78	$\beta_{(1)}$	0.35
$\beta_{(2)}$	0.22	$\beta_{(2)}$	0.65
Φ_{COM}	0.17	Φ_{FUL}	0.37
$\beta_{(1)}$	0.71	$\beta_{(1)}$	0.09
$\beta_{(2)}$	0.29	$\beta_{(2)}$	0.91

$\beta_{(1)}$ = Conventional engine spark ignition engine,
Radial tires,
Standard three speed automatic transmission,
No air conditioning,
55 mph speed limit;

$\beta_{(2)}$ = Same as $\beta_{(1)}$ except with air conditioning.

Case A. θ's and β's are the same as the Base Case, except that the β's include minor aerodynamic changes.

Case B. β's are the same as Case A.

	1975	1976	1977	1978	1979	1980 and on
Φ_{SCO}	0.28	0.35	0.42	0.49	0.55	0.62
Φ_{COM}	0.17	0.21	0.25	0.29	0.34	0.38
Φ_{INT}	0.18	0.14	0.11	0.07	0.04	0
Φ_{FUL}	0.37	0.30	0.22	0.15	0.07	0

Case C.

	1979 and Earlier	1980	1981	1982	1983	1984 and on
Φ_{SCO}	0.28	0.28	0.28	0.28	0.28	0.28
$\beta_{(1)}$	0.78	0.63	0.47	0.31	0.15	0
$\beta_{(2)}$	0.22	0.17	0.13	0.09	0.05	0
$\beta_{(3)}$	0	0.16	0.32	0.48	0.64	0.80
$\beta_{(4)}$	0	0.04	0.08	0.12	0.16	0.20
Φ_{COM}	0.17	0.17	0.17	0.17	0.17	0.17
$\beta_{(1)}$	0.71	0.57	0.43	0.29	0.15	0
$\beta_{(2)}$	0.29	0.23	0.17	0.11	0.05	0
$\beta_{(3)}$	0	0.14	0.28	0.42	0.56	0.70
$\beta_{(4)}$	0	0.06	0.12	0.18	0.24	0.30
Φ_{INT}	0.18	0.18	0.18	0.18	0.18	0.18
$\beta_{(1)}$	0.35	0.28	0.21	0.14	0.07	0
$\beta_{(2)}$	0.65	0.52	0.39	0.26	0.13	0
$\beta_{(3)}$	0	0.07	0.14	0.21	0.28	0.35
$\beta_{(4)}$	0	0.13	0.26	0.39	0.52	0.65
Φ_{FUL}	0.37	0.37	0.37	0.37	0.37	0.37
$\beta_{(1)}$	0.09	0.07	0.05	0.04	0.02	0
$\beta_{(2)}$	0.91	0.73	0.55	0.36	0.18	0
$\beta_{(3)}$	0	0.02	0.04	0.06	0.08	0.09
$\beta_{(4)}$	0	0.18	0.36	0.54	0.72	0.91

$\beta_{(1)}$ = Conventional spark ignition engine,
Radial tires,
Minor aerodynamic improvements,
Standard three speed automatic transmission,
No air conditioning,
55 mph speed limit;

$\beta_{(2)}$ = Same as $\beta_{(1)}$ except with air conditioning;

$\beta_{(3)}$ = Same as $\beta_{(1)}$ but with continuously variable transmission;

$\beta_{(4)}$ = Same as $\beta_{(3)}$ except with air conditioning.

Case D. θ's and β's are the same as Case C except that β's are redefined as follows:

$\beta_{(1)}$ = Conventional spark ignition,
Radial tires,
Minor aerodynamic improvements,
Standard three speed automatic transmission,
No air conditioning,
55 mph speed limit;

$\beta_{(2)}$ = Same as $\beta_{(1)}$ except with air conditioning;

$\beta_{(3)}$ = Same as $\beta_{(1)}$ except for a supercharged stratified rotary engine and a continuously variable transmission;

$\beta_{(4)}$ = Same as $\beta_{(3)}$ but with air conditioning.

Case E. θ's are the same as for Case B; β's are the same as for Case C.

Case F. θ's prior to 1980 are the same as for Case B, except θ_{2PX} is added; β's are the same as for Case C except $\beta_{(5)}$ is added.

	1980	*1981 and on*
θ_{SCO}	0.47	0.32
θ_{COM}	0.38	0.38
θ_{INT}	0	0
θ_{FUL}	0	0
θ_{2PX}	0.15	0.30
(zero prior to 1980)		
$\beta_{(5)}$	1.0	1.0

$\beta_{(5)}$ = Conventional spark ignition engine,
Radial tires,
Minor aerodynamic improvements,
Continuously variable transmission,
No air conditioning,
55 mph speed limit.

Case G. θ's are the same as for Case B; β's are the same as for Case D.

Case H.

	1984 and Before	1985	1986	1987	1988	1989 and on
θ_{SCO}	0.28	0.28	0.28	0.28	0.28	0.28
$\beta_{(1)}$	0.78	0.63	0.47	0.31	0.15	0
$\beta_{(2)}$	0.22	0.17	0.13	0.09	0.05	0
$\beta_{(3)}$	0	0.16	0.32	0.48	0.64	0.80
$\beta_{(4)}$	0	0.04	0.08	0.12	0.16	0.20
θ_{COM}	0.17	0.17	0.17	0.17	0.17	0.17
$\beta_{(1)}$	0.71	0.57	0.43	0.29	0.15	0
$\beta_{(2)}$	0.29	0.23	0.17	0.11	0.05	0
$\beta_{(3)}$	0	0.14	0.28	0.42	0.56	0.70
$\beta_{(4)}$	0	0.06	0.12	0.18	0.24	0.30
θ_{INT}	0.18	0.18	0.18	0.18	0.18	0.18
$\beta_{(1)}$	0.35	0.28	0.21	0.14	0.07	0
$\beta_{(2)}$	0.65	0.52	0.39	0.26	0.13	0
$\beta_{(3)}$	0	0.07	0.14	0.21	0.28	0.35
$\beta_{(4)}$	0	0.13	0.26	0.39	0.52	0.65
θ_{FUL}	0.37	0.37	0.37	0.37	0.37	0.37
$\beta_{(1)}$	0.09	0.07	0.05	0.04	0.02	0
$\beta_{(2)}$	0.91	0.73	0.55	0.36	0.18	0
$\beta_{(3)}$	0	0.02	0.04	0.06	0.08	0.09
$\beta_{(4)}$	0	0.18	0.36	0.54	0.72	0.91

$\beta_{(1)}$ and $\beta_{(2)}$ have the same technical features as $\beta_{(1)}$ and $\beta_{(2)}$ in Case A.

$\beta_{(3)}$ = Stirling engine using gasoline fuel,
   Radial tires,
   Minor aerodynamic improvements,
   Continuously variable transmission,
   No air conditioning,
   55 mph speed limit;

$\beta_{(4)}$ = Same as $\beta_{(3)}$ except with air conditioning.

Case I. θ's are the same as Case B; β's are the same as Case H.

Case 1. θ's and β's are the same as for Case B.

Case 2. θ's and β's are the same as for Case D.

Case 3a. All inputs are the same as Case 2.

Case 3b. β's are the same as for Case A except $\beta_{(3)}$ is added for two passenger cars without air conditioning.

	1979 and Before	1980	1981	1982	1983	1984 and on
θ_{SCO}	0.28	0.44	0.68	0.90	0.62	0.35
θ_{COM}	0.17	0.22	0.32	0	0	0
θ_{INT}	0.18	0.11	0	0	0	0
θ_{FUL}	0.37	0.23	0	0	0	0
θ_{2PX}	0	0	0	0.10	0.38	0.65

Case 3c. β's are the same as for Case C except $\beta_{(5)}$ is added for trunkless subcompact cars with CVT but without air conditioning.

	1979 and Before	1980	1981	1982	1983	1984 and on
θ_{SCO}	0.28	0.40	0.53	0.64	0.76	0.51
θ_{COM}	0.17	0.20	0.26	0.36	0.24	0
θ_{INT}	0.18	0.13	0.07	0	0	0
θ_{FUL}	0.37	0.27	0.14	0	0	0
θ_{RSC}	0	0	0	0	0	0.49

Case 4. θ's and β's are the same as for Case G.

Case 5a, 5b, and 5c. θ's and β's are the same as for Case A except β's do not include radial tires.

Case 6. θ's and β's are the same as for Case B.

Case 7. θ's and β's are the same as for Case D.

Case 8. θ's and β's are the same as for Case G.

NOTES TO APPENDIX D

1. *Energy/Environmental Factors in Transportation 1975–1990*, The MITRE Corporation, April 1973.

2. *Passenger Car Weight Trend Analysis, Vol. II: Technical Discussion*, The Aerospace Corporation, September 30, 1973.

Appendix E

Summary Description of the NAV Model

We designed the New Car Sales/Automobile Ownership/Vehicle Miles Traveled (NAV) Model to do two things. First, we wanted an econometric model that included new car price, gasoline price, and miles per gallon as independent variables, because such a model would enable us to examine policies that involve changes in all these variables in the same context. Second, we wanted an econometric model that would indicate how families would adjust to changes in new car and gasoline prices. Knowing how families adjust to price changes is important for forecasting the economic and social impacts of such changes. For example, if families faced with higher gasoline taxes react by reducing their automobile ownership, rather than by driving fewer miles per car, the economic and social impacts could be quite different.

The NAV Model deals only with automobile ownership, automobile travel, and automobile gasoline use; trucks, buses, and motorcycles are excluded. Also, the model uses only aggregate U.S. data and the relationships obtained apply only at the national level.

The purpose of this appendix is to describe the econometric relationships and procedures used in this report. A description of the theoretical bases of the model and alternative estimating relationships can be found in another study conducted at The Rand Corporation [1].

ADJUSTMENT PROCESSES

We assume the price of new cars and the price of gasoline to be fixed outside the NAV Model. In the United States, automobile manufacturing is an oligopolist industry; consequently, a supply curve

297

cannot be identified and estimated. Supply adjustment processes in U.S. automobile manufacturing are more complex than those of a competitive industry. If we attempted to introduce the supply adjustment processes of U.S. automobile manufacturing, we would have been drawn far from the study's goals. For this reason, we take the price of new cars as fixed outside the NAV Model.

We also assume the price of gasoline to be fixed outside the NAV model. Put in other terms, we assume that the supply of gasoline for *automobile travel in the United States* is perfectly elastic. We made this assumption to simplify and focus our study; as with the previous assumption, if we had attempted to include gasoline supply relationships, our study would have strayed far from its goals and become complicated beyond available analytical resources. It is easy to see the added complexities if we had *not* assumed a perfectly elastic supply. Automobile travel represents only one part of the total demand for gasoline in the United States. Gasoline is only one of many products derived from crude oil; its price is directly related to the price of crude oil. Crude oil is traded in a worldwide market. If we had not assumed the supply of gasoline available for automobile travel in the United States to be perfectly elastic, we would have had to estimate demand relationships for gasoline in other countries and for other petroleum products in the United States and abroad [2]. In addition, we would have had to model supply relationships—a complex task, since crude oil supply has monopolistic elements. With these considerations in mind, we feel that assuming a perfectly elastic supply of gasoline for automobile travel in the United States is reasonable.

Our assumptions mean that the NAV Model cannot be used to forecast future market equilibrium. Rather, it is useful to make conditional forecasts of how American families would adjust to changes in prices of new cars and gasoline. Faced with a change in either price, a family can adjust in one or more of the following ways:

1. Change the *number* of automobiles it owns.
2. Change the miles per gallon it achieves by altering its driving habits and/or changing the *type* of automobile it owns.
3. Change the number of miles it drives per automobile.

Each of these adjustments to price changes would affect the family's gasoline consumption. They can be related to average family gasoline consumption with a mathematical identity:

$$\frac{G}{H} = \frac{A}{H} \cdot \frac{M}{A} \cdot \frac{1}{E} ,$$

where G/H = Automobile gasoline used per household;

  A/H = Automobiles per household;

  M/A = Miles driven per automobile;

  E = Average miles per gallon.

We have attempted to estimate the impacts of new car and gasoline prices on gasoline use per household through their impacts on each adjustment process.

Automobile Ownership Adjustment Process

Figure E-1 indicates how the NAV Model produces estimates for a given year. The boxes numbered 1 to 4 in the figure stand for the automobile ownership adjustment process. They correspond to Equations (1) to (4) in Table E-2. Table E-1 defines the symbols used in the model.

The NAV Model treats new cars and used cars as different but substitutable commodities. New cars are supplied by the automobile manufacturing industry; we assume that American families can buy as many new cars as they want at prices set by automobile manufacturers. Used cars are supplied from last year's automobile ownership; consequently, the supply cannot exceed last year's total ownership.

Table E-1. Symbols Used in NAV Model

Symbols	Definition
P_u	Index of real used car prices
P_n	Index of real new car prices
P_g	Index of real gasoline prices
Y	Permanent income per household
A	This year's automobile stock per household
A_{-1}	Last year's automobile stock per household this year
S	Dummy variable for strikes in automobile manufacturing
N	Annual new car sales per household
U	Used car ownership per household
E	Average miles per gallon in automobile travel
D	Dummy variable for federal regulation
M	Vehicle miles driven in automobiles per household
G	Gasoline consumption by automobiles per household

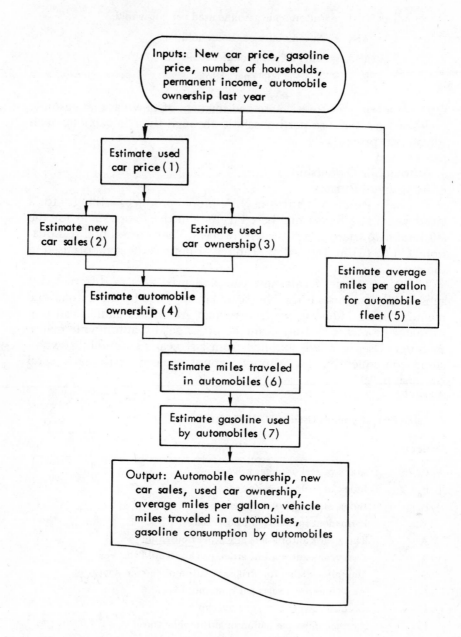

Figure E-1. The NAV Model: Structure.

Table E–2.   NAV Model Equations and Identities *(t–statistics in parentheses)*

Used Car Price

$$P_u = -0.8960 + 1.7268P_n - 0.87122P_g + 0.44809Y - 1.4041A_{-1} - 0.029592S$$
$$\quad (2.052) \quad (5.941) \quad (3.467) \quad (3.892) \quad (2.565) \quad (2.444)$$

$$\text{For } P_u \geq 0 \quad (1)$$

D.F.:13   S.E.:0.03388 $\bar{R}^2$:0.73   F:10.71   D–W:2.21

$P_u = 0$ Otherwise

New Car Sales

$$N = -0.5080 - 0.20869P_n + 0.09318P_u + 0.73050(Y/Y_{-1}) + 0.01733S \quad (2)$$
$$\quad (1.984) \quad (5.512) \quad (1.632) \quad (2.757) \quad (3.406)$$

D.F.:14   S.E.:0.01300 $\bar{R}^2$:0.66   F:9.850   D–W:2.72

Used Car Ownership

$$U = -0.05894 - 0.26645P_u + 0.63665P_n - 0.59339P_g + 0.22529Y - 0.01186S$$
$$\quad (0.264) \quad (2.795) \quad (3.406) \quad (4.526) \quad (10.669) \quad (2.068)$$

$$\text{For } U \leq A_{t-1} \quad (3)$$

D.F.:13   S.E.:0.01429 $\bar{R}^2$:0.99   F:247.45   D–W:1.40

$U = A_{t-1}$ Otherwise

Total Automobile Ownership

$$A \equiv N + U \qquad\qquad (4)$$

Average Miles per Gallon

$$LE = \quad 2.656 \quad + 0.17015LP_g - 0.02228D \qquad (5)$$
$$\quad (1248.74) \quad (3.673) \quad (3.296)$$

D.F.:14   S.E.:0.00699 $\bar{R}^2$:0.90   F:73.55   D–W:1.07

Automobile Miles Driven

Estimated Form
$$LM = \quad 9.176 \quad + 0.86405LA - 0.36853LP_g + 0.02543D \qquad (6a)$$
$$\quad (752.59) \quad (13.360) \quad (3.520) \quad (2.316)$$

D.F.:13   S.E.:0.01130 $\bar{R}^2$:0.99   F:547.29   D–W:1.26

Derived Form
$$LM = 7.996 + 0.86405LA - 0.44409LP_g + 0.44409LE + 0.03532D \qquad (6b)$$

Gasoline Consumption

$$LG \equiv LM - LE \qquad\qquad (7)$$

Note: An "L" before a symbol indicates its logarithmic value.

Used Car Price: Equation (1).[a]   The Used Car Price Equation says that used car prices will increase when new car price and permanent income per household increase and when gasoline price and last year's automobile ownership per household decrease. The last variable on the right is a dummy variable for strikes in the automobile industry; it is set equal to −1 in the year of a strike and equal to 1 in the following year; otherwise it is zero. The strike dummy variable implies that used car prices are higher in strike years. Once a value is estimated for used car price, it is used to estimate new car sales per household and used car ownership per household.

New Car Sales: Equation (2).   New car sales per household increase when used car price, and the ratio of this year's permanent income per household to last year's permanent income per household, increase; new car sales per household increase when new car prices decrease. The sign of the strike variable's coefficient is plus, as one would expect. One would expect the ratio of permanent income to be a measure of change in average household wealth. Note that the price of gasoline is not in this equation. We could not find a significant, direct relationship between gasoline price and new car sales. This suggests that the impact of gasoline price on new car sales results from changes in used car price.

Used Car Ownership: Equation (3).[b]   Used car ownership per household increases if new car price or permanent income increase; it increases as used car price and gasoline price decrease. The strike variable has the expected sign. Note that when the estimated value for used car ownership per household is subtracted from last year's automobile ownership per household, we obtain an estimate of automobiles scrapped per household. This provides a link with the Fleet Mix Model.

Total Automobile Ownership: Equation (4).   This is an identity: new car sales plus used car ownership are equal, by definition, to total automobile ownership.

---

[a]Note that the Used Car Price Equation is defined only for non-negative used car prices. If a negative price is estimated using the equation, the used car price is set at equal to zero in the NAV Model.

[b]Note that this equation is used in the NAV model only when the estimate for used car ownership per household is less than or equal to last year's automobile ownership per household. When estimated used car ownership per household exceeds last year's total automobile ownership, used car ownership per household is set equal to last year's total automobile ownership per household.

Miles per Gallon Adjustment Process: Equation (5). The miles per gallon adjustment process is represented by box 5 in Figure E–1 and Equation (5) in Table E–2. A family produces vehicle miles much as a farmer produces wheat. Both the family and the farmer bring together many inputs to produce an output. The farmer combines land, seed, fertilizer, and labor to produce wheat; the family combines automobiles, gasoline, repair and maintenance, and its own time to produce vehicle miles driven.

Because automobile vehicle miles are outputs of a production process, we can apply production function theory: if the price of an input rises, the producers will substitute other inputs for that input. For instance, if the price of fertilizer increases, a farmer might use more land and less fertilizer to produce his wheat. Similarly, if the price of gasoline increases, a family could use more of its own time and less gasoline to produce vehicle miles—by driving slower. It could also use more maintenance and less gasoline by having tune-ups more frequently. The rate at which gasoline can be substituted for all other inputs is called the elasticity of substitution of gasoline in the production of vehicle miles. In the NAV Model, we assume the elasticity of substitution of gasoline in the reduction of vehicle miles to be constant.

While a family will substitute all other inputs, *as a whole*, for gasoline in the production of its vehicle miles, it might use relatively more or less of particular inputs. Important here is the choice of automobile size and power-assisted equipment options. Between 1959 and 1972, the real price of gasoline fell. During most of the period, not only did average highway speeds increase, but the proportion of new cars with air conditioning, automatic transmissions, and other power assisted equipment also increased [3]. Our estimate includes the dual effects of changes in driving habits and choice of automobile, and we cannot distinguish between them. Consequently, our Base Case forecasts from the NAV Model include some change in the choice of new car size and power accessories. However, the size of our estimate (see below) indicates that the effect will be small.

From the standpoint of production function theory, miles per gallon is an output/input ratio. It is the number of units of output—vehicle miles traveled—for every unit of an input—a gallon of gasoline. We can use it to estimate the elasticity of substitution of gasoline by regressing it against a measure of the real price of gasoline after both variables have been transformed into logarithmic form. Our estimate of the elasticity of substitution of gasoline in the production of vehicle miles is 0.17. This means that if the real price of gasoline increases 10 percent, a set number of vehicle miles will be produced with 1.7 percent less gasoline.

The other variable on the righthand side of Equation (5) is included to account for the effects of federal emission and safety regulations on miles per gallon. It is set equal to one in 1968 and later years; before 1968, it is set equal to zero. The value of the variable is changed in 1968 because both the first federal emission control regulations and the first Federal safety standards for all new cars applied in the 1968 model year [4]. We found that including this variable improves the fit of the equation.

Automobile Miles Driven Adjustment Process: Equations (6a) and (6b). To complete the mathematical identity shown in Table E–2, we could develop an equation for miles driven per automobile, (M/A). Instead, we estimated an equation for miles *per household* $[(M/H) = (A/H) \cdot (M/A)]$, given automobile ownership per household. We established an equation for miles per household because it did not apply the assumption that a family would drive a second car as much as its first car, if the real price of gasoline is constant. The equations for miles per household is represented in box 6 of Figure E–1.

In Equation (6a) of Table E–2, automobile miles per household increase as automobile ownership increases and as the price of gasoline per gallon decreases. The third independent variable is included to account for a structural change that has resulted from federal emissions and safety regulations. Note that the coefficient of automobile ownership per household is less than one; this implies that miles per automobile fall as automobile ownership per household increases; when a family adds a second or third car, each car is driven less.

Because miles per gallon is not an independent variable in Equation (6a),[c] we have to interpret the coefficient of gasoline price to be an estimate when miles per gallon are also adjusting as discussed above. However, we want an equation that separates the effects on miles per household of changes in the price of gasoline per gallon and changes in miles per gallon. We can derive such an equation mathematically using Equations (5) and (6a) [5]; Equation (6b) is used in the NAV Model. Several comments are in order about Equation (6b):

---

[c]Miles per gallon was tried as an independent variable in the equation. It proved to be highly correlated with automobile ownership; consequently, we could not separate the effects of automobile ownership and miles per gallon on vehicle miles traveled. Miles per gallon was dropped from the equation.

1. The coefficient of gasoline price is an elasticity of vehicle miles with regard to gasoline price—when miles per gallon do not change (i.e., when the price of gasoline *per gallon* and the price of gasoline *per mile* change in the same proportion). *Because no offsetting change in miles per gallon occurs, the absolute size of the elasticity is greater in Equation (6b) than in Equation (6a).*

2. *The coefficient of the miles per gallon variable is positive*; an autonomous increase in miles per gallon—with the price of gasoline per gallon constant—lowers the price of gasoline *per mile*. A lower gasoline price per mile will lead to more driving. This means that a 50 percent increase in miles per gallon would result in less than a 50 percent gasoline savings because more miles would be driven.

3. *The coefficient of gasoline price per gallon and the coefficient of miles per gallon differ only in sign.* A 50 percent *increase* in the price of gasoline per gallon (with miles per gallon constant), and a 50 percent *decrease* in miles per gallon (with the price of gasoline per constant) both imply a 50 percent increase in the price of gasoline *per mile.*

4. *Equation (6b) allows us to estimate the impacts of technologies that improve miles per gallon with the NAV Model.* It is another link between the Auto Fleet Mix Model and the NAV Model.

Finally, automobile gasoline consumption per household is calculated in box 7 of Figure E–1. To do this, the log of miles per gallon from Equation (5) is subtracted from the log of automobile miles per household from Equation (6b).

ESTIMATING PROCEDURES AND DATA

The system of equations is recursive; it was estimated using the method of ordinary least squares. The automobile ownership adjustment process was estimated with annual data from 1954 to 1972. The miles per gallon and the miles per household equations were estimated with annual data from 1956 to 1972. Data for the other variables were obtained from the following sources:

1. New car sales, used car ownership, automobile vehicle miles traveled, automobile gasoline consumption, and average auto miles per gallon came from Federal Highway Administration publications [6]. They were adjusted to eliminate vehicle miles traveled and gasoline consumed by motorcycles.

2. Personal disposable income is from the annual *Economic Report of the President.* Permanent income is a weighted average of

present year and past year personnel disposable income; we used weights developed by the National Bureau of Economic Research.
3. New car price, used car price, and gasoline price are measured by components of the national Consumer Price Index.

THE NAV MODEL VERSUS REALITY

How well does the NAV Model perform? We considered two criteria.

How well does the NAV model duplicate the estimating period? How well does it predict?

To test the NAV Model, we tried to duplicate the actual values for the estimating period—1954 to 1972. We started with 1953 automobile ownership and used the actual values for the other exogenous variables each year. The estimate of automobiles per household in one year (after adjustment for growth in the number of households) was used as an input to Equation (1) for the next year. Figure E–2 compares actual values with predicted ones:

1. *Used car price.* NAV captures the sharp increase in used car price in 1959 and the decline since 1967. It underestimates used car prices in 1954 and 1955 and again in 1962 and 1963. The high used car prices in 1954 and 1955 might reflect restricted new car production during the Korean War.
2. *New car sales.* The NAV Model misses the.peaks and troughs during the first part of the estimating period—1955, 1958, and 1961. It does well in the latter part of the period.
3. *Automobile scrappage.* The values predicted by the NAV Model follow the upward movement in automobiles scrapped but fluctuate more. The fluctuation is not surprising because automobile scrappage is calculated as the difference of two other estimates—used car ownership this year and total automobile ownership last year.
4. *Automobile ownership.* Actual and predicted values are close. The NAV Model slightly underestimates automobile ownership during the late 1950s and slightly overestimates it during most of the 1960s. The NAV Model is more sensitive to the economic slowdown of 1969–70 than was actual automobile ownership.
5. *Automobile miles driven.* The actual and predicted values are close. The NAV Model captured the increased growth that began in 1963.
6. *Automobile gasoline use.* The actual and predicted relationships

are close. The NAV Model slightly underestimates the late 1950s and slightly overestimates the early 1960s. In the last part of the estimating period, it is more sensitive to year-to-year changes in income than was actual gasoline use.

The NAV Model tracks automobile ownership as well. Remember that the estimate of automobile ownership for one year—after adjustment for household growth—is an input to the model for the next year. Thus, an error in estimating automobile ownership in one year could throw off estimates for the following year. An error in the automobile ownership estimate that year could throw off estimates for the third year, and so on. In sum, an error in estimating automobile ownership in any one year could throw the model onto the wrong growth path. In spite of year-to-year statistical errors in the estimates of used car price, new car sales, and used car ownership, this does not happen.

A second test is how well the NAV Model predicts. The model used data from 1954 to 1972. Actual 1973 values for the exogenous variables were used to predict 1973 values for endogenous variables. Recently, actual 1973 data for some of the endogenous variables have become available. The actual and predicted values are compared in Table E-3. The prediction of new car sales is close to the actual value. The underestimation of automobile ownership is chiefly due to an underestimation of used car demand. The NAV Model's underestimation of used car demand in 1973 could be due to its inability to incorporate the effects of an increase in inflation.

We have also used the NAV Model to forecast 1974 new car sales. Except for new car price, the assumptions of Chapter Six were used. We assumed a 17 percent increase in nominal new car prices [7]; this is equal to a 10 percent increase in *real* new car prices. The NAV Model forecasts 8.7 million new car sales if the national average pump price of regular gasoline is 59 cents a gallon in 1974 and 9.4 million if it is 52 cents a gallon. The forecasts imply declines of 24 percent and 18 percent, respectively, from 1973 new car sales levels. During the first six months of 1974, new car sales were 25 percent below the same period in 1973 [8].

Table E-3. Actual versus Predicted Values: 1973

	Actual	*Predicted*	*Percent Error*
New Car Sales (in millions)	11.5	11.1	−3.5
Automobile Ownership[a] (in millions)	101.2	99.2	−2.0
Index of Real Used Car Price	0.907	0.820	−8.7

[a]Preliminary estimate provided by Federal Highway Administration.

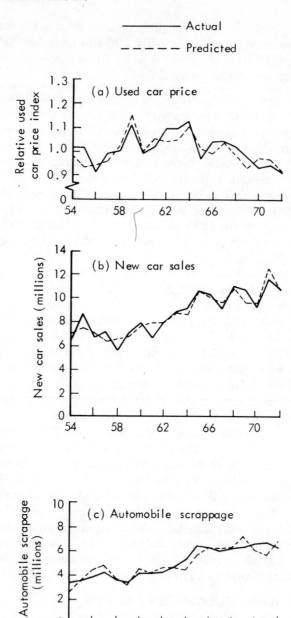

Figure E–2. The NAV Model: Actual versus Predicted.

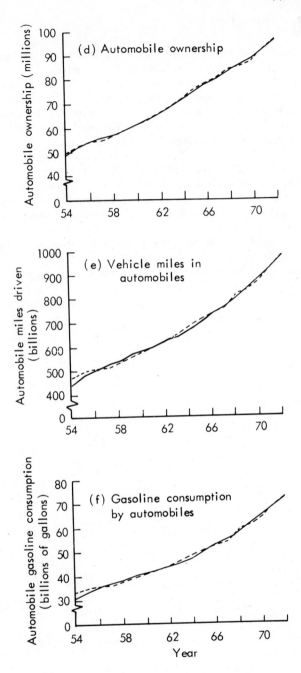

(d) Automobile ownership

(e) Vehicle miles in automobiles

(f) Gasoline consumption by automobiles

NOTES TO APPENDIX E

1. B. Burright and J. Enns, *Econometric Models of the Demand for Motor Fuel*, R–1561–NSF, The Rand Corporation (forthcoming).

2. For an attempt to estimate international demand relationships, see Hendrik S. Houthakker and Michael Kennedy, "Demand for Energy as a Function of Price," unpublished and undated paper. Harvard University, Boston, Mass.

3. *Passenger Car Weight Trend Analysis, Volume I: Executive Summary*, The Aerospace Corporation, September 30, 1973, p. 23.

4. Lawrence I. White, *The Automobile Industry Since 1945*, (Cambridge, Mass.: Harvard University Press, 1971), pp. 233 and 244.

5. Burright and Enns, *Econometric Models of the Demand for Motor Fuel*.

6. U.S. Department of Transportation, Federal Highway Administration, *Federal Highway Statistics* (Washington, D.C.; U.S. Government Printing Office), various issues.

7. "Prices Could Stymie on Auto Comeback," *Business Week*, No. 2335, June 15, 1974, pp. 32–33.

8. Underlying Sales Figures from *Automotive News* (various issues), 1973 and 1974.

Employment Impacts in Five
Auto-Related Sectors

To predict the effect of changes in VMT, new car sales, and auto ownership on employment we estimated regression equations for five auto-related sectors. The definitions of the sectors are based upon the 1967 Standard Industrial Classification (SIC) codes.[a] In 1971 these sectors employed close to 3 million workers or approximately 4.5 percent of the total non-agricultural work force. The five sectors, and the percent of total employment, are (1) motor vehicle manufacturing, less trucks and buses (33 percent), automotive dealers (26 percent), service stations (20 percent), retail and wholesale of parts and accessories (17 percent), and tire manufacturing (4 percent). In addition, of course, other sectors would be influenced by changes in new car production, auto ownership, and gasoline consumption. In particular, the petroleum refining and raw material industries are almost certain to be affected. However, the data concerning employment in these industries are not sufficiently disaggregated to allow an analysis of the auto-related employment impacts. Consequently, the impacts discussed below represent direct effects only and understate the total employment changes that would result from policies adopted to conserve gasoline.

In each case, the dependent variable is total employment—production and clerical/administrative. Annual data for the period 1958 to 1972 were used to estimate the equation coefficients. The following results were obtained:

[a]The five sectors are (1) SIC 3711, 3712, 3714: motor vehicle manufacturing less trucks and buses; SIC 551–2: Automotive dealers; SIC 554: service stations; SIC 501, 553, 559: retail and wholesale of parts and accessories; and SIC 301: tire manufacturing. The data were obtained from *Employment and Earnings: United States, 1909–1972*, U.S. Department of Labor, Bureau of Labor Statistics, Bulletin 1312–9, 1973.

Auto Manufacturing:

(1A) E_M = 1.2 + 0.36 PROD + 0.34 VMT
         (1.6)   (3.6)   (3.4)

   $\bar{R}^2$ = 0.82   DW = 1.91   DF = 10

(1B) E_M = −7.7 + 0.44 PROD + 0.14 VMT + 1.16 WEIGHT
         (−3.6)   (7.2)   (1.9)   (4.5)

   $\bar{R}^2$ = 0.94   DW = 1.5   DF = 9

Auto Dealers:

(2) E_D = 4.4 + 0.137 SALES + 0.289 VMT
         (13.5)   (2.6)   (4.8)

   $\bar{R}^2$ = 0.92   DW = 1.11   DF = 10

Retail and Wholesale Parts:

(3) E_R = −0.70 + 1.03 VMT
         (−7.2)   (69.4)

   $\bar{R}^2$ = 0.99   DW = 1.95   DF = 11

Service Stations:

(4) E_S = −2.39 + 0.77 OWN
         (−7.4)   (27.1)

   $\bar{R}^2$ = 0.98   DW = 1.88   DF = 11

Tire Production:

(5) E_T = 2.1 + 0.39 VMT
         (3.9)   (4.7)

   $\bar{R}^2$ = 0.77   DW = 2.3   DF = 11

where E   = Total employment (thousands);
       SALES   = New car sales (millions) U.S. + foreign;
       PROD   = New car production (millions) assumed
                    to be 85 percent of SALES;
       VMT   = Vehicle miles of auto travel (billions);
       OWN   = Auto ownership (millions);
       WEIGHT   = Average new car production weight (pounds).

Each equation was estimated in the log form; therefore the coefficients represent elasticities. The auto manufacturing equation was estimated in two forms, with and without the weight variable. Including the weight variable improves the equation fit from $\overline{R}^2 = 0.84$ to 0.94; however, the coefficient of WEIGHT is 1.16, suggesting that 1 percent change in new car weight results in a greater than 1 percent change in auto manufacturing employment. This response may be reasonable for the weight changes that occurred in the period 1958 to 1971; in the early 1960s the shift to small cars reduced the average new car weight to around 3,500 pounds while in the late 1960s and early 1970s weight increased to around 3,850 pounds due to federally mandated safety and emission standards. The strong relationship between weight and employment during this period may reflect the fact that in this limited range, weight changes constitute changes in the *complexity* of automobile production; for example, the extra parts required for an advanced emissions control system or stronger bodies directly increases the labor input required.[b] However, for large weight decreases (or increases) it is not apparent that the complexity of the auto will change proportionately. Thus, the one-to-one percentage changes obtained in Equation (1B) probably do not reflect the employment requirements that would obtain if auto weights fell to say, 2,500 pounds. Because of the uncertainty surrounding the relationship between employment and weight for large weight decreases, we estimated the auto manufacturing and weight for large weight decreases, we estimated the auto manufacturing employment equation with and without a weight variable and used both equations to project a *range* of employment changes. The values of auto weight used in Equation (1B) were obtained for each from the Generalized Auto Design Model and the Auto Fleet Mix Model described in Appendixes A and D; the actual weights used are shown in Table F-1.

---

[b]This opinion was expressed to the authors in a personal communication from Mr. John L. Smith, Manager, Car Engineering Division, Product Planning Office, Chrysler Corporation.

Table F—1.   Estimated Average New Auto Weights: 1976–1995
(in pounds)

Case No.	1976	1980	1985	1995
Base	3957	3957	3957	3957
1	3513	2758	2758	2758
2	3715	3448	2397	2397
3a	3715	3448	2397	2397
3b	2715	3329	1548	1548
3c	3715	3467	1971	1971
4	3513	2569	1822	1822
5	Same as Base Case			
6	Same as Case 1			
7	Same as Case 2			
8	Same as Case 4			

Gasoline Price Change Impacts by Earnings Group

In this study, we have dealt with most impacts at the national level without considering how particular groups or regions would be affected differentially. But decisionmakers are interested in particular groups and regions. While we could not estimate the impacts of all potential policies on all affected groups, neither did we want to simply ignore the issue. To provide some insights, we addressed a narrower question: What is the initial impact, with regard to work trips, of changes in gasoline prices on families at different earnings levels? In the body of this study, we concluded that price increases are the only way to reduce automobile gasoline use significantly in the next few years. If our conclusion is correct, this narrower question would be most important.

In answering this question, we used data from the *Panel Study of Income Dynamics*. It is a survey of 4,840 households conducted by the Institute for Social Research at the University of Michigan [1]. We used the 1971 version, which has 1970 income data. To use this data source, we had to make a number of assumptions that could not be checked out. Consequently, *our results must be considered tentative*. Our assumptions and methodology are discussed in the last part of this appendix. First, we discuss the factors leading to differences in work trip gasoline use among earning groups and indicate their overall initial impacts.

DIFFERENCES AMONG EARNINGS GROUPS

We consider only work trips; trips for other purposes—family business, recreation—are not included. Our calculations take into account commuting by both family heads and working wives. Both drivers and carpoolers are counted.

In this analysis, the gasoline used by the average family within an earnings group to get to work is determined by four factors: labor force participation, modal choice, distance to work, and automobile efficiency. How families with different earnings vary with respect to each factor is shown in Table G–1.

The *labor force participation* of family heads and wives is reflected by Employed per Household; see Column (1) of Table G–1. Labor force participation of family heads increases with family earnings. Labor force participation of working wives increases up to the high earnings class and then declines slightly. Both are reflected in the Employed per Household, which increases through the $15,001 to $20,000 earnings groups and then falls. In other words, *one reason that gasoline used for work trips increases with earnings is that, up to the highest earnings group, more family members make work trips.*

Modal Choice patterns can be seen in Column (2)—Percent Work Trips by Automobile. The percentage of work trips made by automobile increases to the middle income range and then declines slightly. The decline in the $15,001 to $20,000 earnings groups is due to the greater number of working wives; working wives commute less frequently by car. The decline in the top earnings group is due to proportionally fewer heads of household commuting by automobile.

The *distance to work* factor is presented in Column (3); average length of work trip increases with earnings for those who drive to work.[a]

The estimates of *average automobile efficiency* can be seen in Column (4). Average automobile efficiency is sharply higher for the less than $5,000 earnings class. Above this level, it declines slightly as income increases.

Table G–1. Comparison by Earnings Group

Earnings Group (1970, $)	(1) Employed per Household	(2) Percent Work Trips by Auto	(3) Average One Way Trip[a] (Miles)	(4) Average Automobile Efficiency (Mpg)
0–5,000	0.58	55	7.6	14.43
5,001 to 10,000	1.35	69	8.6	12.68
10,001 to 15,000	1.61	78	9.2	12.62
15,001 to 20,000	1.70	75	9.3	12.57
Over 20,000	1.53	72	11.4	12.53

[a]Driving only.

[a]For those who carpool, it increases to the $10,001–$15,000 income class, and then declines. The average length of work trip is always greater for carpoolers than for drivers.

In sum, all four factors work to increase gasoline use for work trips up to an above average earnings level. Households with high earnings make fewer work trips in automobiles, but their work trips are longer and in slightly less efficient automobiles.

OVERALL IMPACTS

Our estimates of average gasoline expenditures by earnings groups for work trips are displayed in Tables G–2 and G–3. We made two estimates. One is for families with employed heads; see Table G–2. It reflects the average, initial impact on those families that make most of the work trips.[b] The other estimate is for gasoline expenditures for work trips averaged over all families in the earnings group.

The estimates are compared to total earnings in Table G–4. The two cases give similar results. Initial expenditures on gasoline are roughly proportional to income through the $5,000 to $10,000 earnings groups. (Note that the earnings classes are defined in terms of 1970 dollars; in terms of 1975 dollars, the range would be $6,700 to $13,500.) Above this level, gasoline expenditures on work trips as a proportion of earnings becomes increasingly regressive. In other words, *if we considered only families that make most of the work trips, higher gasoline prices would have the greatest initial impact on those families with less than average household earnings.* Within this group, the impact would be proportional to income.

We have compared gasoline expenditures for work trips with *earnings.* In the case of households with employed heads, this comparison makes sense. In the case of all households, we would have preferred to compare gasoline expenditures for work trips with total income. Total income also includes income from pensions, social security, welfare, and wealth. These other sources of income are most important at the high and low ends of the income distribution. If we had made the comparison with total income, average gasoline expenditures for work trips as a proportion of income would probably have increased to middle-income levels and then fallen. In other words, *if we consider all families and sources of income, the initial impact of higher gasoline prices would probably fall most heavily on (lower) middle-income families.*

ASSUMPTIONS AND LIMITATIONS

The Michigan survey did not have all the data we needed; to do the analysis, we had to make assumptions. Consequently, *the results*

[b]It excludes gasoline expenditures by working wives whose husbands are not employed.

Table G–2. Work Trip Mileage, Gasoline Requirement, and Cost by Earnings Class (Average of households with employed head)

Earnings Class (1970, $)	Average Income (1970, $)	Average Work Trip (Miles)[a]	Average Auto Efficiency (Mpg)[b]	Annual Gasoline Requirement (Gallons)	Annual Gasoline Expenditures At:			
					67¢ Base Price ($)	Plus 15¢ Tax ($)	Plus 30¢ Tax ($)	Plus 45¢ Tax ($)
Less than 5,000	3,243	1,836	14.43	127	63	77	91	105
5,001 to 10,000	7,520	3,929	12.68	310	154	188	223	257
10,001 to 15,000	12,023	5,552	12.62	440	218	267	316	365
15,001 to 20,000	17,410	5,728	12.57	456	226	277	328	378
Over 20,000	27,650	5,981	12.53	477	237	290	348	396

Note: Prices in 1975 dollars; total costs in 1970 dollars using a price index deflator of 1.35.

[a] Assume 240 working days a year. Those that drive are assumed to pay the cost of two trips a day; those that carpool are assumed to pay the cost of one trip.

[b] Obtained from age-fuel economy information contained in Mikolowsky et al., *The Regional Impact of Short-Range Transportation Alternatives: A Case Study of Los Angeles*, The Rand Corporation, June, 1974, Appendix E, p. 117.

Table G–3.   Work Trip Mileage, Gasoline Requirement, and Cost by Earnings Class *(Average of all households in class)*

Earnings Class (1970, $)	Average Income (1970, $)	Average Work Trip (Miles)[a]	Average Auto Efficiency (Mpg)[b]	Annual Gasoline Requirement (Gallons)	67¢ Base Price ($)	Plus 15¢ Tax ($)	Plus 30¢ Tax ($)	Plus 45¢ Tax ($)
						Annual Gasoline Expenditures At:		
Less than 5,000	1,677	962	14.43	67	33	41	48	56
5,001 to 10,000	7,460	3,808	12.68	300	149	182	216	249
10,001 to 15,000	12,255	5,499	12.62	436	216	265	313	362
15,001 to 20,000	17,148	5,659	12.57	450	223	273	324	374
Over 20,000	27,650	5,981	12.53	477	237	290	343	396

Note: Prices in 1975 dollars; total costs in 1970 dollars using a price index deflator of 1.35.

a Assume 240 working days a year. Those that drive are assumed to pay the cost of two trips a day; those that carpool are assumed to pay the cost of one trip.

b Obtained from age-fuel economy information contained in Mikolowsky, et al., *The Regional Impact of Short-Range Transportation Alternatives: A Case Study of Los Angeles*, The Rand Corporation, June 1974, Appendix E, p. 117.

Table G–4.   Gasoline Expenditures for Work Trips as a Percent of Annual Earnings

Earnings Class[a] (1970, $)	Households with Employed Heads				Average of All Households			
	67¢ Base Price	15¢	30¢	45¢	67¢ Base Price	15¢	30¢	45¢
		Plus Tax of				*Plus Tax of*		
Less than 5,000	1.9	2.4	2.8	3.2	2.0	2.4	2.9	3.3
5,001 to 10,000	2.0	2.5	3.0	3.4	2.0	2.4	2.9	3.3
10,001 to 15,000	1.8	2.2	2.6	3.0	1.8	2.2	2.6	3.0
15,001 to 20,000	1.3	1.6	1.9	2.2	1.3	1.6	1.9	2.2
Over 20,000	0.9	1.0	1.2	1.4	0.9	1.0	1.2	1.4

a For 1975, we estimate the inflation factor to be 1.35; thus, a $5,000 earnings in 1970 would be $6,750.

should be considered tentative. The chief assumptions and limitations are the following:

1. Only direct effects are included; no consideration of the indirect effects of gasoline price change through changes in the prices of other goods and services are considered.
2. We assumed that gasoline taxes are entirely shifted forward to purchases.
3. We assumed that household work trip behavior does not change due to higher gasoline prices.
4. Data are available only on the commuting behavior of heads of households and, when the head of household is a husband, on the commuting behavior of working wives. No data are available on tape about additional workers in the household. This means that, if income classes differed greatly in the labor force participation of other family members, our results would be off.
5. No data are available on the modal choices of working wives. To include them, we had to make assumptions. We assume that when the head of household worked and the household owned zero or one automobile, the modal choices of working wives are like the modal choices of heads of households that did not own an automobile. We further assumed that when the head of household worked and the family owned two or more automobiles, the modal choices of working wives were the same as the modal choices of heads of households that owned one or more cars. Parallel assumptions were made for working wives when the head of household did not work. The assumptions were applied to each income group separately.
6. For workers who carpooled, no data were available on the proportion of the cost they paid. We assumed that they paid half. The assumption might be high; it implies that no one carpools with more than one other person. If the assumption is high, we are overestimating the costs of the lower income classes, which make a larger proportion of work trips in carpools.
7. We assumed that families use their newest cars for work trips.
8. We assumed that each employed person goes to work 240 days a year and makes two trips a day.

NOTES TO APPENDIX G

1. *Panel Study of Income Dynamics: Study Design, Procedures, Available Data,* Institute for Social Research, University of Michigan, 1971.

Index

acceleration, 12n, 30, 48, 62; and CVT, 9; and fuel economy, 30, 62–63, 74, 190, 229–231; and horsepower, 6, 62–63; and new engines, 8, 175
adjustment processes, 51–52; and gas prices, 103–104, 110; rate, 17–18, 53
aerodynamic design, 14, 15, 82, 167, 237; costs, 31; and fuel economy, 10–11, 31, 48, 64–67, 68–70, 84, 85, 130, 161, 228–229
Aerospace Corp., 36
air conditioning, 29–30, 48, 58, 83n; and auto industry, 176, 182, 227
Alcoa study, 32
alternative fuels, 15, 28–29; see also hydrogen fuels
aluminum, 32, 67, 182
American Motors: Gremlin, 39; and Rand report, 175–180, 220, 227, 228, 240
Arthur D. Little, 195
Automobile Design Model, 125, 161, 181, 221
Automobile Fleet Mix Model, 12, 47, 49–51, 52n, 81, 164–165; and federal policies, 123–124
automobile industry: capital resources, 7–8, 29, 139, 174, 180, 185–186, 187, 193–195, 202–204, 206, 212, 214, 220, 221; conversion, 124, 129, 139, 217; and emission standards, 179, 181, 182–183; employment, 13, 53–54; market, 81, 120, 127, 128–129, 130–133, 218–220; pricing policies, 10; R&D, 20, 179, 217; and technological change, 7, 126, 128, 173–187, 193–195, 202–204, 206, 212, 239
automobile parts and service, 4, 166

automobile stock: size, 81; turnover, 5, 114–116

bias-ply tires, 58, 64, 82

CVT: see continuously variable transmission
carbon monoxide emissions, 36, 39, 80, 179; standards, 183
Caretto-Sawyer weighting scheme, 13, 49, 57, 78
carpooling, 21, 29, 157, 234
Chamberlain, 106, 107
charge stratification: see stratification
Chase Econometric Associates, 107
Chrysler Corp., 36; and Rand report, 181–186, 227, 228, 240
Clear Air Act, 179, 192
Clean Air Race, 39
coal, 15n, 29, 38, 39
Cochran study, 32
commuters, 4, 6
compact cars: air conditioning, 82; market share, 14, 81, 83, 84, 129
Consumer Price Index, 99
continuously variable transmission, 14–15, 74, 140; and auto industry, 178–181, 195, 223–224; fuel economy, 9, 33, 67, 89, 161, 174; and gas turbine engine, 36; research, 149, 237; and SIE, 84, 129, 136, 140, 167
Curtiss-Wright, 34, 194, 217, 222–223

Data Resources Inc., 107
demand: gasoline, 2, 51, 105, 164; models, 162–167; new car, 51, 104, 213; used car, 124

About the Authors

Sorrel Wildhorn is a senior policy analyst at The Rand Corporation. He received degrees in aeronautical engineering from New York University. Until 1968 his major work at Rand was concerned with applying techniques of systems/analysis to problems of national security. Since 1968, he has headed studies of energy policy issues and policy issues in criminal justice, as well as an exploratory study of the economics of a performing arts center. His work in criminal justice involved a comprehensive study of private police in the United States, a comparative analysis of resource allocation and methods of deploying police patrol, an analysis and evaluation of a large urban prosecutor's office and a study of ways of improving the criminal investigation process in local police departments.

Currently, he heads a new study of ways of measuring performance in the criminal prosecution, defense, adjudication and sentencing process. He is the co-author of two forthcoming books on private police and on the prosecution of adult felony defendants and the author of a number of publications in the fields of national security and criminal justice.

Burke Burright is an economic consultant to The Rand Corporation on energy, environmental, and transportation issues. He has helped formulate approaches for major Rand studies in each area. Mr. Burright is currently completing his Ph.D dissertation in economics at UCLA. His dissertation subject is on an Aggregate Urban Transportation Model.

John H. Enns is an economist in the Management Sciences Department of the Rand Corporation. He has conducted policy research in the areas of energy conservation, military manpower supply, federal revenue-sharing and urban transportation. He is currently Deputy Manager of the Housing Assistance Supply Experiment (Design and Analysis Group), a ten year research program sponsored by the U.S. Department of Housing and Urban Development.

Thomas F. Kirkwood received degrees from Stanford University and the California Institute of Technology. Affiliated with the Rand Corporation for twenty-five years, Mr. Kirkwood's research work has concentrated on military and civil transportation and energy conservation, particularly fuel economy in automobiles. He is currently working on the effects of possible future Federal requirements for emissions, safety, and fuel economy in automobile design and cost.

List of Selected Rand Books

Averch, Harvey A., et al. *How Effective Is Schooling? A Critical Review of Research.* Englewood Cliffs, New Jersey: Educational Technology Publications, 1974.

Baer, Walter S. *Cable Television: A Handbook for Decisionmaking.* New York: Crane, Russak & Company, Inc., 1974.

Baer, Walter S. et al., *Cable Television: Franchising Considerations.* New York: Crane, Russak & Company, Inc., 1974.

Bagdikian, Ben H. *The Information Machines: Their Impact on Men and The Media.* New York: Harper and Row, 1971.

Bretz, Rudy. *A Taxonomy of Communication Media.* Englewood Cliffs, New Jersey: Educational Technology Publications, 1971.

Bruno, James E. (ed.) *Emerging Issues in Education: Policy Implications for the Schools.* Lexington, Mass.: D. C. Heath and Company, 1972.

Carpenter-Huffman, P., G. R. Hall, and G. C. Sumner. *Change in Education: Insights from Performance Contracting.* Cambridge, Mass.: Ballinger Publishing Company, 1974.

Carpenter-Huffman, P., R. C. Kletter, and R. K. Yin. *Cable Television: Developing Community Services.* New York: Crane, Russak and Company, Inc., 1975.

Cohen, Bernard and Jan M. Chaiken. *Police Background Characteristics and Performance.* Lexington, Mass.: D. C. Heath and Company, 1973.

Coleman, James S. and Nancy L. Karweit. *Information Systems and Performance Measures in Schools.* Englewood Cliffs, New Jersey: Educational Technology Publications, 1972.

De Salvo, Joseph S. (ed.) *Perspectives on Regional Transportation Planning.* Lexington, Mass.: D. C. Heath and Company, 1973.

Downs, Anthony. *Inside Bureaucracy.* Boston, Mass.: Little, Brown and Company, 1967.

Fisher, Gene H. *Cost Considerations in Systems Analysis.* New York: American Elsevier Publishing Company, 1971.

Haggart, Sue A., (ed.) *Program Budgeting for School District Planning.* Englewood Cliffs, New Jersey: Educational Technology Publications, 1972.

Hirshleifer, Jack, James C. DeHaven, and Jerome W. Milliman. *Water Supply: Economics, Technology, and Policy*. Chicago, Illinois: The University of Chicago Press, 1960.

Jackson, Larry R., and William A. Johnson. *Protest by The Poor*. Lexington, Mass.: D. C. Heath and Company, 1974.

Levien, Roger E. (ed.) *The Emerging Technology: Instructional Uses of The Computer in Higher Education*. New York: McGraw–Hill Book Company, 1972.

McCall, John J. *Income Mobility, Racial Discrimination, and Economic Growth*. Lexington, Mass.: D. C. Heath and Company, 1973.

McLaughlin, Milbrey Wallin. *Evaluation and Reform: The Elementary and Secondary Education Act of 1965: Title I*. Cambridge, Mass.: Ballinger Publishing Company, 1975.

Meyer, John R., Martin Wohl, and John F. Kain. *The Urban Transportation Problem*. Cambridge, Mass.: Harvard University Press, 1965.

Newhouse, Joseph P. and Arthur J. Alexander. *An Economic Analysis of Public Library Services*. Lexington, Mass.: D. C. Heath and Company, 1972.

Novick, David (ed.) *Current Practice in Program Budgeting (PPBS): Analysis and Case Studies Covering Government and Business*. New York: Crane, Russak and Company, Inc., 1973.

Novick, David (ed.) *Program Budgeting: Program Analysis and The Federal Budget*. Cambridge, Mass.: Harvard University Press, 1965.

Park, Rolla Edward. *The Role of Analysis in Regulatory Decisionmaking*. Lexington, Mass.: D. C. Heath and Company, 1973.

Pascal, Anthony. *Thinking About Cities: New Perspectives on Urban Problems*. Belmont, California: Dickenson Publishing Company, 1970.

Pascal, Anthony (ed.). *Racial Discrimination in Economic Life*. Lexington, Mass.: D. C. Heath and Company, 1972.

Pincus, John (ed.). *School Finance in Transition: The Courts and Educational Reform*. Cambridge, Mass.: Ballinger Publishing Company, 1974.

Quade, E. S. and W. I. Boucher. *Systems Analysis and Policy Planning: Applications in Defense*. New York: American Elsevier Publishing Company, 1968.

Quade, E. S. *Analysis for Public Decisions*. New York: American Elsevier Publishing Company, 1975.

Rivkin, Steven R. *Cable Television: A Guide to Federal Regulations*. New York: Crane, Russak and Company, Inc., 1974.

Turn, Rein. *Computers in the 1980's*. New York: Columbia University Press, 1974.

Williams, John D. *The Compleat Strategyst: Being a Primer on the Theory of Games of Strategy*. New York: McGraw–Hill Book Company, 1954.

Wirt, John G., Arnold J. Lieberman and Roger E. Levien. *R&D Management: Methods Used by Federal Agencies*. Lexington, Mass.: D. C. Heath and Company, 1975.